RELIGIOUS LITERACY IN POLICY AND PRACTICE

Edited by Adam Dinham and Matthew Francis

First published in Great Britain in 2016 by

Policy Press
University of Bristol
1-9 Old Park Hill
Bristol
BS2 8BB
UK
t: +44 (0)117 954 5940
pp-info@bristol.ac.uk
www.policypress.co.uk

North America office:
Policy Press
c/o The University of Chicago Press
1427 East 60th Street
Chicago, IL 60637, USA
t: +1 773 702 7700
f: +1 773-702-9756
sales@press.uchicago.edu
www.press.uchicago.edu

© Policy Press 2016

British Library Cataloguing in Publication Data
A catalogue record for this book is available from the British Library

Library of Congress Cataloging-in-Publication Data
A catalog record for this book has been requested

ISBN 978-1-4473-1666-4 paperback
ISBN 978-1-4473-1668-8 ePub
ISBN 978-1-4473-1673-2 Mobi

The right of Adam Dinham and Matthew Francis to be identified as editors of this work has been asserted by them in accordance with the Copyright, Designs and Patents Act 1988.

Cover design by Clifford Hayes Design
Front cover image: 'Crowd from above' © Mikołaj Tomczak | Dreamstime.com
Printed and bound in Great Britain by CPI Group (UK) Ltd,
Croydon, CR0 4YY
Policy Press uses environmentally responsible print partners

Contents

Foreword

Grace Davie

I am delighted to contribute a Foreword to this important book. I say this for two reasons: first, because I am deeply committed to the notion of religious literacy as such, and second, because the chapters that follow explore this idea in new ways, each of which reflects a particular situation. Religious literacy must be engaged in context: getting it right can make all the difference; getting it wrong can make a tricky situation even worse.

What has led us to talk in these terms? In order to capture what is happening, we need to step back a little and examine the different factors contributing to the religious situation in modern Britain – and indeed, in much of Europe. These are outlined below. Each factor is important in its own right, but the crucial point to grasp is that they push and pull in different directions: some indicate greater secularisation, others the reverse. It is this combination that exposes the need for religious literacy.

The first factor relates to the role of the historic churches in shaping European culture. Other influences were important (notably, Greek rationalism and Roman organisation), but the Judaeo-Christian tradition has, without doubt, had a lasting impact on European society – in, for example, the framing of time and space in this part of the world, and in establishing the categories within which we think about religion. Nobody pretends, however, that the historic churches are able to discipline the beliefs and behaviour of British people in the 21st century – indeed, the very idea is offensive. They remain nonetheless important points of reference at particular moments in the lives of individuals and communities, and indeed, of the nation itself. That said, the number of people who think in these terms is declining, and more secular ways of marking the highs and lows of life (both individual and collective) are becoming increasingly popular. Taken together, these shifts are evidence of secularisation – the process is gradual and uneven, but undeniable.

This is not, however, the whole story. New forms of religious life are beginning to emerge as an observable change takes place in the churchgoing constituencies of Britain. These are operating increasingly on a model of choice, rather than a model of obligation or duty. The implications are important. Churchgoing is declining overall, but those who continue to be active in this sphere do so because they want to rather than because they have to; their motives, moreover, are more likely to be 'religious' than, say, habitual, social or political. And the range of choice is widening all the time and now includes significant other faith communities, brought to this country by the individuals (mostly from the New Commonwealth) who responded to the call for new sources of labour in the mid-postwar decades. This influx established new religious constituencies in Britain, at least some of which have very different aspirations in terms of their religious lives compared with those of the host society. Specifically, the line between public and private is differently formulated.

What has become known as the 'Rushdie controversy' constitutes a pivotal moment in this process, marking important shifts in the religious landscape. It is at this point, for example, that racial and ethnic differences begin to give way to religious ones in public discussions about diversity. This is particularly significant for the Muslim population, whose shared dismay at the publication of *The satanic verses* in 1988 drew them together. Muslim identity became a unifying factor for a community comprising a wide variety of nationalities and ethnicities. The stakes, moreover, were high, as the relative merits of two 'freedoms' were hotly debated: freedom of religion on the one hand, and freedom of speech on the other. The Muslim community invoked the former (faith should be inviolate), while Salman Rushdie and his supporters were claiming the latter (the right to publish freely). Self-conscious secularism is an important consequence of this conflict; indeed, it becomes a factor in its own right, a counterweight to seriously held religion.

A particularly revealing moment occurred at the end of 1990 when Rushdie claimed to have embraced Islam. With every appearance of sincerity, he declared himself a Muslim, apologising to his co-religionists for the problems caused by the book, and acknowledging that some passages were offensive to believers. This was, in effect, an admission of blasphemy. Financial contributions from the book's royalties would be made to those who had suffered injury as a result of the protests – in other words, reparations would be made. Although short-lived, Rushdie's attempt to build bridges seemed genuine enough, and brought some comfort to the Muslim community in Britain. The point to note, however, is that the gesture provoked an equally potent reaction from the opposing camp. The rage of the secular liberals at this point could hardly be contained, revealing an alarming illogicality at the heart of their campaign. Muslims should be tolerant of offensive books, but liberals could not tolerate the writer who became a Muslim. Tolerance, it is clear, was a social construct, to be applied in some cases, but not in others.

Just as troubling was the genuine incomprehension of the British public, who had great difficulty grasping the hurt of the Muslim community after the initial publication. Quite simply, the religious sensibilities of most British people were of a different order. Assuming a relatively relaxed approach to religious issues, it was hard to understand why the publication of a book caused such anger when no one was obliged to read it against their will. So why not leave it at that? Part of being British, it seemed, was to accept a low-key approach to religion, with the strong implication that anyone who comes to live in these islands – for whatever reason – should conform, in public at least, to a similar view. But does this essentially conditional statement provide an adequate basis for a tolerant and pluralist society? The unexpected vehemence of the ensuing controversy indicates that it does not.

In short, the ground was shifting: away from rather casual assumptions about religion being a private matter, operating on a live-and-let-live basis, to something sharper and more confrontational. The implications for religious literacy are multiple. Before looking at these in more detail, however, one final factor must be addressed. That is, a growing realisation that the patterns of religious life in modern Europe should be considered an 'exceptional case' – they are not a global prototype. Britain, like the rest of Europe, is relatively secular; the rest of the world is not – a fact substantiated by looking at the very different patterns of religion in the US, the growth of Pentecostalism in the global South, the huge variety of religious practice within the Muslim world, the intractable situation in the Middle East, the intensities of the Indian sub-continent, the changes on the Pacific rim and, most significant of all, what appears to be happening in China. This is not the moment to deny the significance of religion in the modern world order.

But even in Britain, we need to pay attention. Looking carefully at the factors set out above, it is clear that two things are happening at once. On the one hand are the increasing levels of secularity, which lead, in turn, to an inevitable decline in religious knowledge as well as in religious belief. On the other is a series of increasingly urgent debates about religion in public life, prompted by the need to accommodate new populations, who bring with them very different ways of being religious. This largely unexpected combination is difficult to manage, a fact that is hardly surprising. British people are losing their knowledge of religion (that is, of vocabulary, concept and narrative) just when they need this most, given the requirement, on an increasingly regular basis, to pass judgement on the rights and obligations of the very varied religious actors (individual and corporate) that currently cohabit in this country. The consequent debates all too often are both ill informed and ill mannered, as questions that were considered closed are not only re-opened, but are also engaged with little or no preparation. The Rushdie controversy illustrates every one of the statements; it was, moreover, but one acrimonious affair among many.

There are no easy answers – unsurprisingly, given that the situation requires both an imaginative response and careful attention to detail. The imaginative response lies in moving on from mid-20th century expectations to 21st-century realities, a particularly painful shift for those trained in social science. The roots of this discipline – or more accurately, disciplines – go back to the 19th century; they were part and parcel of the upheavals associated with the industrialisation process in Europe, and the changes in society that followed suit. Transformations in the field of religion were integral to this process as the forms of religious life that fitted so well into pre-industrial ways of living came under severe strain as populations moved away from rural areas to the rapidly growing cities of 'modern' Europe. At the same time, the onslaughts of the Enlightenment took their toll. All too often, however, the wrong inference was drawn: namely, that all forms of modern society were necessarily inimical to religion, whether at home or further afield – an attitude that reached its peak in the 1960s, the decade in which social science expanded exponentially. Was this or was it not a coincidence?

Whatever the case, the world-changing events of the late 20th century came as something of a shock. No one was expecting the Iranian Revolution in 1979, the fall of communism in 1989 or the devastating attack on the Twin Towers in 2001. These are complex, multicausal events that require careful analysis. Religion, however, was a central factor in all of them, and clearly able to motivate widely different groups of people. At the very least, it was proving itself more durable than many had imagined possible. But once again, the wrong inference was drawn. The tendency this time was to assume that religion was resurgent or back, reasoning that we are now in a post-secular – rather than a post-religious – situation. To argue thus, however, is to conflate two rather different things. Was it really the case that religion (or God) was back? Or was it simply that the disciplines of social science, along with a wide variety of policy-makers, had now become aware (or re-aware) of something that had been there all the time? In other words, is it perceptions that have altered rather than reality? It is, in fact, a mixture of both: new forms of religion have asserted themselves in unexpected ways in different parts of the world.

That is clear. It is incorrect, however, to assume that these emerged from a vacuum. In almost all global regions, the presence of religion has not only been continuous but taken for granted; only in Europe might this statement be questioned, and then only partially.

It is, however, the partial and complex reality discovered in 21st-Britain that the Religious Literacy Leadership in Higher Education Programme seeks to address. As we have seen, Britain is becoming more secular – steadily so. At the same time, new arrivals have brought to this country very different ways of being religious (predictably enough, given their provenance), leading at times to painful confrontations. Third, British people who look outwards are aware that the situation elsewhere is markedly different from that at home. For all these reasons, a more developed knowledge of religion, together with the ability to speak well about this subject, is becoming a requirement rather than an option. It is to the credit of the programme that they had both the vision to see this and the energy to tackle the problem – beginning with their work in higher education. Universities, they rightly maintain, have a special role in shaping the environment in which learning and development unfold, influencing in turn the attitudes and understandings of a generation who will guide society for the foreseeable future.

Since then, the programme has 'diversified', in the sense that it is beginning to penetrate a variety of sectors, including the media, the workplace, welfare providers, advice and equality bodies and government officials. This volume extends the remit even further, addressing a range of topics under three headings: theory, policy and practice. It is here, moreover, that the attention to detail matters, as each story develops in its own way. It is not a case of one size fits all. It is, rather, a question of finding exactly how to address the difficult questions that arise with respect to religion in a particular institution or profession, aware that each of these has its own history, culture and ways of working. It is with this in mind that I recommend this volume with enthusiasm; in both concept and detail, it impresses.

Grace Davie
Professor Emeritus of Sociology
University of Exeter

Acknowledgements

This volume is prompted by the work of the Religious Literacy Leadership in Higher Education Programme, which one of the authors, Professor Adam Dinham, directed and the other author, Dr Matthew Francis, managed for a time, supported by a wide range of generous colleagues. We would like to express thanks for their extraordinary contributions: to Professor David Maughan-Brown, Deputy Vice-Chancellor, York St John University, and Dr Jeremy Clines, Chaplain, University of Sheffield, who were critical to the founding and framing of the programme; to the wider Advisory Board: Dr Husna Ahmed, CEO, FaithRegen; Professor Grace Davie, Professor Emerita, Sociology of Religion, University of Exeter; Professor Richard Farnell, Emeritus Professor, Coventry University; Professor David Ford, Regius Professor of Divinity, University of Cambridge; Mr Gary Loke, Equality Challenge Unit; Ms Kat Luckock, National NUS Interfaith Coordinator; Professor Peter Lutzeier, Principal, Newman University College; Ms Nadira Mirza, Dean of the School of Lifelong Learning, University of Bradford; Professor Martin Stringer, Deputy Pro Vice-Chancellor, University of Birmingham; Ms Kath Thomson, Higher Education Funding Council for England (HEFCE); Professor Linda Woodhead, Professor of the Sociology of Religion, Lancaster University; Mr Ewart Wooldridge CBE, CEO, Leadership Foundation for Higher Education and Professor Michael Worton, Vice-Provost, University College London. They, and many others, have provided boundless enthusiasm and support for which we are deeply grateful.

Likewise, we are grateful to a wider range of friends of the programme who have supported it in a variety of other ways, including by co-facilitating religious literacy workshops. Eileen Fry, from the Multifaith Centre at the University of Derby, deserves special mention for her many appearances in the workshops, but there are many others who will know who they are.

We are grateful, too, to the various researchers who worked on the programme at various times, including Stephen Jones, Martha Shaw, Notis Pentaris and Tim Stacey. Above all, we thank the Higher Education Funding Council for England (HEFCE) for providing generous funding and strategic support for the Religious Literacy Leadership in Higher Education Programme, from which the wider initiative has sprung.

Notes on contributors

Michael Barnes SJ is Professor of Interreligious Relations at Heythrop College in the University of London, UK, where he is also Dean of Research Students. He studied Theology in the University of London and Indian Religion and Culture at the University of Oxford. His PhD, from the University of Cambridge, was an application of the thought of Paul Ricoeur and Emmanuel Levinas to the theory and practice of interreligious relations. He lectures, researches and writes on a number of interreligious topics – especially the hermeneutics of cross-religious reading and Comparative Theology.

Rebecca Catto is a Research Fellow at Coventry University, UK. She is Convenor of the British Sociological Association Sociology of Religion Study Group and co-editor of the Ashgate AHRC/ESRC Religion and Society series. Publications include 'What can we say about today's British religious young person?' (*Religion*, vol 44, no 1, 2014) and *Religion and change in modern Britain* (Routledge, 2012, co-edited with Linda Woodhead).

Jeremy Clines is the Anglican chaplain at the University of Sheffield, UK, and author of the 2008 *Faiths in higher education chaplaincy* report. He has contributed to the Religious Literacy Leadership in Higher Education Programme since its inception, it having arisen, in part, from the findings of his report. He researches in chaplaincy practice, spiritual development, liberation and contextual theologies and church liturgy.

James C. Conroy is Vice-Principal (Internationalisation) at the University of Glasgow, UK, where he has been Professor of Religious and Philosophical Education since 2005. His most recent book (with others), *Does Religious Education work?* (Bloomsbury, 2013), was based on a three-year AHRC/ESRC ethnographic study of religious education in British schools. The Scottish government has also funded him to develop an innovative 'clinical' model of teacher placement. Prior to teaching in universities James worked as a Religious Studies teacher in secondary schools and sixth form colleges in the UK.

Beth R. Crisp is Professor of Social Work at Deakin University in Melbourne, Australia. She has been involved in health and human services research for 25 years, initially in programme development and evaluation in the areas of substance misuse, HIV/AIDS and health promotion, and more recently in the area of professional development and the transfer of professional knowledge. From 2004 until 2008 she was involved in the evaluation of the new social work degree in England. She is interested in the interface between religion and spirituality and social work practice, and has published the books *Spirituality and social work* (Ashgate, 2010) and *Social work and faith-based organizations* (Routledge, 2014).

Adam Dinham is Director of the Faiths and Civil Society Unit at Goldsmiths, University of London, UK, where he is Professor of Faith and Public Policy. He holds degrees in Theology and Religious Studies as well as being a qualified social worker. He is policy adviser to a number of faith-based agencies and policy bodies, and has advised central government on issues of public faith. He has published widely on faith in the public realm and religious literacy, and was Director of the Higher Education Funding Council for England (HEFCE) Religious Literacy Leadership in Higher Education Programme in the UK.

Amanda van Eck Duymaer van Twist is Deputy Director of Inform, a non-profit information centre specialising in minority religious movements, spiritualities and fringe political movements, based at the London School of Economics and Political Science (LSE) in London, UK. As part of her work, she has encountered and researched a range of topics and issues dealing with minority and/or new religions. Her publications include contributions on topics such as beliefs in spirit possession and witchcraft, socialisation of children in sectarian new and minority religions, and the methodological challenges of researching and providing information on 'cults and extremism'.

David Ford is the Regius Professor of Divinity at the University of Cambridge, UK. His current research interests in the area of contemporary Christian thought are focused in two directions: first, in the direction of hermeneutics, the interpretation of scripture and substantive issues in contemporary Christian thought and practice; and second, in the direction of interfaith theology and relations, particularly the issues of interfaith scriptural interpretation and the relation of faiths to secular cultures, traditions and forces. Among his other research interests are the shaping of universities and of the field of Theology and Religious Studies within them; political theology; theology and poetry; ecumenical theology; and Christian theologians and theologies.

Matthew Francis is a Senior Research Associate in the Department of Politics, Philosophy and Religion at Lancaster University, UK. He was previously manager of the Higher Education Funding Council for England (HEFCE) Religious Literacy Leadership in Higher Education Programme in the UK, and a researcher at the charity Inform, focusing on fringe political and religious movements. He has researched the role of beliefs and values in the move to violence in religious and non-religious groups, and is currently researching how ideologies have an impact on decision-making at times of uncertainty. He founded the website www.RadicalisationResearch.org which summarises academic research on radicalisation, extremism and fundamentalism, and has commented on these topics for a number of media outlets.

Sophie Gilliat-Ray is Professor of Religious Studies at Cardiff University, UK, and Director of the Islam-UK Centre. Her recent publications include: *Understanding Muslim chaplaincy* (with Mansur Ali and Stephen Pattison, Ashgate, 2013); *Muslim childhood* (with J. Scourfield, A. Khan and S. Otri, Oxford University Press, 2013); *Muslims in Britain: An introduction* (Cambridge University Press, 2010). Alongside these books, Sophie has published numerous book chapters and journal articles about religion in public institutions and the work of chaplains. Sophie is currently Chair of the Muslims in Britain Research Network, and a founding member of a new European association for chaplaincy research.

Mike Higton is Professor of Theology and Ministry at Durham University, UK. He is a Christian theologian who previously taught at the University of Exeter. In 2010, he took up a three-year secondment to the Cambridge Interfaith Programme, to develop research programmes bringing together scholars of Judaism, Christianity and Islam, and to help develop associated public education projects. His research examines the relationships between doctrine and practice, and explores what it means to teach doctrine today in the churches and in university. His recent publications include *A theology of higher education* (Oxford University Press, 2010) and (with Rachel Muers) *Modern theology: A critical introduction* (Routledge, 2012).

Stephen H. Jones is a Research Associate at the Centre for Trust, Peace and Social Relations at the University of Coventry, UK. He previously held research positions at the University of Bristol and at York St John University, where he worked as a researcher on the Religious Literacy Leadership in Higher Education Programme.

He has research interests in religion and social change, faith-based political participation and the impact of policy-making on religious organisations.

Lauren R. Kerby is a PhD candidate at Boston University, USA. Her dissertation studies Christian tourism in Washington, DC, and its role in constructing Christian American identity. Her other research interests include religious literacy, religion in public schools, American evangelicalism, religious material culture, and religion and American law. She is also interested in practical approaches to religious tolerance and pluralism, and in 2013 was a fellow at the Balkan Summer School on Religion and Public Life. Lauren has previously been a teaching fellow and a lecturer for the Boston University Department of Religion.

Diane L. Moore is Senior Lecturer in Religious Studies and Education at Harvard Divinity School, Cambridge, USA. She is currently engaged on a multiyear collaboration with educators and other professionals to create resources to better understand the intersections of religion, conflict and human rights in contemporary world affairs. She is Director of the Harvard Religious Literacy Project, and served as the chair of the American Academy of Religion's Task Force on Religion in the Schools, which conducted a three-year initiative to establish guidelines for teaching about religion in public schools. Her book, *Overcoming religious illiteracy: A cultural studies approach to the study of religion in secondary education*, was published by Palgrave in 2007.

David Perfect is a Visiting Research Associate at the University of Chester, UK. He works for the Equality and Human Rights Commission (EHRC) as Research Manager, and is part of the team working on the implementation of its strategy on religion or belief in public life. His publications on religion or belief issues include a 2011 EHRC briefing paper, which analysed the available statistical data, and a 2013 *Public Spirit* article, which discussed the EHRC's legal, research and policy work in this area. He is writing in this book in a personal capacity.

Stephen Prothero is a Professor in the Department of Religion at Boston University, USA, and author of numerous books, most recently *The American Bible: How our words unite, divide, and define a nation* (HarperOne 2012), *God is not one: The eight rival religions that run the world – and why their differences matter* (HarperOne, 2010) and *Religious literacy: What Americans need to know* (HarperOne, 2007). He has consulted and written for several media outlets, and in 2010 was invited to speak about religious literacy at the White House. During 2012-13 he was a fellow at the Smithsonian's Museum of American History.

Jonathan D. Smith works at the intersection of faith and social action in multicultural societies. He managed a multi-year project (for the Lokahi Foundation) on developing best practice in good campus relations at seven UK universities. He taught for four years at universities in Lebanon and the Palestinian Territories, where he supported student groups engaged in interfaith dialogue and non-violent action for peace and justice. He holds MA degrees in Applied Linguistics and in International Peace Studies from the University of Notre Dame and a BA in Biblical Studies. He has conducted research and written on interfaith solidarity in South Africa and Christian–Muslim relations in the Middle East.

Nick Spencer is Research Director at Theos, the religion and society think tank. He is the author of several books, most recently *Atheists: The origin of the species* (Bloomsbury, 2014) and *Freedom and order: History, politics and the English Bible* (Hodder & Stoughton, 2011). He has also written a number of Theos reports, including *Doing God: A future for faith in the public square* and *Neither private nor privileged: The role of Christianity in Britain today*, and contributes to various publications, including *The Guardian*, *Tablet* and *Church Times*. He is currently engaged in doctoral research on the theology of the state.

Michael Wakelin is Director of the Cambridge Coexist Programme, which is a partnership between the University of Cambridge's interfaith programme and the Coexist Foundation. He is also a consultant to various projects and organisations including the Council of Christians and Jews. Michael worked as Head of Religion and Ethics at the BBC from 2006 to 2009. During his tenure he sold and oversaw the production of numerous programmes across the television and radio networks. He also worked as a producer and director on *Songs of Praise* for 10 years before becoming series producer in 2001.

Section One
Theory

ONE

Religious literacy: contesting an idea and practice

Adam Dinham and Matthew Francis

The aims of the book are multiple but simple, as revealed by the chapters that follow. We challenge the idea of religion as a problem, and recast it as something pervasive, nuanced and pressing in the contemporary world – something to be engaged with, not feared. We re-examine the perceived boundary between the secular and the religious, recognising that the world is complexly both. We explore the challenge to really understand the secular, as well as the religious, because this is the context in which religion and religious illiteracy play out. And we argue for a proper engagement with cutting-edge data and theory that reveal a real religious landscape which is quite different to the one frequently imagined in school Religious Education (RE), university Religious Studies, and in the popular and media imagination. Exploring various understandings of religious literacy in different contexts is a key aim of the book. In doing so, we hope to move towards an understanding of religious literacy as both generalisable and context-specific, exploring how it plays out in a variety of public practices and settings in the real contemporary world.

Why is religious literacy needed?

We were each brought up in a generation that believed one shouldn't speak about either religion or politics in polite company, and this book breaches that etiquette by doing both. This childhood rule is instructive of something that has really come to characterise contemporary thinking about religion in modern Western settings – that it is controversial, difficult somehow, and can only lead to rows. We want to challenge that idea of religion, and to suggest some ways in which we can – and should – move religion away from this anxiety and tension, and look at it instead as something far too pervasive, far too interesting, and far too nuanced to simply write off as too risky to talk about.

This reflects an observation we have been making all our adult lives – that contemporary British people are usually in a muddle about religion and belief (see Dinham and Jones, 2012). They're not sure what religion is, how much of it there is, what it looks like, what it's for, or what to do about it. That probably goes for most Europeans, and for a great many North Americans and Australians too. The question is, however, does this actually matter?

Our answer is, absolutely, yes, because, as is widely being recognised, religion and belief are everywhere. But as this book will show, decades of relativistic, non-confessional religious education (RE) in schools, and a shift in welfare from churches to states, have left religious language out of public talk for at least a generation. When we do now try to talk about religion and belief, we find we've pretty much lost the ability to do so. What we tend to have instead is a muddled conversation, often mired in anxieties about extremism or sex, and frequently leading to knee-jerk reactions, which tend to focus on issues such as the wearing of the veil or forced marriage. They are also often driven by legal cases, such as a case where a British Airways employee was told she couldn't wear her cross to work, and took the airline to court and won; and another, where a Christian Bed and Breakfast owner refused to allow a same-sex couple to stay, and again, this went to court, where the same-sex couple won. These are examples of public treatments of religion that have produced more heat than light.

Media reporting and public discourse also tend to assume that we live in a somehow secular age, and this vague idea of secularity is frequently equated with neutrality. But as we have observed elsewhere, 'Nobody starts from nowhere', and there is no such thing as neutrality (Dinham et al, 2009). Secularity itself arises from a distinctive world view, and is, in any case, far more nuanced and contested than common treatments would suggest. The conversation about religion is impeded by the paucity of the conversation about the secular. In short, on religion we find ourselves, as Grace Davie observes in her Foreword to this book, with a lamentable quality of conversation, just as we need it most.

We are not going to suggest that the answer lies in a return to the past – more confessional RE in schools, a re-valorised Church of England, and a return to predominantly church-based welfare services. The clocks are not going back, even if we wanted them to (which, for the record, we don't). But we do want to challenge a number of assumptions which have taken hold about religion and belief in the public sphere during the second half of the 20th century – although it turns out that they haven't taken root very deeply, at least in the settings in which we have been researching – push at them firmly, and the assumptions soon fall away. What is left, we have found, is frequently a positive, healthy space for a far better quality of conversation about religion and belief than we thought had become the case. We have found that the problem is not people's willingness to have the conversation; it is their ability to do so. This book is an attempt to address this.

It is pressing to engage in this space: there is widespread understanding that religion and belief are pervasive. As Grace Davie points out, religion and belief haven't disappeared, as many had predicted. Billions of people – 84 per cent in fact – around the world remain religious, despite assumptions of secularity (PEW Research, 2012). Millions are in the UK and Europe, and millions more in North America and Australia. Globalisation and migration expose us all to daily encounter with this diversity and plurality of religion. And as Chapter Six later shows, increasingly mixed economies of welfare right across the West are re-admitting faith-based actors into the public sphere as they are called on to plug the gaps in welfare as states withdraw.

Yet public discourse – such as it is – tends to resonate with the assumptions we want to challenge: that the West is largely secular; that religions tend to cause wars, oppress women and gay people; that they want to hold people in orthodoxies that constrict their freedoms and creativities. Likewise, it is generally supposed, as we have said, that the public sphere is a secular sphere, by which is usually meant a somehow neutral sphere when it comes to religion and belief: believe what you want, but don't bring it to the public table where it can only cause arguments.

Thus, in their book, *Religion and change in modern Britain*, Linda Woodhead and Rebecca Catto write about:

> ... a characteristic assumption of the post war period: that religion has become a purely private matter with no public or political significance. So long as this idea prevailed, both in scholarship and in society, it was possible to treat religions as discrete entities which could be analysed solely in terms of their inner logics.... (Woodhead and Catto, 2012, p 2)

They challenge this assumption, saying that religion is not an *aside* to economics, politics, media and the law '... and other arenas' (Woodhead and Catto, 2012, p 2), but is, indeed, integral to them. 'Private religion, public sphere' is an antinomy that makes less and less sense as the religion and belief landscape becomes increasingly apparent once more.

Nevertheless, the assumption that religion is a private matter is consolidated by the notion that there are somehow separate secular and religious realms. This, too, is being challenged in contemporary contexts (Knott, 2013). The world was never simply religious nor simply secular, but has always been complexly both (see, for example, Ford, 2011). We agree, and this book is an attempt to explore the integrity of these realms, as opposed to their separation, and the implications for public thought and action.

Religious Literacy Leadership in Higher Education Programme

The approach to religious literacy that prompted this volume emerges out of the framing of a large project to improve the quality of conversation about religion and belief in higher education (HE) in the UK, a project on which both authors have worked, as director (Adam Dinham) and researcher and manager (Matthew Francis). Many of the other authors in this volume have also played a significant part. The project, called the Religious Literacy Leadership in Higher Education Programme, was funded by the Higher Education Funding Council for England (HEFCE), and its appeal was in large part underpinned by anxiety within (and about) the HE sector regarding extremism on university campuses, an issue that had appeared a great deal in the media and was 'hot' at that time, as indeed it continues to be. In framing the project, this was one of a number of assumptions that presented themselves and needed to be challenged. A process of recasting itself threw up some of the dilemmas and difficulties of religious literacy and illiteracy.

The first point to challenge was the focus on the issue of extremism itself. This mirrors a widespread anxiety about religious extremism right across society and the world. But as Chapter Seven in this volume shows, it is, in reality, a problem caused by a tiny minority, although it is absolutely right to take it seriously because the consequences can be catastrophic when things go wrong. Yet the rhetoric in general, and the conversations that were at first framing this project in particular, would suggest that the problem was far more extensive and widespread than it really is. There seemed to be a loss of perspective, feeding and fed by an anxiety that religion is something to be frightened of – or at least suspicious of. No approach to religious literacy will start well from the assumption that religion and belief are primarily a problem, and that the task at hand is the prevention of extremism. This is not the pressing issue and it is not the pressing need.

It was also important to point out that extremism – on campuses and elsewhere – is not only rare but also notoriously hard to judge, as it is in the rest of society. Right-wing political parties across Europe are one example of alternative and potent sources of extremism, about which there has been far less policy and media attention. In any case, universities are supposed to be places for the exploration of difficult ideas and the formation of identities. There is a very real sense in which radicalism and contestation are precisely what universities *should* be for, as students grapple with new and competing ideas, so where should the line be drawn?

But most importantly, an approach based on anxiety about extremism casts religion and belief as a problem first and foremost, and the programme – and this book – argues that this need not nor should not be the starting point. We aim to explore an alternative: we suggest that it would be much more effective – and much more realistic – to set religion and belief in their proper context as normal, mainstream and widespread, and to seek engagement *with* them rather than solutions *for* them. After all, religion and belief are not 'something else somewhere else', despite many of the assumptions that exoticise it, as we will see.

This leads to the question, why focus on universities? It may not be immediately obvious, but there are, we believe, several reasons why they make particularly good places to start. As Grace Davie says in her Foreword, although the programme has since diversified to work in other sectors and settings, HE was an excellent place to begin. Why?

First of all, universities are places of peculiarly intense encounter, especially, but not exclusively, between young people. They are often even more plural and mixed than the rest of society around them, although sometimes the exact opposite is true – which brings a different set of problems. And they are precisely designed to encourage debate about interesting and difficult issues. Although there remains a long way to go, we have become quite good at discussing race, gender and sexual orientation in universities and in wider intellectual life, for example. So where does religion fit in to this?

Second, universities embody what liberalism takes to be a range of essential freedoms – namely, freedom of speech and freedom of thought. These are the basis of academic freedom. But religions are sometimes seen as an obstacle to such freedoms, and indeed, a distraction from the intellectual endeavour itself. This can put the conversation about religion and belief on the back foot before it even begins.

Third, we have argued elsewhere (Dinham and Jones, 2012) that universities are perpetuators – perhaps even guardians and reproducers – of a particular post-religious way of thinking that tends to reject religion as distracting nonsense. As these assumptions are produced and reproduced in university settings, they are part of the formation of minds underpinning the conversation in wider society.

So it turns out to matter very much what universities think about religion, even though they may have thought of themselves as post-religious, secular and somehow neutral on the matter. Indeed, as Stephen Jones shows in Chapter Ten, the research he helped carry out in the programme, with vice-chancellors and other staff in universities in 2009-10, found two helpful things. The first was about the sort of stances universities think they take in relation to religious faith. This led us to a typology in four parts, which sheds light not only on how universities treat religion and belief, but also on how wider society does too: soft neutral, hard neutral, repositories and resources and formative collegial groups.

For some, religion is seen as a problem to be solved. Society is conceived of as a secular space where public institutions remain neutral, as far as possible, and education avoids mentioning religions or belief. Faith itself is seen as a largely private matter, spilling into the public domain only when it gives rise to problems, which are resolved on a case-by-case basis. This was a stance adopted by some of the vice-chancellors we spoke to, and we called this group *soft neutral*.

A similar but harder line actively seeks the protection of public space from religious faith, asserting a duty to preserve public bodies, such as universities, as secular, and to reject religious discourse in all its forms. Religion is often considered not fully rational and is therefore seen as threatening, particularly to institutions of higher learning. One vice-chancellor we spoke to expressly described his institution (and others that were similar) as "secular and therefore needing to defend that". We called this group *hard neutral*.

On the other hand, many – including many policy-makers – see religious faith as a resource on which society can draw (Dinham et al, 2009). They understand it as offering possibilities and opportunities for encounter, enrichment and enjoyment, as well as financial, social and human capital. For them, keeping questions of religious faith to some sort of private sphere means missing opportunities and bracketing – even annihilating – potentially rich aspects of self and society. Instead of rejecting public faith, or reluctantly accommodating it piecemeal, advocates of this outlook tend to support engagement with religious faith as an opportunity for beneficial encounter and enrichment. A larger number of the vice-chancellors we spoke to took this view, with many stressing the point that their campus is friendly to all religious traditions and comfortable with religious diversity. We called this group *repositories and resources*.

Such an outlook tends to be more sceptical of the claim that religion is necessarily irrational, instead regarding religious belief as relating to important – and maybe inescapable – dimensions of human experience, while at the same time questioning the rationality of 'rationalism' itself in intellectually interesting ways. In a university context, this stance may translate into the fourth approach we identified, which aims to offer education 'for the whole person' in ways that incorporate a specifically religious or belief dimension. In practice, this perspective is more common in universities that were founded as religious institutions, although in our study it was not exclusive to them. (At least two of the vice-chancellors we spoke to led universities that take this sort of 'whole person' perspective without being religious foundations.) We called this group *formative collegial*.

We also asked a second set of questions about what sorts of issues concerning religion and belief seem most important to vice-chancellors. This revealed four key areas: equality and diversity law; providing a highly thought-of and good quality student experience; widening participation and reaching international markets; and preventing violence and extremism. These seem like reasonable and practical concerns for a leader in any sector or setting to have, and as they apply to universities, they certainly reflect the HE market, as it has become. They also reveal something of the concerns of wider society in relation to religion and belief, and this, too, makes them valuable places for the investigation to begin, as proxies for wider society. (The issues are set out later, in Chapter Ten.) It is not difficult to imagine how these play out in other settings outside of HE too, and in this sense, HE stands as something of a microcosm of the challenges and assumptions that inhere right across society.

Finally, we conducted case study research in three universities to understand the narratives of religious faith as experienced by students and staff, and this enabled us to dig down into the many practical ways in which faith plays out in universities much more widely. We found students who hadn't felt able to attend interviews, or exams, or Saturday lectures because of clashes with religious events. There were anxieties about public speakers and what to 'allow' them to say on topics such as Israel and Zionism. Timetabling staff were worried about how to handle the exam periods for the four or five years after 2014 when Ramadan falls in the middle of it. Canteens and bars were taking all sorts of stands for or against halal food, alcohol-free events and single-sex socials, and there were bitter rumours in one institution that 'the Muslims' were receiving subsidised lunches. There were sports societies whose members were ribbing a Sikh for wearing the five k's (*kesh* – uncut hair; *kara* – armband; *kangha* – comb; *kacchera* – knee-length shorts; and *kirpan* – dagger). Residences were struggling with kosher kitchens and women–only halls. Campus banks either could or couldn't handle the requests of Muslim students for halal borrowing for student fees. And counselling services felt they couldn't talk about religion with religious students.

These may present as pressing reasons for taking religion more seriously in university operations, but this still left the tricky question of whether and how to take religion seriously in the curricula. How, if at all, should the intellectual life of universities respond? This goes for education all the way down to primary level too, as James Conroy explores later, in Chapter Nine. And it is also instructive of wider debates and disputes. In some subjects, of course, religion is simply a topic of relevance, as in History and in Religious Studies itself. In others, it is a cultural legacy to be decoded and understood, as revealed in the growing tendency to teach 'Introduction to the Bible' to English Literature students so they can manage Milton or Donne. In others, it embodies the opposite of the rational, scientific method that has emerged in the modern era. As such it is an utter irrelevance, as in Richard Dawkins' comparison between Astrology and Astronomy. In some cases this produces hostility against all religious ideas. This can surely feel painful for students who, as some of our research shows, can feel uncomfortable hearing lecturers be quite rude or offensive about their beliefs, or about belief in general. And in the Social Sciences, religion has rarely been a variable at all, like race, gender or sexual orientation. It simply doesn't often count as a thing to be counted.

The Religious Literacy Leadership in Higher Education Programme has translated its analysis and findings into programmes of training within universities, designed to help them engage better and in very practical ways with religion and belief. It was always the intention to diversify in due course to other sectors and settings, on the assumption that the issues presenting within HE would be reflected in wider society, and could therefore be subject to similar analyses and interventions. This began in a project in 2012 with the UK's Equality and Human Rights Commission (an independent arm's-length government-funded body tasked with facilitating the equality and human rights agenda) to work with employer organisations, including trades unions, the third sector and private sector bodies, and with service providers. The rationale was that the Equality Act 2010 extended protection against discrimination on the grounds of religion and belief, and was applied specifically to employers and service providers.

A series of public dialogues revealed two key findings: first, that employers and providers did not feel that the law had clarified matters. In fact, they found it was adding to the confusion. A court's finding in one legal case did not point to the answer – even the likely answer – in the next. And second, that employers and providers had observed that a turn to law was leading to an assertion of rights over and above an engagement in dialogue, and that this was generally unhelpful. Strategic work with policy-makers is underway as we write to address these dilemmas. Other religious literacy projects are progressing in the areas of school education and in health and social care, both topics addressed in the chapters that follow.

The challenge of pinning down 'religious literacy'

So, religious literacy is a pressing need across society, in the full range of sectors and settings. Religion and belief, the private and the public, religion and the secular, are not separate but are inescapably bound up – in law, in identities, in beliefs and in practices, not to mention the physical landscape, with its spires, mosques and temples. We believe that it is impossible to talk fully about the public sphere without talking about religion and belief, although we have become very used to doing so.

Religious literacy begins with an understanding of this – that religion or belief pervade as majority, normal and mainstream, whatever one's own position or stance. Clarity about the category of religion and belief is the beginning of religious literacy – it requires a willingness to recognise it as relevant. This precedes knowledge about specific religions and beliefs themselves, which can only effectively follow on from intelligent, thoughtful, informed understanding of ideas about religion and the secular – an understanding of how the conversation is framed. In this sense, it is useful to note that 'religion' is a useful shorthand to refer to a range of beliefs, rituals, symbols, institutions and communities, and that 'secular' does not mean a neutral opposite to religion, however much it is often erroneously assumed to be. Further, religious literacy need not (and we would argue should not) exclude non-religious identities which are equally complex, but we focus on religion because there is a need for a far more nuanced understanding of the real religious landscape than has usually been the case, and this is a second element in the religious literacy endeavour. It is also important to say that the term itself is also contested: religion, faith, belief, the spiritual – all (or none) are possible sobriquets for the task at hand. The advisory board of the Religious Literacy Leadership in Higher Education Programme has debated this extensively, and the conversation could have gone on (and on) if we had let it. In one sense, it does indeed continue, and this book is one expression of that conversation. At the same time, we recognised a need for a practicable term that would be generally recognisable, if complexly debatable, that would encapsulate roughly what we are attempting to do. All of these debates apply to the 'literacy' word too, and our response has been the same: 'religious literacy' is not a perfect term, but it is the best we have found for our purposes, and for the debates that play out in this book.

The real religious landscape

Religious literacy does not end at recognising the legitimacy of the conversation. Grasping the shape of religion and belief is a key part of the religious literacy journey too. The UK 2011 Census is helpful on this, although it is, of course, by no means the only source, or the definitive one. The headlines are that, despite falling numbers, Christianity remains the largest religion in England and Wales, with 33.2 million (59.3 per cent of the population). Muslims are the next biggest religious group, with 2.7 million (4.8 per cent of the population), and this group has grown in the last decade. In fact, this group has increased the most (up from 3.0 per cent in 2001). Meanwhile, the proportion of the population that reported they have no religion has now reached a quarter in the UK – 14.1 million. This is an increase (from 14.8 per cent in 2001 to 25.1 per cent).

There is also more religious diversity in general, and there are pockets of religious and non-religious intensity around the UK too. For example, Knowsley was the local authority with the highest proportion of people reporting to be Christians (at 80.9 per cent), and Tower Hamlets had the highest proportion of Muslims, at 34.5 per cent (over seven times the average England and Wales figure).

Likewise, in England and Wales, while church attendance has fallen to 6.3 per cent of the population (Christian Research, 2005), the breakdown of attendees has also changed – less than one third are now Anglican, less than one third Catholic, and over a third (44 per cent) charismatic and independent. This is a massive internal realignment within Christianity alone, which is hardly ever commented on.

According to other sources and other questions, *what* we believe has also changed. Belief in 'a personal God' roughly halved between 1961 and 2000 – from 57 per cent of the population to 26 per cent. But over exactly the same period, belief in a 'spirit or life force' doubled – from 22 per cent in 1961 to 44 per cent in 2000 (see Woodhead, 2012). There is also evidence of consumerist behaviours in religion as people pick religions and ideas within religions to build their own frameworks of belief, often separate of creed and organisation.

Of course, the data are hugely debatable, and other sources say different things, but the trends are clear enough. They point to how religious forms have been changing in this period, as well as the religious mix and the mix of religion and non-religion. It is really important to grasp this because there appears to be a *real* religious landscape and one imagined by policy-makers and publics, with a growing gap between them (see Dinham, 2012). This is likely to affect how policy-makers seek to shape services and practice, and how providers provide them. There is a serious risk that they will all shoot wide of the mark. Society is religiously more nominal – that is, people report an affiliation without actively attending a church or equivalent. Society is also more plural and less formal: more and more of us believe in nothing, or something (but we're not sure what), or many things, as in Jewish atheism or Christian Hinduism. Many people hold spiritual, non-creedal, non-organisational beliefs and views. Others, for that matter, have non-religious beliefs that are also deeply important to them, as in humanism, secularism and environmentalism.

It is important for religious literacy, therefore, to ask ourselves, what's going on? One account is found in Grace Davie's idea that we are 'believing without belonging' (Davie, 1994). This has also been inverted by Hervieu-Leger, who suggests the phenomenon of 'belonging without believing' (Hervieu-Leger, 2000). David Voas and Abby Day, on the other hand, say that what we are seeing is a corruption of proper religious forms into a sort of 'fuzzy fidelity' (Voas and Day, 2007). Linda Woodhead, on the other hand, says that, 'it is a wrongly fundamentalising interpretation to say that *real* dogmatic religion is declining, leaving people with a muddled and fuzzy residue' (Woodhead, 2013). She thinks the exact opposite is true: 'Turn it on its head and you see it the right way round: real religion – which is to say everyday, lived religion – is thriving and evolving, while hierarchical, dogmatic forms of religion are marginalised' (Woodhead, 2013). We could compare it to changing forms of communication – for example, the use of telegrams has declined to a vanishing point. But we don't take this to mean that communication has ceased; we simply look for it in other places, such as email, Twitter and Facebook.

So where are we now? We find a sort of 'fuzzy secularity' alongside a general muddle, often tinged with indifference and sometimes with hostility. Many people have a vague sense that religion ought not to matter, while grasping, at the same time, that it somehow does. But the majority are largely unable to articulate the debate – as we have said, there is a lamentable quality of conversation about religion. Liberalism's solution – to confine religious debate to Habermas's (2011) public reasons and somehow rise above the fray in some sort of public neutrality – does not seem adequate, and even if it were conceptually appropriate, law would no longer permit it. There is indeed a pressing need for a better quality of conversation in order to avoid knee-jerk reactions that focus only on 'bad' religion and bad ideas about religion. As the HE programme shows, universities know they have got to get better at providing really excellent student experience on these matters. What is starting to emerge is a bigger debate about the role of religion in teaching and learning and, by proxy, in intellectual life more broadly. This reflects a crucial contention in the rest of society about the re-emergence of religious faith as a public category at all: is society and its institutions secular or religious, or complexly both? To what extent should religion be private or public? Can we leave religious identity at the door? And if so, which door?

We have argued that religious literacy resides, then, in an improved quality of conversation about the category of religion and belief itself, which first of all irons out the muddled binaries and assumptions explored here – about religion versus the secular, private versus public, and perceptions of religion as a threat or a risk to an otherwise rational modern world. It is an exercise in pulling together these perspectives and getting ready for the engagement. But it doesn't stop at being ready and willing to have the conversation. It needs to go on into the conversation itself. In this sense, religious literacy engages in the depths of religions and beliefs, as they present in theology, tradition and lived experience and practice. It is about the specificity as well as the generality. It is obvious that nobody can know everything about every religion and belief, and religions and beliefs are not homogeneous slabs of knowable 'stuff' in any case. The reality is of religion and belief as shifting aspects of contested identity. But engagement in the detail and the reality of at least some religion and belief, and an ability to ask appropriate questions with confidence about others, is an essential part of the journey. Scriptural reasoning has emerged as one approach to this – a deep, prolonged engagement with sacred texts, undertaken by people from a variety of traditions, or none, sometimes in the original languages. For others, religious literacy is a less cerebral undertaking, in the form of interfaith dialogue, or multifaith social action. For most, it will be driven by instrumental factors such as law and best practice, which compel an engagement with religion and belief as aspects of the identities of service users and employees.

But religious literacy can go further. At its most exciting, it promises a re-engagement with religion and belief, not only in compliance with law or in deference to the realisation that the world is religiously infused after all. As David Ford and Mike Higton suggest in Chapter Three, religious literacy can enable a renewed encounter with the wisdoms that reside therein, which can be enriching of individual and social life. These are, after all, 'wisdom traditions'. This approach draws attention to how strange it seems that millennia of insight, experience, drama and poetry should be set aside in favour of the natural scientific paradigm of modernity. For them, one does not displace the other. Rather, they can coexist, they say. Religions and beliefs have interesting things to say about life, the universe and everything! We may not agree with all – or even much – of what they say, but since they resonate in so many different ways, in so many different lives, and down through the ages, right across the globe, acting as though they are irrelevant or insignificant to many everyday conversations hardly seems appropriate.

Outline of the chapters

The book is arranged in three connecting sections: theory, policy and practice. The boundaries between are, of course, blurred, but the framework is useful for reflecting a real world that involves them all.

The book starts with an exploration of contrasting conceptual approaches to religious literacy, whose variance illustrates the fluidity and contestability of the concept, and highlights how similar challenges can be differently construed in different spaces and places. As we say in the concluding chapter, we regard this as a strength of the concept – so long as it is treated as a framework for thinking through the implications and challenges of religious literacy in particular contexts, not as a 'one size fits all'.

In her Foreword, Grace Davie draws our attention to the rise of 'self-conscious secularity' in response to controversies and events including the Rushdie controversy in 1988, the Iranian Revolution in 1979, the fall of the Berlin Wall in 1989, and the attack on the Twin Towers in 2001. These followed on from a period when people had been paying little or no attention to religion and belief, and this made it all the more difficult to predict, recognise, or address them when they happened. It has resulted, she says, in a bad tempered and ill informed conversation, and a pressing need for religious literacy that recognises and deals with a religion scene in the UK that is at once more secular *and* more religious.

Davie lays the foundation for an exploration in the first section of the book of the ideas underlying the religious literacy approach, and these are variously discussed and set out in what follows. We have begun by introducing the idea of religious literacy in this chapter, drawing on our experience of running the Religious Literacy Leadership in Higher Education Programme. For us, and drawing on Dinham's earlier work with Jones (2010), religious literacy is a civic endeavour, over and above a theological or religious one, aimed at enabling people of all faiths and none to engage with the increasing plurality of religion and belief encountered by everyone as a result of migration and globalisation. As noted, it is made all the more difficult by decades of non-confessional RE in schools, the marginalisation of Theology and Religious Studies in universities, and the traction of assumptions of secularity.

Diane Moore takes a similar approach in Chapter Two, but with a US inflection. She wants religious literacy to 'provide resources for *how to recognise, understand, and analyse* religious influences in contemporary life'. She draws attention to many common assumptions which are unhelpful to a good quality of conversation – ignorance of the distinction between devotional expression and non-sectarian study of religion; controversy about women and Islam; the multiplicity, as opposed to homogeneity, of traditions and beliefs; change over time; and the cultural specificity of religions which make the same traditions differ from place to place (sometimes even within the same town). The understanding of religious literacy she works towards is very close to that of the Religious Literacy Leadership in Higher Education Programme, emphasising an ability to perceive the connections between a complexly religious world and the social, political and cultural.

In Chapter Three, David Ford and Mike Higton take a different approach, although driven by the same sorts of concerns – that is, a lamentable quality of conversation about religion just as we need it most. They explore the role Theology and Religious Studies might play in religious literacy, and how it might enable people to 'navigate a complexly religious and secular landscape'. They – and we – are clear that Theology and Religious Studies are not the same as religious literacy, but want them to be used as tools to achieve it. This renders it a necessarily intellectual and therefore somewhat elite endeavour, likely to appeal to and work for a limited number of participants. This makes it no less valuable a part of the religious literacy jigsaw, and their emphasis on the depth that can be achieved through this kind of rigorous intellectual engagement can certainly underpin those approaches with a broader base and appeal, especially if what they reveal is translated into tools and methods with a more user-friendly face. Although Ford and Higton focus on Christianity, they are firm that their approach can apply to other traditions too, and pose an invitation to do so. Notably, however, they do not address their efficacy for non-religious and non-traditional beliefs, while in our approach to religious literacy we certainly would. Clearly, their idea of Theology is clearly not amenable to those modes of religion and belief that are less formal and systematic. What Ford and Higton have in mind is a serious dialogue between a prevalent and ancient world phenomenon – in this case, Christianity – and a public realm that simply cannot do it, or itself, justice while ignoring it. For them, talk within and about a public realm is simply not possible without taking seriously the pervasive religion within it, regardless of one's own religious beliefs, or none. In any case, they say, to stop short of Theology is to assume that there are conversation-stopping beliefs – what they call 'erratic boulders' – that cannot ever be engaged with. Whereas they perceive 'argumentative structures' in all the traditions, and their debaters, which Theology can actively assist in uncovering. In this way it is, in some senses, essential to the sharpening of the conversation. It is precisely engagement in what they call this 'conversational mode' that is most likely to lead to religious literacy, they argue, even if the methods for doing so vary. Most importantly of all, Ford and Higton's approach reminds us that a dry approach, rooted in the attempt to be neutral and to somehow rise above the fray, is intellectually inadequate as well as practically ineffective, as so many of the heated controversies of recent years reveal.

Stephen Prothero and Lauren Kerby make a different sort of argument in Chapter Four. They assume that religious literacy lies specifically in a loss of knowledge about traditions, *not of religion itself*, and they trace this loss in the US, first in Christianity, through legal cases from the 1960s (which are not, in their view, the root of religious illiteracy) back to the minimising of Christian denominational differences in the 19th century for the sake of Christianising the nation in a sort of coalition of the Christian willing. For them, historical efforts to strengthen Christianity have had the effect of weakening it, and this underlies the decline of religious literacy. A drive towards common denominators continues, they think, into the 20th century, culminating in the 'Moral Majority' movement of the 1970s which, in taking all-comers, diminished and removed their doctrinal differences. They argue that this has translated in to a 'spiritual marketplace that is America in the 21st century', citing books, for example, with titles such as *Buddhism without beliefs*. Now, they say, 'doctrine is ignored in favour of a shared commitment to a shared conservative brand of morality' which rejects liberalism and the non-religious. For them, this plays out in the contemporary US in the language of the 'multireligious' or at least 'Abrahamic' America, where 'the similarities ... matter, while their differences do not'. Today, they say, this blurring of Protestant beliefs is so embedded that the public square cannot but make use of its language, and Americans must know something about Protestant beliefs and the Bible if they are to participate in it. This argument highlights the context-dependency of the idea of religious literacy, in this case, rooted in a specific historical outworking (inflected, too, of course, by the American Constitution, as Prothero and Kerby point out). One size does not fit all. The compulsion to understand religious 'others' is secondary, for them, to the need to know the Bible, although both are present and pressing. In the end they arrive at a different place in response to similar contemporary issues – 9/11, increased religious plurality, and the desire to produce 'good citizens'. Likewise, the complexion of the solutions varies, and they advocate 'to add the topic of religion to public school curricula', reflecting another context specificity – this time, the place of school RE. Compare this with the UK where it is not the place but the purpose of school RE that is contested.

Chapter Five concludes the section, focusing on ideas of religious literacy, this time exploring religious literacy as 'harmony'. Michael Barnes and Jonathan Smith return us to a broadly multifaith perspective, and marry this with Ford and Higton's emphasis on depth, Moore's concern with peace, and Prothero and Kerby's concern about the unhelpfulness of the elision of difference. They say that it is the very specificity of faith commitments that gives them life, and that the task is not to elide but to value difference. For them, religious literacy resides, not just in reflection on the cultural and historical roots of difference, but on the processes internal to the community. This is a deep engagement, not quite with the theological, as Ford and Higton propose, or with the cultural and historical, as for Moore and Prothero and Kerby, but with the lived. At the same time, and also in common with Ford and Higton, they point to a dialogue between the contemporary and the wisdoms that reside in religious traditions themselves.

In the second section, on policy, the book explores the policy imperatives that are driving, shaping and sometimes misshaping religious literacy. As Dinham has observed elsewhere, these revolve around three primary areas: welfare and service provision; cohesion, radicalisation and extremism; and a turn to law and rights (see Dinham, 2009).

In Chapter Six, the first of the policy chapters, Adam Dinham bridges theory and practice in an analysis of how recent policy-making history (circa post the Second World War) has affected religious literacy, and how it now specifically presents challenges to improve it. The welfare sphere, it is argued, first accidentally rendered British society less religiously literate than it had been when churches were majority providers of care, then accidentally drove an urgent need for the recovery of religious literacy by repopulating the welfare field with faith-based providers after 1980, and in particular, after 1997.

The second central area of policy attended to in this section is broadly associated with extremism, and Matthew Francis and Amanda van Eck Duymaer van Twist address this in Chapter Seven, taking in radicalisation and cults in the process. They start by exploring the connections and disconnections between the political and the religious, and the frequent confusion between the two. From there they draw attention to the focus in policy on Islam as a problem, which they see as overblown and unhelpful – a prominent expression of religious illiteracy. They bring us back to the theme of fluidity that pervades this book, pointing out that religion and belief are messy and shifting aspects of identity, not monolithic blocks, easily amenable to simple political tropes and their corresponding actions in violence. Yet the 'securitisation' of British Muslims, and their brothers and sisters around the world, does precisely this, and this is noted and lamented. They also observe a classic case of perverse outcomes of policy in their section on 'division from cohesion': policies designed to produce cohesion between different faiths, while laudable for recognising plurality, have been blunt in their shape and application. In places they have served to puff up distinctions, and have been seen as excluding some while privileging others, alienating non-religious belief movements struggling to get a voice. Their example of Buddhism to explore the complexities of ideas, definitions, muddles and debates in the sphere of extremism is left field, and all the more illuminating for it. The point they want to make is that there are 'many such disputes within religious traditions in Britain that go unnoticed to the ... media and the ... public'. There is insufficient religious literacy to grasp it. We might conclude from this, first, that it is wrong to single out Islam as a problem, as many have said; and second, that religious literacy must include 'an understanding that these kinds of complexities exist'. They conclude that 'in the high stakes games of preventing violent radicalisation, these arguments from exception have had disproportionate policy results'. For them, 'it is not Islam … which makes someone violent, but a belief that violence is legitimate…'.

The third policy area with a strong religious literacy agenda is law itself. In Chapter Eight, Rebecca Catto and David Perfect bring this right down to earth in a forensic analysis of some of the key cases, and their implications. This repays close reading, closely analysing the implications of judgments and disputes for religious literacy. They remind us that a new legal settlement in the UK after 2010 puts an onus on judges and lawyers, as well as employers and service providers to whom law applies, to be religiously literate, although largely they are not. Their reference to Sandberg's suggestion that 'judges could benefit from more sociological as well as legal training' presents both a delightful image and an important broader challenge – how do public professionals of all kinds engage well with religion and belief as categories, and as lived identities, which they increasingly encounter? This is a theme that is also picked up in the 'practice' chapters that follow. In particular, Catto and Perfect draw attention to an important controversy revealed in debates about religion and the law about the place of Christianity in Britain – one that echoes Prothero and Kerby's exploration in the US context: while some may think Christianity is privileged over the faiths which are newer to Britain, others are concerned that it is marginalised by a political correctness which bends over backwards to avoid that. In these ways, law in this area both reveals the paucity of religious literacy across society, and highlights the pressing urgency for it. Catto and Perfect conclude that there is 'a growing consensus that litigation ought to be a last resort', yet, as pointed out earlier in their chapter, there is a growing sense that it is increasingly the first.

In the third section, on 'practice', we explore some of the ways in which religious literacy is being done, and how it plays out, in practice settings and sectors. A key focus is on education, in schools and in universities. Two other chapters in this section address social work, and the media, presented as examples of spaces and places in which religious literacy is playing out. But we would note that it was always the intention of the Religious Literacy Leadership Programme that core work in HE (where we started) would be translated into a wide range of other sectors and settings, and this has begun, as Grace Davie says, with employer groups, law, and in new work with schools and in health and social care (more widely than social work). In this light, we could have included many more settings and sectors besides. The list could extend, for example, to work with the armed forces, hospitals, the police, probation and prisons, community and youth work, and a plethora of others. It could also relate to international relations and international development, and to foreign policy. The sectors and settings that appear here do so because of notable work and analyses that are already under way. They are not intended to imply that the parameters of religious literacy stop with them, and we anticipate future volumes that will take these others forward.

Here the third section begins with education, which, of course, plays a particular role in religious literacy, being both crucially formative and informative on matters of religion and belief. Ford and Higton set out a compelling case for depth in their chapter, as we have said. Stephen Jones builds on this to examine the contexts that inform the practice of religious literacy in higher education institutions (HEIs). He makes the case in Chapter Ten that HEIs are good places to tackle religious literacy, although they are also precisely the places that often think they should not. His focus is on university operations in relation to religion and belief – the things they do – although he also engages with questions about the place of religion and belief in curricula.

The curricula in school education (specifically for 14- to 16-year-olds in the UK) is similarly problematised by James Conroy in Chapter Nine. He argues that both the teaching and examination of religion in schools simplifies, trivialises and makes irrelevant religious histories and thought. For example, schools are wary of considering truth claims, and so reduce religious arguments to personal, and therefore unchallengeable, interpretations. This contributes to a lack of critical insight and to religion not being taken seriously. It is further harmed by the way religious education (RE) is examined, which focuses on grades at the expense of an engagement with the issues, reducing complex issues such as discourses on abortion to simplistic pre-coached answers. Perhaps most significantly, religion, as it is taught in schools, is frequently unrecognisable to students of faith, with teachers unable or unwilling to engage in issues of thought and practice that are not contained within the syllabus. The combined effect of these deficiencies, Conroy argues, is that RE in school reduces religious practice to a private practice, and religious sentiment into private sentiment. The corollary of this argument is that, as argued by Ford and Higton earlier, religious literacy is only possible where a meaningful engagement with religion takes place, not a light-touch postmodern relativisation of religious thought.

Between Jones and Conroy (and with Ford and Higton), they make compelling cases for better education about religion and belief. They also raise questions about what RE, Religious Studies and Theology can and should be for, as well as how religion and themselves should be treated and engaged in the educational endeavour. This picks up on a pressing debate about RE in England, outside of the main chapters of this book, which revolves around the question of what RE is for. It notes that RE has been accidentally populated with proxies such as citizenship and cohesion within the UK, and with notions such as 'intercultural education' in the European Union (EU) and Canada. The focus on RE as the teaching of monolithic traditions – sorts of slabs of knowledge about the world religions – is criticised for treating religion as something 'out there' or 'in the past', rather than lived and living now. It is also challenged for being too narrow, failing to extend to notions of belief and non-religious belief. A really important challenge is not only to address a better quality of conversation about religion and belief in HE, and in schools, but to connect it up and on into the lifelong learning that people do after school and university. Just as Hervieu-Leger's 'chain of memory' (Hervieu-Leger, 2000) has been broken, in her view, on religion and belief, so, too, is there a 'chain of learning' which can enable people to grow an ability to engage well with religion and belief throughout their lives. Perhaps in due course this will look something like the complex but widely known discourses on gender, race and sexual orientation (although all still have some way to go).

In Chapter Eleven, Beth Crisp turns our attention to social work, through an examination of curricula and education for social work students. She describes this as having for many years been 'a curriculum of omission' as far as religion and belief are concerned. Nevertheless, she argues that social work needs religious literacy for at least two reasons: to engage well with the religion and belief identities of service users; and because large numbers of social workers are themselves employed in organisations that have a religious foundation. Crisp draws attention to a tendency in social work to use 'spirituality' instead of or interchangeably with religion or belief; indeed, she notes a marked preference for the former. This reflects a wider tendency to be more comfortable with proxies for religion than with the word itself. This in itself is a challenge of religious literacy since spirituality is a term with its own specific meanings. Crisp also describes how religious literacy 'is now policy in Australia', although adds that 'it is still unclear as to what is meant, or practically how we do this'. This reflects the challenge for social work – and other health and social care professions – around the world. She attempts to pin this down, identifying three rationales for religious literacy in social work: to enable good working with others; for working with faith-based organisations that provide social work services; and for social workers employed by such faith-based organisations. She argues that 'religiously literate social workers won't necessarily have all the answers, but they will be able to work from a framework which enables them to ask questions ... and identify ... options and resources ...'.

In Chapter Twelve, Michael Wakelin and Nick Spencer present an account of the challenges of religious literacy for media, rooting their exploration in a case study of the UK's BBC, where Wakelin was formerly Head of Religion. This begins to open up a crucial area for religious literacy that is both hindered and helped by how it is mediated in journalism, news, drama and entertainment. The chapter touches on a broad and well-established field of research that indicates that things have not always gone well in the relationship between religion, religious literacy and the media. The challenges here echo many of those in the other sectors and settings considered. It is likely that they are magnified when it comes to media by the sheer exposure it can command.

Finally, Chapter Thirteen turns to the challenges as they play out in chaplaincies. These are not always obvious or particularly visible spaces at all, yet Jeremy Clines and Sophie Gilliat-Ray show how they play important roles in the lives of the organisations they belong to. In hospitals and universities they are prevalent, likewise in prisons and the armed forces. Often they are the focus for whole institutions of all the religion and belief which they think is 'taking place', and much besides. This chapter explores the challenges of and for religious literacy, and proposes strengths, weaknesses and improvements to chaplaincy practices and conceptions.

Whatever one's motivation for pursuing religious literacy, we believe the case is pressing and clear. The chapters that follow expand on this, building on and exploring the framework we have set out, in theory, policy and practice.

We hope this book will demonstrate that religious literacy is a multifaceted endeavour. It is not didactic. It asks that faith in the public realm be taken seriously by everyone, regardless of one's own religion, belief or none, and that the engagement be informed, intelligent and open. Assumptions are to be flushed out and tested. Above all, religious literacy is not about more religion, but a better quality of conversation about the religion and belief that is already there. We hope this book will provide a helpful beginning for a conversation that Western societies have largely forgotten how to have.

References

Christian Research (2005) *The English Church Census*, UK Data Archive Study Number 6409, (www.thearda.com/archive/files/codebooks/origCB/Engish%20Church%20Census%202005%20User%20Guide.pdf).

Davie, G. (1994) *Religion in Britain since 1945: Believing without belonging*, Oxford: Blackwell.

Dinham, A. (2009) *Faiths, public policy: Problems, policies, controversies*, Basingstoke: Palgrave Macmillan.

Dinham, A. (2012) 'The multifaith paradigm in policy and practice: problems, challenges, directions', *Journal of Social Policy and Society*, vol 11, issue 4, October, pp 57787.

Dinham, A. and Jones, S. (2012) 'Religious literacy in higher education: brokering public faith in a context of ambivalence', *Journal of Contemporary Religion*, vol 27, issue 2, pp 185-201.

Dinham, A., Furbey, R. and Lowndes, V. (eds) (2009) *Faith in the public realm: Controversies, policies and practices*, Bristol: Policy Press.

Ford, D. (2011) *The future of Christian theology*, Oxford: Wiley-Blackwell.

Habermas, J. (2011) '"The political": the rational meaning of a questionable inheritance of political theology', in E. Mendieta and J. Vanantwerpen (eds) *The power of religion in the public sphere*, New York: Columbia University Press, pp 15-33.

Hervieu-Leger, D. (2000) *Religion as a chain of memory* (translated by Simon Lee), New Brunswick, NJ: Rutgers University Press.

Knott, K. (2013) 'The secular sacred: in-between or both/and?', in A. Day, C. Cotter and G. Vincett (eds) *Social identities between the sacred and the secular*, Aldershot: Ashgate, pp 145-60.

PEW Research (2012) *The global religious landscape: A report on the size and distribution of the world's major religious groups as of 2010*, Washington, DC: Pew Research.

Voas, D. and Day, A. (2007) 'Secularity in Great Britain', in B.A. Kosmin and A. Keysar (eds) *Secularism and secularity: Contemporary international perspectives*, Hartford, CT: Trinity College Institute, pp 95-112.

Woodhead, L. (2012) 'Mind, body and spirit: it's the de-reformation of religion', *Guardian online*, 7 May (www.theguardian.com/commentisfree/belief/2012/may/07/mind-body-spirit-dereformation-religion).

Woodhead, L. (2013) *Religion in Britain has changed, our categories haven't* (http://faithdebates.org.uk/wp-content/uploads/2013/09/1335118113_Woodhead-FINAL-copy.pdf).

Woodhead, L. and Catto, R. (2012) *Religion and change in modern Britain*, Abingdon: Routledge.

TWO

Diminishing religious literacy: methodological assumptions and analytical frameworks for promoting the public understanding of religion

Diane L. Moore

Religions have functioned throughout human history to inspire and justify the full range of agency, from the heinous to the heroic. Their influences remain potent in the 21st century in spite of modern predictions that religious influences would steadily decline in concert with the rise of secular democracies and advances in science. Understanding these complex religious influences is a critical dimension of understanding modern human affairs across the full spectrum of endeavours in local, national and global arenas. An important dimension of diminishing religious illiteracy is to provide resources for *how to recognise, understand, and analyse* religious influences in contemporary life. This chapter provides a methodological framework for understanding religion in contemporary human affairs through the overarching theme of conflict and peace.

For a variety of reasons dating back to the Enlightenment (including Christian-influenced theories of secularisation that were reproduced through colonialism) there are many commonly held assumptions about religion in general and religious traditions in particular that represent fundamental misunderstandings. Scholars of religion are well aware of these assumptions, and have articulated some basic facts about religions themselves and the study of religion that serve as useful foundations for inquiry (see AAR, 2010).

First and foremost, scholars highlight the difference between the *devotional expression* of particular religious beliefs as normative, and the non-sectarian *study of religion* that presumes the religious legitimacy of diverse normative claims. The importance of this distinction is that it recognises the validity of normative theological assertions without equating them with universal truths about the tradition itself. Unfortunately, this distinction is often ignored in public discourse about religion. For example, religious leaders and practitioners are often looked to as 'experts' of their tradition. This is problematic because their experience as devotees is limited to a particular theological or interpretive strand of the tradition as represented by their sect and community. Unless they have *also* pursued education about their tradition from a non-sectarian Religious Studies framework, they will not be exposed to the diversity of interpretations represented among other sects and even within their own.

In a second example, there is a great deal of contemporary debate about 'what Islam teaches' regarding the proper dress and behaviours for women. In truth, there are a variety of theological interpretations of the tradition that lead to different, sometimes antithetical, practices and assertions. Equally common is that differing communities will have similar practices but with diverse theological justifications. For instance, there are self-proclaimed feminist Muslims who dress modestly and work as homemakers *and* self-proclaimed conservatives who serve as professionals in a variety of fields and dress in what is known as Western business attire. Although there are many theological claims about the proper roles for women in Islam, functionally, there are a variety of often competing interpretations within the tradition (and within *all* religious traditions) about the 'proper' gendered roles for both sexes.

In both examples, it is appropriate for members of a particular community to assert the orthodoxy or orthopraxy of their theological interpretations of the tradition, but it is important to recognise the difference between a theological assertion of normativity and the factual truth that multiple legitimate perspectives exist. The latter represents the non-sectarian study of religion. This is the approach promoted here, and the one most appropriate to advance the public understanding of religion.

There are three other central assertions about religions themselves that Religious Studies scholars have outlined, and that flow from the recognition of the distinction between devotional expression and the non-sectarian study of religion outlined above: first, religions are internally diverse as opposed to uniform; second, religions evolve and change over time as opposed to being ahistorical and static; and third, religious influences are embedded in all dimensions of culture as opposed to the assumption that religions function in discrete, isolated, 'private' or separable contexts.

Religions are internally diverse

This assertion is a truism, but requires explanation due to the common ways that religious traditions and practices are frequently portrayed as uniform. Aside from the obvious formal differences within traditions represented by differing sects or expressions (for example, Roman Catholic, Orthodox, Protestant for Christianity; Vaishnavism, Shaivism, Shaktism for Hinduism, etc), there are differences within sects or expressions because religious communities function in different social/political contexts. One example is the debate mentioned above regarding the roles of women in Islam. The following assertions are also commonly repeated: 'Buddhists are non-violent', 'Christians oppose abortion', 'Religion and science are incompatible', and so on. All of these comments represent particular theological assertions as opposed to factual claims representing the tradition itself.

Religions evolve and change

This is another truism, but again, requires explanation due to the common practice of representing religious traditions without social or historical context, and solely (or primarily) through ritual expression and/or abstract beliefs. Religions exist in time and space and are constantly interpreted and reinterpreted by believers. For example, the Confucian concept of the 'mandate from heaven' evolved within dynasties, geopolitical regions and historical eras, and continues to evolve today. Another example is that the practice of slavery has been both justified and vilified by all three monotheistic traditions in differing social and historical contexts. Finally, in a more specific example, the Southern Baptist Convention in the US passed a series of resolutions in the 1970s supporting the moral legitimacy of abortion, and reversed those resolutions in 2003 (for a full text compilation of all the Southern Baptist resolutions on abortion from 1971 to 2005, see www.johnstonsarchive.net/baptist/sbcabres.html).

Religious influences are embedded in cultures

Religions are collections of ideas, practices, values and stories that are all embedded in cultures and not separable from them. Just as religion cannot be understood in isolation from its cultural (including political) contexts, it is impossible to understand culture without considering its religious dimensions. In the same way that race, ethnicity, gender, sexuality and socioeconomic class are always factors in cultural interpretation and understanding, so, too, is religion.

Whether explicit or implicit, religious influences can virtually always be found when one asks 'the religion question' of any given social or historical experience. For example, political theorists have recently highlighted the ways that different interpretations of secularism have been profoundly shaped by varied normative assumptions about Christianity (Taylor, 2007; Casanova, 2012; Hehir, 2012). This is just one representation of a fundamental shift in political theory that is challenging the legitimacy of the longstanding assertion that religion both *can be* and *should be* restricted to a private sphere and separated from political influence.

Modernist claims predicting the steady decline of the transnational political influence of religion that were first formalised in the 17th century have been foundational to various modern political theories for centuries. In spite of the ongoing global influences of religions in political life throughout this time period, it is only in the aftermath of (1) the Iranian Revolution in 1979, (2) the fall of the Berlin Wall in 1989 and the subsequent rise versus the widely predicted demise of religion, and (3) the 9/11 and 7/7 terrorist attacks in 2001 and 2005 that political theorists in the West began to acknowledge the highly problematic ways that religions and religious influences have been marginalised and too simplistically rendered.

This shift paves the way for multi- and cross-disciplinary collaborations with Religious Studies scholars across the full range of social science investigations in order to explore the complex and critically important roles that religions play in our contemporary world.

Definition of religious literacy

The following definition of religious literacy is one that I articulated in 2006 and has been adopted by the American Academy of Religion (AAR) to help educators understand what is required for a basic understanding of religion and its roles in human experience (see Moore, 2006, p 1 and AAR, 2010, p 4):

> Religious literacy entails the ability to discern and analyze the fundamental intersections of religion and social/political/cultural life through multiple lenses. Specifically, a religiously literate person will possess 1) a basic understanding of the history, central texts (where applicable), beliefs, practices and contemporary

manifestations of several of the world's religious traditions as they arose out of and continue to be shaped by particular social, historical and cultural contexts; and 2) the ability to discern and explore the religious dimensions of political, social and cultural expressions across time and place.

Critical to this definition is the importance of understanding religions and religious influences *in context* and as *inextricably woven into all dimensions of human experience*. Such an understanding highlights the inadequacy of understanding religions through common means such as learning about ritual practices or exploring 'what scriptures say' about topics or questions. Nevertheless, these are some of the most common approaches to learning about religion, and lead to simplistic and inaccurate representations of the roles religions play in human agency and understanding.

Cultural studies

The cultural studies approach to understanding religion that forms the analytical and methodological foundation for the approach promoted here assumes the basic elements of the study of religion outlined above, and frames them within a postmodern world view with the following specific characteristics. First, the method is multi- and interdisciplinary, and recognises how political, economic and cultural lenses are fundamentally entwined rather than discrete. For example, economic or political dimensions of human experience cannot be accurately understood without understanding the religious and other ideological influences that shape the cultural context out of which particular political or economic actions and motivations arise. This is the methodological framework related to the third tenet of Religious Studies above: that religions are embedded in culture, and that 'culture' is inclusive of political and economic influences.

Second, the method assumes that all knowledge claims are 'situated' in that they arise out of particular social/historical contexts and therefore represent particular rather than universally applicable claims. This notion of 'situatedness' is drawn from historian of science Donna Haraway's assertion that 'situated knowledges' are more accurate than the 'god-trick' of universal or objective claims that rest on the assumption that it is possible to 'see everything from nowhere' (1990, p 191). Contrary to popular opinion, the recognition that all knowledge claims are 'situated' is not a manifestation of relativism whereby all interpretations are considered equally valid. Rather, 'situated knowledges' offer the firmest ground on which to make objective claims that are defined not by their detachment, but rather by their specificity, transparency and capacity for accountability.

Regarding the study of religion, this understanding of 'situatedness' offers a tool to recognise that religious claims are no different than other forms of interpretation in that they arise out of particular contexts that represent particular assumptions as opposed to absolute, universal and ahistorical truths. (For example, claims such as 'Islam is a religion of peace' and 'Islam promotes terrorism' are equally problematic and need to be recognised as particular theological assertions as opposed to ultimate truths.)

Third, this notion of situatedness applies to the texts and materials being investigated, the scholarly interpreters of those materials, and all inquirers regardless of station. The method recognises that all forms of inquiry are interpretations filtered through particular lenses. By acknowledging this fact, an essential dimension of the inquiry itself is to identify those differing lenses and make transparent that which would otherwise be hidden.

Fourth, the method calls for an analysis of power and powerlessness related to the subject at hand. Which perspectives are politically and socially prominent, and why? Which are marginalised, or silenced, and why? Regarding religion, why are some theological interpretations more prominent than others in relationship to specific issues, in particular, social/historical contexts? For example, what are the factors that led to the Taliban's rise to power in Afghanistan, and why did their interpretation of the role of women in Islam, for example, gain social legitimacy over other competing claims within the tradition itself?

In another vein, what are the converging factors that lend social credibility and influence to some religious traditions over others, and which dimensions of those traditions are interpreted as orthodox and which heretical, and by whom? What were the conditions that allowed Muslims, Christians and Jews to live together in relative harmony in medieval Spain, and what are the religious influences that have contributed to shaping contemporary tensions in the Middle East and more globally regarding the 'War on Terror' and the 'Arab Spring'?

Fifth, this approach highlights what cultural anthropologists know well: that cultural norms are fluid and socially constructed, even though they are often interpreted as representing uncontested absolute truths. This dynamic tension is powerfully demonstrated in social science theorist Johan Galtung's three-pronged typology of violence/peace.[1] This framework also provides an excellent foundation for discerning and representing the varied ideological influences of religions in human affairs. What follows is an overview of his typology and examples of how it can be useful for highlighting the significance of religious influences in human experiences across time and place.

Johan Galtung: direct, structural and cultural forms of violence and peace

Often referred to as the 'Father of Peace Studies', Norwegian theorist Johan Galtung has developed a three-pronged typology of violence that represents how a confluence of *malleable* factors merge in particular cultural/historical moments to shape the conditions for the promotion of violence (and, by inference, peace) to function as normative:

- *Direct violence* represents behaviours that serve to threaten life itself and/or to diminish one's capacity to meet basic human needs. Examples include killing, maiming, bullying, sexual assault and emotional manipulation.
- *Structural violence* represents the systematic ways in which some groups are hindered from equal access to opportunities, goods and services that enable the fulfilment of basic human needs. These can be formal, as in legal structures that enforce marginalisation (such as Apartheid in South Africa), or they could be culturally functional, but without legal mandate (such as limited access to education or healthcare for marginalised groups).
- *Cultural violence* represents the existence of prevailing or prominent social norms that make direct and structural violence seem 'natural' or 'right' or at least acceptable. For example, the belief that Africans are primitive and intellectually inferior to Caucasians gave sanction to the Transatlantic African slave trade. Galtung's understanding of cultural violence helps explain how prominent beliefs can become so embedded in a given culture that they function as absolute and inevitable and are reproduced uncritically across generations.

These forms of violence are interrelated and mutually reinforcing. Galtung provides a representation of these intersecting forces in the following commentary on slavery:

> Africans are captured, forced across the Atlantic to work as slaves: millions are killed in the process – in Africa, on board, in the Americas. This massive direct violence over centuries seeps down and sediments as massive structural violence, with whites as the master topdogs and blacks as

33

the slave underdogs, producing and reproducing massive cultural violence with racist ideas everywhere. After some time, direct violence is forgotten, slavery is forgotten, and only two labels show up, pale enough for college textbooks: "discrimination" for massive structural violence and "prejudice" for massive cultural violence. Sanitation of language: itself cultural violence. (1990, p 295)

Galtung's typology provides a helpful vehicle to discern the complex roles that religions play in all three forms of violence as well as in their corresponding forms of peace. The formulations of cultural violence and cultural peace are especially helpful and relevant. *In all cultural contexts, diverse and often contradictory religious influences are always present.* Some will be explicit, but many will be implicit. Some influences will promote and/or represent socially normative beliefs while others will promote and/or represent marginalised convictions.

For example, in Galtung's illustration cited above, religions functioned to both support and challenge the moral legitimacy of the Transatlantic slave trade, and religions continue to function to support and thwart structural and direct forms of contemporary racism. Similarly, religions currently function in particular ways to shape and support as well as to challenge prominent economic theories and their policy manifestations. In a final example, normative cultural assumptions about gender roles and sexuality in particular social-historical contexts are always shaped as well as contested by diverse religious voices and influences. One has to simply look for these voices and influences in any context and about any issue to find the ways that religions are embedded in all aspects of human agency and experience.

Implications

This method challenges many commonly reproduced assertions about religion that are widespread. Below are two of the most common.

The assertion that 'extremist religion is a perversion of faith' is one of the most common and implies (1) that 'extremist' is both negative and uniformly definable; and (2) that 'faith' is 'good' unless corrupted. This is an excellent example of a theological as opposed to factual assertion. How both 'extremist' and 'perversion' are defined is a matter of theological interpretation and always contested. Faith is not always used to promote human wellbeing, and 'extremism' is not always negative. For example, Martin Luther King, Jr, was accused by white Christian clergymen in Birmingham, Alabama in 1963 of being an 'extremist' for agitating against racial injustice. His response was framed in his famous 'Letter from a Birmingham jail', and reads, in part, as follows:

> So I have not said to my people: "Get rid of your discontent." Rather, I have tried to say that this normal and healthy discontent can be channeled into the creative outlet of nonviolent direct action. And now this approach is being termed extremist. But though I was initially disappointed at being categorized as an extremist, as I continued to think about the matter I gradually gained a measure of satisfaction from the label. Was not Jesus an extremist for love: "Love your enemies, bless them that curse you, do good to them that hate you, and pray for them which despitefully use you, and persecute you." Was not Amos an extremist for justice: "Let justice roll down like waters and righteousness like an ever flowing stream." Was not Paul an extremist for the Christian gospel: "I bear in my body the marks of the Lord Jesus." Was not Martin Luther an extremist: "Here I stand; I cannot do otherwise, so help me God." And John Bunyan: "I will stay in jail to the end of my days before I make a butchery of my conscience." And Abraham Lincoln: "This nation cannot survive half slave and half free." And Thomas Jefferson: "We hold these truths to be self evident, that all men are created equal...." *So the question is not whether we will be extremists, but what kind of extremists we will be. Will we be extremists for hate or for love? Will we be extremists for the preservation of injustice or for the extension of justice?* (Martin Luther King, Jr, 'Letter from a Birmingham jail'; emphasis added)

In another example, world leaders across the globe are using the good/ bad binary that this assertion represents to justify state-sanctioned violence against those they deem to be 'terrorists' or 'extremists'. Following the 9/11 attacks on US soil, former President George W. Bush famously designated the leaders of Iran, Iraq and North Korea as representing the global 'axis of evil' in his 2002 State of the Union Address (see Bush, 2002). This rhetoric was used to designate those who 'harbour terrorists' and 'promote terrorism' in contrast with those who promote 'justice and freedom'. He used this rhetoric to justify the US-led invasion of Iraq in 2003.

In March 2011, Syrian President Bashar al-Assad justified his violent crackdown in Dara'a against peaceful Arab Spring-inspired protestors by stating through a spokesperson that demonstrators had been infiltrated by 'extremists' who were threatening the state (see Abouzeid, 2011). At the time of writing, he continues to maintain that rebel fighters are 'terrorists' and 'extremists' as justification for his violent actions that have been condemned by the United Nations (UN), the Arab League and the European Union (EU).

Whatever one may believe about the legitimacy of violence, the use of these binaries serves to mask the conditions that make extreme action feel credible to significant numbers of people. I return to Martin Luther King, Jr, in another salient excerpt from the same letter quoted above:

> You deplore the demonstrations taking place in Birmingham. But your statement, I am sorry to say, fails to express a similar concern for the conditions that brought about the demonstrations. I am sure that none of you would want to rest content with the superficial kind of social analysis that deals merely with effects and does not grapple with underlying causes. It is unfortunate that demonstrations are taking place in Birmingham, but it is even more unfortunate that the city's white power structure left the Negro community with no alternative.

The assertion that a given religious group or religiously associated activity represents 'extremism' is a theological claim, not a statement of fact. So, too, is the assertion that 'extremism' represents a 'perversion' of faith. This distinction does not mean that normative claims are invalid; it simply challenges the legitimacy of equating normative theological assertions with universal truths. Understanding this point leads to other questions regarding the social/political contexts and conditions that inspire both religious 'extremists' and those who label them as such. This can, in turn, lead to a better understanding of how religions function in particular contexts and as embedded in social/political/cultural life. Simplistic binaries mask many things, including the complex and diverse roles that religions play in human experience.

Many commentators and analysts continue to draw distinctions between what they deem a 'political' representation of religion as opposed to a 'religious' representation. This distinction is based on the assumptions that (1) religion is defined as ritual practice; and (2) that religion as ritual practice is distinct from other forms of political, economic and cultural experience. The basic tenets of Religious

Studies outlined above challenge this distinction and don't require repetition here. It is important to note, however, that when this distinction is employed in discourse or analysis, it serves to reinforce the notion that 'religion' is not and should not be sullied by political instrumentalities. It promotes an inaccurate and problematic view of religion, thus masking the more complex roles that religions do play (and have always played) in all dimensions of human agency.

Conclusions

This framework represents the following methodological and analytical assumptions about religion:

- there is a fundamental difference between the devotional expression of a religious world view as normative and the study of religion which recognises the factual existence of diverse devotional assertions;
- religions are internally diverse;
- religions evolve and change;
- religious influences are embedded in all aspects of human experience;
- all knowledge claims (including religious ones) are socially constructed and represent particular 'situated' perspectives;
- there is nothing inevitable about either violence or peace; both are manifest in three intersecting formulations: direct, structural and cultural, and both are shaped by conscious and unconscious human agency where religious influences are always operative.

Religion remains one of the most misunderstood and misrepresented dimensions of human expression, yet it has a tremendous impact on human behaviour and self-understanding. Much of this misrepresentation and misunderstanding stems from Enlightenment definitions of secularism that spread widely through colonialism and remain deeply embedded in cultures throughout the globe. The framework for understanding religion in contemporary life summarised here helps identify those misrepresentations while simultaneously offering a way to better understand the multivalent dimensions of how religions function in contemporary life. These foundations provide the best tools to understand the complex roles that religions play in human experience, and understanding them will help diminish the negative consequences of widespread religious illiteracy.

Note

[1] Although his own representation of religion is problematic in that he falls victim to making universal claims about religion based on a specific interpretation of one tradition, the typology itself is extremely useful when a more sophisticated and complex understanding of religion is employed.

References

AAR (American Academy of Religion) (2010) *The American Academy of Religion guidelines for teaching about religion in K-12 public schools in the United States*, Atlanta, GA: AAR.

Abouzeid, R. (2011) 'Syria crackdown escalates: Assad dispatches tanks, snipers to Dara'a', *Time*, 25 April (http://content.time.com/time/world/article/0,8599,2067357,00.html).

Bush, G.W. (2002) State of the Union Address, Miller Center, University of Virginia, 29 January (http://millercenter.org/president/speeches/speech-4540).

Casanova, J. (2012) 'Rethinking public religions', in T.S. Shah, A. Stepan and M. Duffy Toft (eds) *Rethinking religion and world affairs*, New York: Oxford University Press, pp 25-35.

Galtung, J. (1990) 'Cultural violence', *Journal of Peace Research*, vol 27, no 3, August, pp 291-305.

Haraway, D.J. (1990) 'Situated knowledges: the science question in feminism and the privilege of partial perspective', in D.J. Haraway, *Simians, cyborgs, and women: The reinvention of nature*, New York: Routledge, pp 183-202.

Hehir, J.B. (2012) 'Why religion? Why now?', in T.S. Shah, A. Stepan and M. Duffy Toft (eds) *Rethinking religion and world affairs*, New York: Oxford University Press, pp 15-24.

King, Jr, M.L., 'Letter from a Birmingham jail' (www.africa.upenn.edu/Articles_Gen/Letter_Birmingham.html).

Moore, D.L. (2006) 'Overcoming religious illiteracy: A cultural studies approach', World History Connected, November (http://worldhistoryconnected.press.illinois.edu/4.1/moore.html).

Shah, T.S., Stepan, A. and Duffy Toft, M. (eds) (2012) *Rethinking religion and world affairs*, New York: Oxford University Press.

Shakman Hurd, E. (2012) 'The politics of secularism', in T.S. Shah, A. Stepan and M. Duffy Toft (eds) *Rethinking religion and world affairs*, New York: Oxford University Press, pp 36-54.

Taylor, C. (2007) *The secular age*, Cambridge, MA: Harvard University Press.

THREE

Religious literacy in the context of Theology and Religious Studies[1]

David Ford and Mike Higton

Theology and Religious Studies

In the UK 'Theology and Religious Studies' has become a catch-all phrase for the academic study of religion. Several universities have a Department of Theology and Religious Studies (King's College London, Nottingham, Leeds, Chester, Glasgow, and several others), advocacy for the field is carried out by a body called Theology and Religious Studies UK (TRS UK, formerly the Association of University Departments of Theology and Religious Studies, or AUDTRS), and in 2000 representatives of British university departments of divinity, theology, religion, religious studies, biblical studies and various combinations of those terms met under the auspices of the Quality Assurance Agency (QAA) and agreed on a benchmarking statement for the field using the phrase 'Theology and Religious Studies' as their heading.[2]

The document that the QAA process produced showed the great variety in the field, but also the mutual recognition among different types of department and approach. For some who took part in the process of consultation it felt like the 'coming of age' of a new paradigm, of Theology *with* Religious Studies, which had been slowly worked out over many years. As one summary noted: 'There is less tension between the disciplines in Britain than there is elsewhere' (Ross, 2007).

Nevertheless, the phrase 'Theology and Religious Studies' is sometimes still taken to paper over a strong contrast. On one side of the contrast, 'Theology' might be said to assume the faith of the person doing the studying, while 'Religious Studies' might be said to bracket the student's faith or lack of faith, and to be a self-consciously neutral discipline. Or 'Theology' might be said to be the internal discourse of a specific religious community, properly at home in that community's seminaries, while 'Religious Studies' is a discourse belonging to the public at large, properly at home in a secular university. Or Theology might be said to be about God, while Religious Studies is about the practices and beliefs of religious people.[3] These contrasts are sometimes summarised by saying that Theology is 'confessional' while Religious Studies is 'non-confessional'. Indeed, the two sides sometimes seem to be thought to be united only by their focus on questionable objects of study, with Theology only making sense as an academic discipline if one assumes the existence of God, and Religious Studies only making sense as an academic discipline if one assumes that 'religion' is a well-formed category.

In recent years in the UK, however, it has become possible to construe the relationship between Theology and Religious Studies rather differently, and at the same time to see more clearly the role that Theology might play alongside Religious Studies in advancing a religious literacy agenda, that is, in providing a whole variety of learners with the forms of knowledge and understanding, the practices of engagement, that might enable them to navigate a complexly religious and secular landscape. In this chapter we set out something of this construal of the relationship between Theology and Religious Studies, and of the contribution that Theology can play alongside Religious Studies to a religious literacy agenda, and then say something about the institutional locations in which Theology and Religious Studies appear to be flourishing together.

We focus primarily on Christianity. Even if Religious Studies might typically be defined in a similar way regardless of the religious community or tradition being studied, the nature of 'Theology' is harder to generalise. There are discourses whose relationship to other religious traditions is analogous to Christian Theology's relationship to Christianity, but the analogies can't be assumed without further investigation to be drawn tightly enough to allow our arguments to walk lightly across them. The practices of reasoning, the social location of those practices, the materials on which they draw, and the effects that they might have differ markedly from case to case. We therefore talk about Christianity, about Christian Theology, about Religious Studies insofar as it takes Christianity as its subject matter, and about 'the churches' as a way of naming a range of Christian communities and traditions that might be the focus of such study. Far more space would be needed to do justice to other traditions, but we are confident, based on experience of what happens in settings where a Theology and Religious Studies approach has had time to mature, that analogous positions to that we propose in relation to Christian Theology can be maintained convincingly with regard to other religions. This chapter might be seen as an invitation to develop such positions in relation to religious literacy.

The first step in our argument is to note that, as a matter of fact, Christian Theology is an academic discipline undertaken by students and scholars who have a wide variety of relations to Christian belief and practice, from those who would count themselves believers and practitioners to those who would not, with any number of variations and complexities in between. Undertaking academic study in Christian Theology certainly does make some demands on what those who undertake it believe, but what it requires first of all is that its students come to believe, at least for the sake of argument, in the existence of Christianity – that is, the existence of a rich and complex weave of communities, traditions and identities that can be identified as Christian. Beyond that, it requires that they come to believe that, among the many Christian forms of life, there are some reasonably prominent strands that have ordered their lives in part by means of sustained and disciplined deliberation about Christian beliefs and practices, and about their bases, interconnections and implications. It requires that students come to believe that, at least in some cases, these practices of deliberation are discourses within which it is possible to reason, to make and respond to arguments, to adduce evidence, to explain and to question. And it requires that they come to believe that the outcome of those patterns of reasoning has had and still can have some purchase in ordering the life of that community, if the reasoning is carried out in the appropriate locations and forms. Finally, it requires of students that they come to believe that, at least in some cases, these community-shaping, argument-sustaining, belief-focused practices of deliberation cannot wholly be reduced to other discourses: they have their own solidity and integrity, and can bear assiduous and serious attention.

If all this is true, then students can learn to *follow* such distinctive Christian practices of deliberation, to learn the kinds of moves by which they proceed, and to discover how they have been and how they might be deployed, in forms recognisable to members of the community in question, as contributions to that community's own conversations. Students can, in other words, learn about Christian reasoning by learning to reason Christianly.

Theology and public argument

If we ask what place such learning might have in a secular university context, the first answer will simply be that the communities in question, the churches, are a significant part of the world that we share, with an estimated two billion or so members worldwide. They make a public difference, and the difference that they make is affected by the practices of deliberation that they sustain. A university promoting the varied forms of literacy that will enable students to understand and navigate the world well will, of course, want to pay disciplined attention to the discourses that shape it, to explore and test them. If it is interested in promoting better quality public argument, it will, of course, be interested in bringing more fully into public argument the reasons people have for their forms of public participation. Such a university therefore *has* to be interested in theological discourses; it has to be interested in understanding those discourses in their own terms; it has to be interested in understanding the arguments that can and cannot be mounted in them, and in understanding what possibilities of development those discourses do and do not possess. None of that requires a stance of faith; none of it requires belief in God – but it does involve serious attention to a discourse developed and sustained by those who do so believe.

Without such attention, there can be a tendency for reference to religious belief in public life to be an argument stopper. If one looks, say, at media commentary on a neuralgic topic like the religious right's attitudes to abortion, quite a lot of it appears to assume that, because various forms of opposition to abortion are based on religious conviction, they are therefore inevitably *undiscussable* – they are erratic boulders that simply have to be navigated around. Yet if those forms of opposition are indeed based on religious conviction, this will often actually mean that they are supported by an argumentative structure – even if it will probably not be an argumentative structure that rests only on axioms that all rational people are likely to share (but on ethical matters, how many such axioms are there?). And in at least some Christian contexts, these forms of opposition are genuinely supported by that structure, such that alterations in that structure would affect the stance members of the relevant religious community take in public.

In some contexts, of course, the kind of argument in play in a Christian community might appear to allow little scope for engagement. It might appear to run: 'The Bible says "Don't do this!"; the Bible is authoritative guide for all right belief and conduct; therefore we will not do this and will seek to prevent other people doing this.' But the reason for picking abortion as an example is that even this stock example of an adamant public stance struck by conservative Christians turns out to be much more complex than that, not least because there are hardly any straightforwardly relevant biblical materials to which appeal can be made.

Far from stopping with the discovery of religious convictions, a theological investigation will be committed to digging deeper, and uncovering the kinds of argument that can underpin such a stance, uncovering the arguments that underpin the stances of Christians who argue differently on this matter, uncovering the ways in which Christians who disagree about this might reason with one another, and uncovering the deep assumptions and the patterns of evidence involved in their arguments. Far from being an argument stopper, discovering that religious convictions are in play in some public controversy can be a doorway into a whole world of argument and deliberation. And it is only by exploration of the arguments involved that one can understand not only the public stance of religious people, but the forms of malleability, of responsiveness, that are built into those stances in their own terms, and so what it might take for them to change.

Just because the arguments explored are Christian arguments, and do not necessarily rest on axioms shared with those of other traditions, this does not mean that understanding them has nothing to contribute to public argument – across and between traditions. To understand this point more clearly, it is worth considering a rather different example. Both of us have an interest in thinking theologically about the purpose and health of universities, including of secular universities (see Ford, 2007a, chapter 9; Ford, 2007b; Higton, 2012). We participate in the life of such universities, alongside many others that are shaped by multiple different traditions, religious and secular, but we are aware that our participation, and our vision of what is and could be good about university life, is shaped by our Christian theological commitments. Part of the task of public participation, for us, is to become *articulate* about that – to find ways of explaining the commitments and practices of reasoning that underpin our contributions to university life. That doesn't mean that we will necessarily be able to trace the routes by which our ideas about university life arose psychologically or sociologically, but we do hope aptly to describe the way in which we now make sense of those ideas in the light of our tradition.

What kind of conversation does this enable, however, with someone who does not share our religious commitments? However valid the arguments that we make from those commitments to our conclusions, those arguments cannot compel agreement from someone who does not share our commitments. This does not mean that the only option is to accept that the matter is beyond reasoned argument, nor that the non-Christian's response can only take the form of a simple comparison between their views and ours, or a purely pragmatic agreement that takes disagreement for granted, unargued, and simply looks for overlaps big enough to build shared projects on.

Rather, if we have succeeded in articulating the argumentative structure within which our ideas about university life now sit, others can *experiment* with that structure – they can learn, in the sense set out above, to follow the kinds of argument we use, and to deploy them in ways that they hope will be recognisable to us. So they can argue with us about what really follows from the commitments we have identified as basic. They can see whether they can argue on our grounds towards something closer to what they want to say about academic life. They can ask us what we can say about various aspects of academic life that we have not covered, and try to provoke us to envy by expounding the things that they can say about those things within their tradition of argument.

Such discussion can have many possible results. It might lead to us changing our minds about the nature of university life; it might lead to us significantly extending the area within which our conclusions about academic life resemble those of our conversation partners. It might, on the other hand, lead to us understanding more deeply the nature of our disagreement with them, and so the limits on our possible cooperation. And it can (and almost certainly will) lead to everyone involved amending their articulations. They were only *attempts* at articulacy in the first place, and it is hard to imagine a serious conversation that would not show us routes to better articulations: more faithful identification of our commitments, more careful explanation of how those commitments relate to questions about academic life, more precise delineations of the limits and uncertainties of our conclusions about that life. In other words, this process of arguing can lead to the securing of extended agreement, to richer and more interesting disagreement, and to deeper mutual understanding and deeper self-understanding – and on the basis of all that, to the discovery of new patterns of shared and unshared action, a new shape of academic life together.

Such public argument does not require us all to stick to the argumentative territory marked out by the axioms we happen to share. Rather, it involves members of various traditions of argument learning each other's languages well enough to experiment in them, to speak recognisably in them – becoming *literate* in them. Religious literacy properly includes Christian Theology, and analogous discourses in other traditions.

There is one more thing to say, however, about the benefits of theological literacy. That literacy can properly be pursued for the sake of deeper and richer relationships between the people involved – deeper understanding of each other's positions and practices of argument, of the differences between them – but it is also pursued for the sake of deeper and richer understanding of the objects about which we reason. And because we are talking about religion, this means a deeper and richer understanding of life, the universe and everything. After all, as well as the questions that arise *between* the religions, there are questions raised *by* the religions. The traditions of deliberation and argument that we investigate in Christian Theology are, in the broadest sense, wisdom traditions – they involve exploring the different possibilities of discernment and action that become visible when the world is seen as created and redeemed by the God who raised Jesus and who shares his Spirit. One does not need to share the beliefs on which that tradition of reasoning rests to be prompted to think differently by engagement with it. One only needs to be willing to explore and to experiment with the ways of thinking that it makes possible.

Theology and description

Theology, in this understanding, is closely related to Religious Studies, but not identical with it. It is close, because description is central to both approaches – description of the practices and beliefs of religious communities (we might say that our approach to questions raised *between* the religions, and questions raised *by* the religions, begins with questions raised *about* the religions). At the heart of Theology is a descriptive claim roughly of the form, 'Christians believe x' or better, 'Christians deliberate and argue about x in such and such a way' – and Theology as a discipline takes off from that description. In particular, Theology is interested in the deployment within certain forms of Christianity of claims of the form 'we believe x, *and therefore* ...' or 'we believe x, *because* ...' – and it is interested in those claims insofar as they genuinely shape Christian life. It has tended to be interested in these claims insofar as they appear within the more-or-less official teaching processes of churches, in the education of ministers, in intra- and interdenominational debates about controversial practice, and with the extended conduct of such teaching and debates in various academic contexts, including seminaries and universities. Theology takes off from attentive description of the kinds of deliberation and argument that take place in those contexts – attentive description that borrows from other descriptive disciplines, often from History, but also, to an extent (a growing extent), from Social Anthropology, although it is fair to say that it still tends to be dominated by the careful analysis of *texts* that circulate in these contexts. To the extent that Theology is descriptive in this way, one could think of it as a specialist branch of Religious Studies.

However, Theology does not stop with description, even though this is the starter motor for theological investigation. Take, for instance, Theology's relation to History. Academic theologians spend a good deal of time undertaking a certain kind of intellectual history, patiently uncovering some argumentative discourse that has shaped Christian communities, or circulated among those seeking to shape those communities. Historical investigation uncovers the vocabulary in play, the moves made, in those deliberations and debates – and theologians are undertaking a specialist form of historical investigation while they pursue this. But theologians then take a turn likely to irritate historians: they take the discourse they have uncovered, and after asking, 'What *was* done with this, and how, and why?', they ask, 'What *can be* done with this?'. What ways of thinking does it make possible? How might it be possible to use these forms of deliberation and argument creatively?[4]

There is certainly a distinction here between Theology and Religious Studies, but it is not (or need not be) an opposition.[5] In fact, if our account is right, it means that the fundamental divide in the area of the academic study of religion is not going to be between Theology on the one hand and Religious Studies on the other, but between Theology *with* Religious Studies on the one hand, grounded as they both are in description, and on the other, any kind of approach that tries to answer questions about God and other 'big questions' without reference to the life, beliefs and discourses of actual religious communities. For both Theology and Religious Studies, it seems to us that they becomes less academic, less justifiable as part of a secular university, and less intellectually respectable the less they are engaged in detail with the life of particular religious communities.

Institutional contexts

The proper critical edge of the academic study of Christianity (and other traditions) is not best secured by turning away from engagement with the churches (or other religious communities), nor by adopting a stance of supposed neutrality, but by bringing multiple engagements, multiple perspectives, the discourses of multiple traditions (religious and secular) into conversation with one another. It is Theology and Religious Studies in this engaged and conversational mode that have most to offer to the promotion of rich religious literacy in a plural democracy.

In the remainder of this chapter, we briefly look at a range of institutional settings where the kind of study we have been describing is flourishing, continuing to focus on the theological end of the 'Theology and Religious Studies' spectrum. The first three examples below are all institutions that support forms of Christian theology that are engaged with the churches and yet thoroughly conversational, where descriptive work coexists with the more exploratory, experimental work of constructive theological thinking. These examples were chosen because they illustrate a wide range of possibilities, and because we have first-hand knowledge of them; we could easily have chosen a very different (and far longer) list, but these give an initial sense of some of the locations in which Theology and Religious Studies is making a contribution to religious literacy in the UK today. The fourth and final example, the only one in which we have been employed together, is a programme that has been attempting to contribute directly to the spread of religious literacy from within a Theology and Religious Studies environment.

Society for the Study of Theology

We start on the conference circuit. The Society for the Study of Theology was established in 1952, and has been running annual conferences on themes in Christian theology ever since. The conferences attract both academics working in Theology and related fields, and people with academic expertise and interests working in the Christian churches, from around the UK. The conferences have grown to the point where they normally attract more than 200 attendees. One of us has been attending annual meetings of the society for nearly 40 years, the other for more than 20, and we have seen it go through several phases – although none, perhaps, so vibrant as the present. We do not know of another society quite like it, and in part this is because of the society's ways of relating church and academy. A general description might be that the society is hospitable to members of a range of churches and to many academic approaches, and encourages theological discussion between them and about them. It creates a conversational space where differences as well as similarities can be explored through academic discussion, and critical and constructive theological positions put forward. Meetings of the society gather theological thinkers not only from universities and theological colleges or seminaries, but also from among those who are in various church ministries and in secular employment – and while a willingness to engage seriously with the questions raised by the Christian churches is required of those who attend, there is no restriction on what participants themselves believe or practice.

The society is *de facto* an ecumenical gathering, but it is not a representative gathering where churches are in official dialogue or negotiating their differences, and there is no attempt to reach consensus on the matters discussed. It is, at its best, a venue for intense and argumentative theological conversation, in which the discourses of the churches (past and present) are brought into interaction with one another, with a range of academic disciplines, at the hands of scholars and practitioners and many who live in the overlap between those two circles. There is certainly scope for the widening of its conversations in all these respects, but the liveliness and increasing size of the meetings make it one sign of the vitality of theological exploration in the UK today, and a generator of wider theological literacy.

Durham University

A very different example is provided by Durham University. Durham is an unashamedly secular, plural institution (see Higton, 2013) that is hospitable to unashamedly Christian academics, students and affiliated bodies. Its Department of Theology and Religion is one among many examples of the flourishing of the UK paradigm of Theology and Religious Studies. This combination creates a space where those of different faiths and none can study and think together, and issues of truth and practice, besides those of meaning, description, analysis and explanation, can be addressed both critically and constructively. The questions raised by and between the religions, as well as those raised (in both Religious Studies and theological modes) about the religions, can be pursued together.

The department currently has an annual undergraduate intake of around 70, and a postgraduate population of around 150, but it also works in various ways directly with various churches. This space held open within a secular, plural institution has turned out to be an attractive one for various churches to be linked into, since it connects their Christian theological concerns with those of other faiths and with many academic disciplines, and is an arena where diverse positions in our multireligious and secular society can engage with each other. In recent years the department has endowed a professorship in Catholic Theology and developed a Centre for Catholic Studies, and in this and other ways has cultivated partnerships with churches and their institutions – Roman Catholic, Anglican and Methodist. The Church of England, for instance, has recently awarded Durham the 'Common Awards' contract for validating most of the institutions training people for Anglican ministry in England (and for ministry in other churches working in ecumenical partnership alongside them). In 2015, more than 1,000 students will be taking Common Awards programmes validated by Durham, and that number is projected to rise above 2,000 over the following two years. (One of us now works as the academic lead on Durham's activity in this area.) At the same time, its academic engagement with other faiths, especially Judaism, has grown, as has its sociology and anthropology of religion, and all within a university that has placed considerable emphasis on the sort of interdisciplinary work that suits Theology and Religious Studies well. The stated ethos of the department sums up key characteristics of the UK paradigm at its best: 'We nourish a vibrant community of all faiths and none.... We aim to lead our students to think rigorously and independently both within and beyond their own traditions, and to train students at all levels to think as researchers.'[6]

As regards church and academy, Durham's relationship with more than one church is in line with being home to the Receptive Ecumenism movement, one of the most promising Christian ecumenical developments of recent decades (Murray, 2008). Its initiator, Professor Paul Murray, Director of the Centre for Catholic Studies, has convincingly described the conditions for the Durham developments in terms that are important for this chapter. His key point is that it represents a convergence of factors that have come to maturity. These include the long-term partnerships of the university with churches and other bodies; the transformation in the relationship between Catholic theology (especially lay theology) and the public universities in the UK over the past 40 years; the more general process of maturation of Christian theology in relation to UK universities, mostly in the context of Theology and Religious Studies; and constructive responses by departments of Theology and Religious Studies to contemporary cultural and religious plurality (Murray, 2013).

St Mellitus College

If the Society for the Study of Theology provides a context where church and academy mix, and if Durham provides an academic context that is hospitable to engagement with the churches, our third example is a church initiative that is hospitable to academic engagement. The year 2007 saw the foundation of St Mellitus College, combining St

Paul's Theological Centre, founded in 2005 by Holy Trinity Brompton Anglican Church, and the Church of England Diocese of Chelmsford's North Thames Ministerial Training Course. It is an Anglican initiative that has students and staff from many Christian traditions. It educates Anglican ordinands, church leaders and lay workers in many churches, and independent students interested in Theology. In 2014 it was training about 100 Anglican ordinands, with 500 people taking courses.

Many of its students are full time and also based in local churches so that their theology can be integrated with their work there, theology and ministry being learned together. In some ways, it might be seen as following through on Holy Trinity Brompton's Alpha Courses that have initiated many into Christian faith, by offering further theological education at a number of levels, some more academic in character than others. Like Alpha, it has a global horizon for its theological work, with ambitious plans for online and multimedia forms of education that can be accessed around the world, with a special concern for theology in local churches in many countries. St Mellitus College has already built up a well-qualified staff, attracted some leading UK theologians and scholars to give lectures or courses, introduced academic theology to new constituencies, and found funding for rapid development and for buildings.

We would make two points about this development. First, it is a feat of innovative institutional imagination; it is the outcome of complex negotiations, especially between Holy Trinity Brompton and the Dioceses of London and Chelmsford, and is closely related to their London contexts; it has entailed risks of many sorts, from educational and theological (with some in the church having strong reservations about it) to financial; its wisdom-seeking has sought to combine the more academic and the more practical (while, indeed, recognising the dangers of that distinction), and it has tried to relate Theology to the Arts, the Sciences, Economics, and many spheres of contemporary life; finally, it has reflected theologically on the ecclesial rationale for what it is doing.[7] Second, the flourishing of St Mellitus and St Paul's is heavily dependent on universities, particularly in this country, and especially on their departments of Theology and Religious Studies, for its staff and lecturers, for some of its students, for the literature studied on its courses, and for the general theological climate in which it flourishes.

Cambridge Inter-faith Programme

Our final example is of how Theology and Religious Studies can directly inspire religious literacy initiatives. The Cambridge Interfaith Programme, within which both of us have worked, has its home in the Faculty of Divinity in the University of Cambridge, where the main undergraduate and Master's courses are in Theology and Religious Studies. This faculty has been shaped by a commitment to three responsibilities, primarily towards academic Theology and Religious Studies, and, through that, towards the religious communities and towards society as a whole. Religious literacy is especially part of the latter concern, and has been pursued mainly through two sets of initiatives.[8]

One is the practice of Scriptural Reasoning, for which Cambridge has been one of the chief centres since it began in the mid-1990s. It has mostly involved studying and discussing in small groups the Jewish, Christian and Muslim scriptures, with the scriptures of other traditions being increasingly included in some settings.[9] Scriptures are intrinsic to literacy in these traditions, and the practice of joint study and conversation around them contributes to broadening and deepening understanding, not only of the scriptures of others, but also of one's own. It can also enable forms of collegiality across differences that help in living with long-term problems (of which there are many in the sphere of religions), improving the quality of disagreement. Having begun among academics, Scriptural Reasoning is now practised in many local congregational settings, and in schools, prisons, leadership courses, peacemaking projects, festivals, and so on. There have, for instance, been community Scriptural Reasoning groups in recent years in Birmingham, Blackburn, Bolton, Bradford, Dundee, Durham, Edinburgh, Exeter, Kirkby Stephen, London, Manchester, Preston, St Andrews and York, and the Three Faiths Forum has been running a schools programme reaching around 5,000 students in 70 schools each year. Scriptural Reasoning has flourished best when the connections with the academic practice have been maintained, and so far, the main university resources for it have come through departments of Theology and Religious Studies.[10]

The second is a project aiming at creating in London an inter-faith centre, Coexist House, for public education, exhibitions, meetings and events. Five institutions – the University of Cambridge, the City of London Corporation, the Coexist Foundation, the Inner Temple (one of the Inns of Court where lawyers and judges are educated and based) and the Victoria and Albert Museum – have come together to explore this possibility. At the time of writing it is still in the feasibility study stage, but it has already engaged in religious literacy in several forms, including reaching out to younger generations through festivals and films, building partnerships with cultural and artistic organisations, sponsoring training and learning programmes, and engaging with the Equality and Human Rights Commission, in a partnership led by the Religious Literacy Leadership Programme at Goldsmiths, University of London, in order to take conversations on religious literacy into government, the law, the arts, the media and society at large.

Conclusions

Religious literacy is not simply a matter of learning about the religions. It involves learning patterns of fruitful interaction – engaged, conversational, perhaps argumentative. It involves learning how religious communities argue, and how to join in with those arguments in order to explore agreements and disagreements, and the dynamics by which they can change. It involves engagement with questions raised about, between, by and with the religions.

If this is what real religious literacy involves, then it requires engagement with Theology as well as with Religious Studies – or, better, with Theology and Religious Studies working together, with only a porous and messy boundary between them. And the kind of Theology it requires is the kind we have describing: an academic discourse driven by engagement with the life of the churches – and, analogously, with the life of other religious communities too. The good news is that such Theology is flourishing in the UK at present, in multiple contexts – and the work being done in those contexts has much to offer to those pursuing a religious literacy agenda.

Notes

[1] Earlier versions of parts of this chapter were delivered in David Ford's plenary paper for the 2013 Society for the Study of Theology Conference in Nottingham, and in Mike Higton's paper at the Open University's Conference on 'Contemporary Religion in Historical Perspective: Engaging Outside Academia', also in 2013. See also Ford (2011, chapter 8); and Ford et al (2005).

[2] The current version is QAA for Higher Education (2007).

[3] A glance at the Wikipedia pages for both 'Theology' and 'Religious Studies' and their edit histories (at least up to 23 September 2013) provides some evidence that this is a popular and resilient way of dividing the territory.

[4] Matters are made still more complex by the fact that the discourse being explored might itself encourage or allow various kinds of appeal to history – reference, say, to the history of God's ways with the world, or to God's incarnate presence in history – but

the rules governing those appeals in the context of this discourse are not necessarily the same as the rules governing *Wissenschaftlich* academic history. Nevertheless, the investigation of those appeals – what kinds of appeal are permissible in this discourse, how they work, what might be done with them, how they relate to other forms of attention to history, including the work of academic historians – are a proper task of the theologian.

[5] There can certainly be something of a tension between Religious Studies' tendency to focus on popular practice and belief and Theology's tendency to focus on official discourses, or those that circulate in highly educated circles – but the latter has been significantly qualified by the growth of liberation Theology, and of interest in 'ordinary Theology', and so on.

[6] See the department's web page at www.dur.ac.uk/theology.religion

[7] We are grateful to Dr Graham Tomlin, Dean of St Mellitus and Principal of St Paul's Theological Centre, for sharing a draft paper, 'Theological education and the church', containing his latest theological thinking on its rationale. His main points are that the primary home of Christian Theology is in the church, that theology and church ministry should be learned together while rooted in a local church, and that it requires non-competitive partnerships between church and academy.

[8] For more on the Cambridge Inter-faith Programme, see www.interfaith.cam.ac.uk

[9] For example, in the Institute for Comparative Scripture and Interreligious Dialogue in Minzu University of China, Beijing, where Scriptural Reasoning is done with texts of Judaism, Christianity, Islam, Confucianism, Daoism and Buddhism; elsewhere Hindu and non-religious wisdom texts are used.

[10] In the US the main centre, with doctoral and Master's courses in Scriptural Reasoning, has been the Department of Religion in the University of Virginia, which is unusual in being a state university where Theology and Religious Studies come together. For further reading see www.interfaith.cam.ac.uk/resources/scripturalreasoningresources

References

Ford, D.F. (2007a) *Christian wisdom: Desiring God and learning in love*, Cambridge: Cambridge University Press.

Ford, D.F. (2007b) *Shaping theology: Engagements in a religious and secular world*, Oxford: Blackwell.

Ford, D.F. (2011) *The future of Christian theology*, Oxford: Wiley-Blackwell.

Ford, D.F. Quash, B. and Soskice, J.M. (eds) (2005) *Fields of faith: Theology and Religious Studies for the twenty-first century*, Cambridge: Cambridge University Press.

Higton, M.A. (2012) *A theology of higher education*, Oxford: Oxford University Press.

Higton, M.A. (2013) 'Theological education between the university and the church: Durham University and the Common Awards in theology, ministry and mission', *Journal of Adult Theological Education*, vol 10, no 1, pp 25-37.

Murray, P.D. (ed) (2008) *Receptive ecumenism and the call to Catholic learning: Exploring a way for contemporary ecumenism*, Oxford: Oxford University Press.

Murray, P.D. (2013) 'The shaping of Catholic theology in the UK public academy', in T. Greggs, R. Muers and S. Zahl (eds) *The vocation of theology today: A Festschrift for David Ford*, Eugene, OR: Cascade, pp 330-42.

QAA (Quality Assurance Agency) for Higher Education (2007) *Theology and Religious Studies*, Subject Benchmark Statement, London: QAA (www.qaa.ac.uk/Publications/InformationAndGuidance/Documents/Theology.pdf).

Ross, G.M. (2007) 'Theology and Religious Studies Benchmark Statement Summary', Higher Education Academy Subject Centre for Philosophical and Religious Studies, British Association for the Study of Religions (www.basr.ac.uk/trs_resources/pubs_and_resources/documents/384.htm).

FOUR

The irony of religious illiteracy in the USA

Stephen Prothero and Lauren R. Kerby

In 2010, Pew Research on Religion & Public Life published the results of a survey that had one very clear finding: Americans, for all their religiosity, know very little about their own religions, and even less about those of their neighbours'. While more than 70 per cent of Americans surveyed could identify Mother Theresa as Catholic and Bethlehem as the birthplace of Jesus, only about half of those surveyed could identify Ramadan and the Qur'an as the Islamic holy month and holy book, respectively. Fewer than half knew the religious affiliation of the Dalai Lama, the day of the week on which the Jewish Sabbath begins, and the names of the four Christian Gospels. The lowest scores came on questions concerning the American theologian Jonathan Edwards and the Jewish philosopher Maimonides – only 11 per cent of those surveyed could associate Edwards with the First Great Awakening, while only 8 per cent could identify Maimonides as Jewish. The average respondent answered 16 out of 32 questions correctly, for an average score of 50 per cent (see Pew Research, 2010).

How did such a deeply religious nation sink into such religious illiteracy? At least part of the answer lies in another question on this *US Religious Knowledge Survey*: while 89 per cent of those surveyed know that US law prohibits public school teachers from leading their classes in prayer – the question most frequently answered correctly – only 23 per cent know that the same public school teacher can read from the Bible as an example of literature. This ignorance of the US Constitution when it comes to religion in public schools no doubt contributes to religious illiteracy today, but its roots can be found in many other arenas of American life. Churches, voluntary societies, political organisations and public (state) schools have all played a role in the decline of religious knowledge in America. However, the irony is that each step taken toward the current state of ignorance was a side effect of efforts to strengthen the church. The cumulative effects of these steps toward religious illiteracy have been felt in recent years in the Branch Davidian fiasco in Waco, Texas, in 1993, and in attacks on Sikhs after 9/11. Many leading scholars and educators have realised the adverse effects of religious illiteracy and are working to combat it. This chapter traces the rise of American religious illiteracy, and offers an overview of efforts to repair the damage.

Origins of American religious illiteracy

When asked about the source of religious illiteracy, some Americans point to a pair of Supreme Court decisions from the early 1960s as the main culprits. Those cases, *Engel v Vitale* (1962) and *Abington School District v Schempp* (1963), ruled school-sponsored devotional prayer and Bible reading unconstitutional. Although the Supreme Court prohibited only state-sponsored devotional religious practices in schools, many Americans have erroneously taken this to mean that discussion of religion in any form has been banned from the classroom. But the Supreme Court did not cause American religious illiteracy. While it banned *promotion* of religion by public schools, it did not ban the *study* of religion. In fact, in a famous passage from *Schempp*, it explicitly encouraged this sort of academic study: 'It might well be said that one's education is not complete without a study of comparative religion or the history of religion and its relationship to the advancement of civilization.' In other words, the Court went out of its way to underscore the constitutionality of the academic study of religion. The problem is that far too many American public schools have failed to embrace the Court's suggestion.

A second reason we cannot date American religious illiteracy to the early 1960s is that the processes that produced it were already set in motion more than a century before *Abington v Schempp*. Beginning in the early 19th century, in the midst of the revivals of the Second Great Awakening, evangelical Protestants minimised the importance of their denominational differences for the sake of Christianising the nation. In doing so, they set a pattern that Americans would continue to follow, even as the country became more religiously diverse. This pattern of downplaying differences in order to promote a shared goal manifested again in the 20th century, as Protestants, Catholics and Jews united against 'atheistic communism' during the Cold War, and as Christians, Jews and Muslims reimagined themselves as participants in the Judeo-Christian-Islamic tradition after 9/11. With each of these developments, religious literacy declined. But much of the damage had already been done by 1963. Americans may have mourned the loss of prayers in public schools, but they did not become religiously ignorant overnight.

If we want to understand contemporary American religious illiteracy, we must first understand its origin, and in particular the ways in which the devotion of Americans to tolerance and inclusiveness have caused them to forget much of what they once knew about their own religious traditions.

Protestant America

The first step toward religious illiteracy came in the early 19th century, during the Second Great Awakening. A variety of factors contributed to a dramatic change in how religion was practised, including what Nathan Hatch has called 'religious populism' (Hatch, 1989, p 5). In the aftermath of the American Revolution, Hatch argues, the democratic values that had informed the new American government were now applied to American Protestantism. The will of the people was paramount in both the legislature and the pulpit. Disestablishment of religion in the US gave congregations power over their ministers. The practice of any religion (or none) was now voluntary, and Americans could attend – and tithe to – any church they pleased. Without state support (which ended with the disestablishment of Congregationalism in Massachusetts in 1833), ministers were wholly dependent on their congregations for their salaries; thus, the satisfaction (and entertainment) of churchgoers gained unprecedented importance (Hofstadter, 1969). Like George Whitefield before them, Charles Grandison Finney and the preachers of the Second Great Awakening relied on theatrics to keep their congregations entertained, emphasising stories over doctrine in their sermons, and making churchgoing as emotionally lively as possible. While these techniques may have kept attendance high, they did not make for congregations well versed in the Bible. As a result, the doctrines and practices that once served to differentiate the sects of Protestant Christianity from one another retreated from public consciousness.

By the middle of the 19th century, religious experience had taken precedence over both doctrine and ritual for many American Protestants. One impetus for this, in addition to disestablishment, was a theological shift from Calvinism to Arminianism – from a religion of the head to a religion of the heart. According to historian Richard Hofstadter, the Puritans were the first American intellectuals, and they dismissed as mere 'enthusiasm' any emotional form of religion (1969, p 85). But the evangelicals who emerged in the early 19th century rejected Puritan thought in favour of emotional and experiential religion, and they saw traditional authority and theological training as just one more form of tyranny to be escaped. The result was a movement that Hofstadter calls modern culture's 'most powerful carrier of ... religious anti-intellectualism' (Hofstadter, 1969, p 59). In their quest for religious as well as political liberty, 19th-century evangelicals took pride in their ignorance of the finer points of doctrine, focusing their energies instead on pragmatic efforts to uplift their fellow citizens and to Christianise the nation. Preachers such as Peter Cartwright, a Methodist revivalist who boasted of his own lack of education, encouraged their audiences to feel and to act rather than to think, and to employ ministers who did the same. Too much seminary training would only impede a minister's ability to save souls by bringing them into an authentic, heartfelt relationship with Jesus Christ. Nor was this pervasive anti-intellectualism limited to 'lowbrow' audiences. Such great American intellectuals as Ralph Waldo Emerson and Walt Whitman also saw doctrine as an impediment to true religious experience (Lasch, 1965). Across all strata of American society, the head was subordinated to the heart, and doctrine was pushed aside in favour of experience.

In lieu of doctrine, a new centre was needed for American Protestants. What made a person a Christian if not holding certain beliefs or knowing certain Bible passages? The answer, first for evangelicals and later for liberal Protestants, was loving Jesus, and not the Jesus of tradition, known through catechisms and creeds, but a malleable Jesus who could take on whatever shape was needed at any particular historical moment. Liberals, unsure of the authority of the Bible in the wake of biblical criticism, turned to Jesus as their exemplar; as Kathryn Lofton has argued, Christian modernists employed Jesus as a 'strategic manual' for Christian action in the world (Lofton, 2006, p 381). Similarly, evangelicals and fundamentalists, although they did not reject the authority of scripture, focused more of their energies on building a relationship with Jesus, valuing that relationship above all else (the Bible included). In this way, religious literacy among both liberal and conservative Protestants declined, as it was deemed to be peripheral (or detrimental) to a Christian life that put relating to the person of Jesus at its centre.

In addition to these changes, two other developments helped to institutionalise religious illiteracy in 19th-century America. The first was the emergence of voluntary societies – parachurch organisations dedicated to converting sinners and reforming American society. These societies ranged from the American Home Missionary Society to the

Women's Christian Temperance Union, and almost all of them operated on the principle of non-denominationalism – doctrinal differences between Protestant denominations were left at the door. Members were united by their shared sense of purpose in their society's mission and by their commitment to Protestant essentials, stripped of any and all denominational specifics. Debates over doctrine or rituals were seen as superfluous and distracting from the real work of Christianising the nation. In this way, morality replaced theology as the sine qua non of American Protestantism, which was reduced to simply doing good rather than believing any particular creed or performing any particular ritual. This development, more than any other, helped to foster American religious illiteracy.

Public schools also forced American Protestants to put aside their denominational differences, for both legal and practical reasons. In the 1830s, when public schools were first widespread, Christianity was seen as indispensable to the education of good citizens. By virtue of the Establishment Clause of the First Amendment, these schools could not be sectarian or preach the beliefs or practices of any particular denomination. However, 'non-sectarian' at that time did not mean 'non-religious'. The watered-down Protestantism that served as the official theology for voluntary societies was sufficiently religious to serve the moral needs of students and sufficiently generic that it would not offend the First Amendment as it was interpreted in this period. Basic prayers and readings from the Protestants' King James Bible were encouraged in some classrooms and mandated in others, and the widely used McGuffey readers were replete with biblical language. The key to the acceptability of these religious components in the public schools was their 'non-sectarian' nature. In the eyes of Protestants in power, the religion being taught in schools was hardly religion at all, but rather, basic morality on which all good Americans could agree. Only when denominational particularities intruded did this form of religion become unsuitable for the classroom.

Further fuelling the Protestant tendency to ignore denominational differences in favour of pragmatic unity was the influx of Catholics to America in the mid-19th century. As the number of Catholic immigrants to America skyrocketed, Protestants grew nervous, seeing in Catholicism the union of religious and political power that America's founders had sought to avoid by separating church and state (on Catholic immigration, see Finke and Stark, 2002; on Catholicism and the separation of church and state, see Hamburger, 2002). The principle of religious liberty was thought to be anathema to Catholics and their authoritarian Pope, and the first line of defence against this encroaching tyranny was the supposedly non-sectarian public school, in which Catholic children might be educated (via the King James Bible, no less) into properly American attitudes toward religion and government. When Catholics protested this arrangement as unfair, un-American and unduly Protestant, Protestants felt that their fears had been justified. Riots erupted in Philadelphia in 1844 as Catholics protested the mandatory use of the King James Bible in public schools and Protestants took to the streets to defend it. Although less violent than this Philadelphia conflict, the Cincinnati 'Bible wars' of the 1840s and 1850s were equally emotional, as Protestants accused Catholics of attacking not only the Bible, but the 'Republican institutions and liberties' of America itself. Cincinnati Catholics had proposed that either Catholic schools receive public funding or that the public schools be 'secularised'. In 1870, the Cincinnati Superior Court ruled that the schools should be neither sectarian nor secularised; the middle ground the Court found was a generic Protestantism that used the King James Bible in the guise of non-sectarianism. This pattern then proceeded across the US: in order to maintain public schools that taught 'American' values, Protestants were compelled to minimise their denominational differences in order to tread a middle path between sectarianism and secularisation. The long-term result of these Bible wars was that religious illiteracy, disguised as non-sectarianism, was institutionalised in the public schools over the course of the 19th century.

By the end of the 19th century, American Protestantism had undergone a dramatic change: from established to voluntary, from heady to heartfelt, and from Bible-centric to Jesus-centric. Even as these developments made Protestantism more accessible and entertaining, they further diminished the importance of distinctive doctrines and practices; and as they were institutionalised through voluntary societies and public schools, knowledge of one's own religious tradition – not to mention those of others – was no longer seen as essential. The changes that had been intended to strengthen Protestantism had the side effect of teaching future generations that religious particularities simply did not matter.

Triple Melting Pot

In the 20th century, religious illiteracy was further reinforced by a new form of non-sectarianism, the 'Judeo-Christian tradition', that emerged first in the 1930s, driven in part by the desire of American Jews and Christians to ally against 'the Antichrist trinity of Hitler, Stalin, and

Mussolini' of John Cournos' *Open letter to Jews and Christians* (Prothero, 2002). In the postwar period, this alliance united against a new enemy: 'godless communism'. Just as denominational differences between Protestants had been downplayed in the previous century, the doctrinal and ritual differences between these three religions were now deemed less significant than their agreement on monotheism, the authority of the Bible, and morality as enshrined in the Ten Commandments. Religion in general was seen as essential to American citizenship, but the particularities of any one religion were seen as irrelevant (so long as they fit under the Judeo-Christian canopy). President Eisenhower famously captured this theme when he stated that, "our form of government has no sense unless it is founded in a deeply felt religious faith, and I don't care what it is." While this triple melting pot, as sociologist Will Herberg described it, is more inclusive than an exclusively Protestant America, the melting pot approach in all its varieties requires that the distinctions between religions be publicly (and perhaps privately) ignored. If all that matters are the few similarities between traditions, Americans have no motivation to learn the unique content of their own religions and of those around them.

This same lowest-common-denominator approach to religion pervaded American public schools until the 1960s. Religion was a regular part of school in many states, as students began their school day by reading the Bible 'without note or comment' and reciting vaguely monotheistic prayers. Morality was the important thing; the specifics of any one religion were unimportant so long as schoolchildren learned how to be good people and moral citizens. This meant that religious exercises in the classroom could be all but content-free in an effort to please all the Christians and Jews involved. The prayer at issue in *Engel v Vitale* (1962) provides a perfect example of this variety of religion reduced to its lowest common denominator: 'Almighty God, we acknowledge our dependence upon Thee, and we beg Thy blessings upon us, our parents, our teachers and our country.' These bland 22 words were intended to be acceptable to 'all men and women of good will', which at the time obviously excluded American polytheists and atheists. The prayer, controversial as it turned out to be, did not teach students any sort of substantive content about any religion. Religious exercises of this sort, far from maintaining religious literacy, actually contributed to its decline by attempting to find common ground free of all particularities. In this way, students were taught that the theological and ritual facts of any religion were incidental and unimportant.

A third development contributing to religious illiteracy in 20th-century America was the close association between religion and politics that began in the 1970s and remains powerful today. The so-called Moral Majority (established in 1979) defined itself by its conservative politics and its Judeo-Christian beliefs, in that order. Although it was spearheaded predominantly by evangelical and fundamentalist Christians, the Moral Majority was also open to conservative Catholics and Orthodox Jews who shared the political goals of its evangelical leaders. While this was a politically effective move, it, too, came at the cost of attention to Protestant, Catholic and Jewish particularities. Like 19th-century voluntary associations working to Christianise the nation, the Moral Majority emphasised political goals over doctrinal differences.

Since the heyday of the Moral Majority in the 1980s, Americans have increasingly correlated politics with religion. As sociologist Robert Wuthnow has shown, liberal Protestants have more in common with liberal Catholics than with conservative Protestants, and conservative Catholics share more with conservative Protestants than with liberal Catholics (Wuthnow, 1988). In short, the 'fault line' in American religion is now political rather than denominational (Putnam and Campbell, 2010). This tendency to ally with those who share political but not religious principles further reinforces the tendency to avoid or ignore religious differences in the name of political pragmatism. The result is a politically active but religiously illiterate population.

Multireligious America in the 21st century

The characteristics that fostered religious illiteracy in the 19th and 20th centuries still pervade American religion today. Evangelical megachurches, the largest religious groups in the US, are typically 'seeker-friendly', that is, not so full of doctrinal jargon as to be off-putting to the newcomer, and their worship services are increasingly inclined toward entertainment over Bible study, although to varying degrees. And in the competitive spiritual marketplace that is America in the 21st century, non-Christian groups find themselves competing, too, offering 'Buddhism without beliefs' (in the name of one popular book) on the theory that Americans don't want to take their Asian religions neat.

Meanwhile, the desire to present a unified political front across religious groups has not diminished, although the opponent has changed. Where Protestants once united in the face of a perceived Catholic threat, conservatives from a variety of American religions now unite in the face of perceived persecution from a secular government and from liberals and the non-religious. The means of unification, however, look the same. Since doctrinal differences would shatter any coalition if they were ever deemed sufficiently important to be emphasised, doctrine is ignored in favour of a shared commitment to a conservative brand of morality and a shared vision of religion's proper role in society. Most recently, in the 2012 battle over insurance coverage of contraceptives, conservative Protestants joined with conservative Catholics to oppose President Obama's mandate that religious institutions such as hospitals, universities and charities offer contraceptive coverage to their female employees. Although American evangelicals have rarely opposed contraception (unlike their fervent opposition to abortion), they took the side of Catholics against the government because of their shared view that religious liberty was under attack. Doctrine was never the unifying issue; conservative Protestants and Catholics were joined by a shared moral and political agenda.

A similar instance of valuing political and moral similarities over doctrinal and ritual differences is the unlikely alliance of Mormons and evangelical Christians that brought Mitt Romney the Republican nomination in the 2012 presidential election. Mormonism had been listed as a cult on the website of celebrity American evangelist Billy Graham, until a timely visit from Romney in October 2012 garnered Graham's endorsement and caused Mormonism to be removed from that list. Further evidence of Republicans' desire to downplay religious differences among conservatives came in the surprising lack of attention paid during the campaign to Romney's faith. One might think that a Mormon run for the White House would be an opportunity to educate Americans about Mormonism, given the fact that only half of Americans can identify Joseph Smith as a Mormon. However, throughout his campaign, Romney remained tight-lipped about the beliefs and practices of Latter-day Saints (Mormons), focusing instead on the 'family values' he shares with the evangelicals who dominate the GOP (Republican Party). The strategy seems to have worked: although Romney lost the election, he won the vote of 79 per cent of white American evangelicals, the same percentage won by George W. Bush in 2004. This expedient ignorance of religious differences, although politically useful, remains a powerful contributor to religious illiteracy today.

Finally, just as the desire for inclusiveness fostered religious illiteracy in the 19th and 20th centuries, so, too, does the language of 'multireligious America' or 'Abrahamic America' in the 21st. The players may have changed since the days of non-sectarianism and the triple melting pot, but the principle is the same: the similarities among America's religious citizens matter, while their differences do not. Some might argue that attempts to include America's religious minorities, such as President Obama's mention of America as 'a nation of Christians and Jews, Muslims and Hindus – and non-believers' in his first inaugural address, are more important than calling attention to the religious differences that could potentially divide Americans. Although such statements readily discard the particularities of each tradition in favour of a vague moral uniformity, perhaps, in the end, the benefit of religious tolerance is worth the price of religious illiteracy. Sociologists Robert Putnam and David Campbell have recently referred to this approach as 'America's grace', since it allows Americans to make their judgements about those of other faiths based on social interactions rather than religious teachings. Such arguments on behalf of religious illiteracy can sound compelling; after all, few long to return to the days of sectarian strife and interreligious warfare.

Despite this, religious literacy does not have to come at the price of religious harmony. As current efforts across the United States show, religious literacy can foster tolerance, too. The remainder of this chapter details how certain American organisations are teaching about religion in a way that encourages respect for religious differences and for religious liberty, ideally producing citizens who are both informed and tolerant at the same time.

Improving American religious literacy in the 21st century

In the US today, the driving force behind religious literacy is the conviction that Americans must know something about Christianity and other religions if they are to be effective citizens. According to advocates for religious literacy, in order to responsibly participate in the democratic process and in civic life, Americans must know something about the beliefs and practices of their neighbours, and about the Protestant Christianity that continues to occupy a large portion of the public square. It is commonplace – almost necessary – for politicians to quote the Christian Bible in speeches, and nearly every presidential address ends with some version of 'God Bless America'. In spite of the separation of church and state, the Protestant legacy lingers – not least in presidential rhetoric. So effective citizenship requires a basic knowledge of the Bible and of Protestant beliefs and practices. At the same time, it is equally important for citizens to be informed about a much wider range of world religions, from Sikhism to Sufism. As pluralism scholar Diana Eck has pointed out, Muslims and Hindus are no longer far away in Pakistan and India, but next door, in Boston and Des Moines. Moreover, in our increasingly interconnected world, religious literacy is required to make sense of events abroad as well as at home. As voters and citizens, Americans need to be able to understand the dynamics of world events, which often requires knowing something about Judaism, Christianity and Islam in the Middle East, for example, or about Hinduism and Islam in Kashmir. In short, advocates for religious literacy are convinced that whether Americans are at the polls or at the supermarket, they need to be conversant in Christianity and the world's religions.

These goals are complicated, however, by the ongoing culture wars. Conservative Republicans and liberal Democrats routinely disagree on how the Bible or the world's religions should be taught in public schools, or if it should be taught at all. Religious conservatives fear that their children will be exposed to relativism and led astray, while liberals fear that fundamentalists will hijack Religion courses in order to indoctrinate unsuspecting students into conservative Christianity. These fears surface in every debate about religious education in public schools, and it is a difficult task to please both sides. Yet, if the right approach is taken, both conservatives and liberals can be satisfied with a Religious Studies course. Conservatives want children to study the Bible, even if it is in Religious Studies rather than a devotional context, while liberals want children to learn about the world's religions in order to foster tolerance. Including both approaches in a single course (on, say, scriptures of the world) has the benefit of pleasing both the religious right and the secular left, despite the volatile atmosphere of the American culture wars.

Since 9/11, American educators and scholars of religion have become increasingly concerned with religious illiteracy. While there is no single way to solve this problem, one of the most direct ways to address it is to take the Supreme Court's suggestion from 50 years ago to include the study of religion in public schools. Across the country, several efforts are already underway to add the topic of religion to public school curricula, either in stand-alone courses or as supplements to existing courses. There are many challenges to be overcome, however, including budget cuts in schools, the proliferation of high-stakes testing, and a troubled economy that causes students and parents to think of education as simply a means to a job. Teachers and administrators must also combat the lingering sense that such efforts are unconstitutional, since only 36 per cent of Americans know that a public school teacher may teach a course comparing world religions, and only 23 per cent know that a public school teacher may read from the Bible or another scripture as an example of literature.

Yet another obstacle is the fact that there are so few resources available to public school teachers who do want to teach about religion. Although there are competing curricula for Bible as Literature courses, there is no nationally distributed curriculum for a high school course on the world's religions. Teachers face the dual challenge of being unsure of how to broach this topic without running foul of the First Amendment and of having taken few Religious Studies courses of their own in college or graduate school. In order to improve their students' religious literacy, teachers must first improve their own, which takes time and resources that are not always readily available. Since the 1960s, a variety of efforts have been made to fill this gap by providing literature addressing legal concerns about religion in the classroom as well as curriculum content and resources for lesson planning.

In the years following *Abington v Schempp*, America saw a wave of interest in teaching about religion in public schools, since, as Justice Clark had said, no proper education could be said to be complete without it. Liberals and conservatives reached an uneasy compromise: conservatives realised that Religious Studies was the closest they could come to the Sunday School-style religion education of the pre-1963 era, while liberals were willing to endorse the academic study of religion in the name of diversity, so long as it remained strictly academic. Several states implemented Religious Studies courses as electives, including Florida and Pennsylvania. The National Council on Religion and Public Education was founded in 1971 to promote the academic study of religion in public schools and to disseminate materials for that purpose. In 1972, Harvard Divinity School founded its Program in Religion and Secondary Education (PRSE) as a training programme for teachers. Nonetheless, the movement lost momentum. Tepid support from liberal and conservative groups, each of whom would have preferred a different approach to religion in public schools, faded, and by the 1980s, the movement had largely died out.

In the late 1980s, a new wave of interest in Religious Studies emerged, according to religion and education expert Dr Charles Haynes of the First Amendment Center. Two textbook trials called attention to the lack of religion in the curriculum, sparking several studies that demonstrated just how absent religion had become (*Mozert v Hawkins County Board of Education*, 1987, and *Smith v Board of School Commissioners of Mobile County*, 1987). Paul Vitz famously found that 'pilgrim' was defined in one textbook as 'someone who makes long trips' (Vitz, 1986, pp 18-19). This renewed interest, coupled with the passing of the Equal Access Act in 1984, allowing religious clubs in schools, demanded a major rethinking of how religion figured in public schools. In 1988, the first edition of *Finding common ground: A guide to religious liberty in the public schools* appeared, written and edited by Charles Haynes and Oliver Thomas of the First Amendment Center. This consensus statement was signed by a diverse range of groups, including the National Association of Evangelicals, the Church of Jesus Christ of Latter-day Saints, Americans United for Separation of Church and State, the American Federation of Teachers, and the National Parent-Teacher Association. *Finding common ground* shares some of the language of the Williamsburg Charter, another consensus document published in 1988, and the guidelines it lays out continue to be used by school districts and the courts.

Efforts continued throughout the 1990s to publish a definitive set of guidelines for teaching about religion in American public schools. In 1999, every principal in the US received a memo from the Department of Education reminding them that 'public schools may teach about religion – for example, in classes on history, music, the arts, or comparative religion, the Bible (or other scripture)-as-literature, the role of religion in history – but public schools may not provide religious instruction'. The terrorist attacks of September 11, 2001, further galvanised interest in this topic as teachers and administrators realised overnight that Islam was an important subject to study, no matter what religion you happened to practice. Yet there remains a growing need for detailed guidelines regarding what is and is not permissible to teach in public schools, as well as for resources providing content for a Religious Studies curriculum.

One organisation that has worked to provide teachers with the training and resources they need to teach about religion is the Religion and Public Education Project (RPEP) at California State University, Chico (Chico State). The primary focus of RPEP, founded in 1995 by Dr Bruce Grelle, is providing resources and training for teachers regarding the legal and ethical concerns involved in teaching about religion in public schools. The First Amendment's two clauses about religion – prohibiting establishment and guaranteeing free exercise – are applied to specific situations teachers will face in a classroom in order to help them understand how to provide effective instruction while remaining within constitutional boundaries. RPEP helps to prepare current teachers through professional development seminars and future teachers through pre-service training at Chico State. Since 1997, Chico State has offered a course titled Religion in American Public Schools, designed to familiarise future teachers with legal guidelines for teaching about religion and to teach them the basics of several major world religions. Because California standards specifically require attention to the role of religion in American and world history classes, the need for properly prepared teachers is clear.

RPEP at Chico State is also active in California's version of the 3 R's Project, a programme sponsored by the First Amendment Center that currently exists in California and Utah. The programme is designed to address the challenges of religious diversity by teaching the 3 R's – rights, responsibility and respect. Based on the 1988 *Finding common ground* guidelines, this programme offers training sessions for public school teachers, administrators and community members. Religious liberty is the centrepiece of the project – educators are taught how to engage students in constructive dialogue so that they learn to defend their own religious liberty and that of others. The California version of the project also offers online curriculum resources for teachers looking for help in adding religion to their lesson plans. The 3 R's Project offers a constructive way to engage religious differences in the classroom. The resources and training they provide are invaluable in helping teachers in California and Utah to navigate the legal labyrinth of Religious Studies that too many other states simply avoid.

Despite these efforts and the increasing interest in religion in public schools, it was not until 2007 that the American Academy of Religion (AAR), the trade association for Religious Studies in the US, began work on a set of guidelines that would apply the expertise of Religious Studies scholars to primary and secondary education, as is typical in many other fields, including History and Literature. The AAR's *Guidelines for teaching about religion in K-12 public schools in the United States* (2010) is based on the premises that religious illiteracy is widespread; that it leads to antagonism and prejudice and hinders respect for diversity; and that teaching about religion in public schools is an effective way to address these challenges. After making this concise case for why religion should be taught, the report lays out the boundaries of what is and is not constitutionally permissible in a public school classroom. These boundaries include 'encouraging student *awareness* of religions, but *not acceptance* of a particular religion; studying *about* religion, but *not practicing* religion; *exposing* students to a diversity of religious views, but *not imposing* any particular view; and *educating* students about all religions, but *not promoting or denigrating* religion' (AAR, 2010, p i). These are the guiding principles that religion scholars can recite from memory with little effort; however, precisely what teachers must do to remain on the constitutional side of each binary may not be so clear to someone with no Religious Studies training (AAR, 2010).

To fill that gap, the AAR report suggests specific strategies for teaching about religion. For instance, it recommends beginning a discussion by asking students (and teachers) to acknowledge the assumptions they already make about religion, and whether those assumptions are accurate. This can help students to move away from a familiar, devotional approach to religion to a more objective Religious Studies approach. Other concrete strategies are revealed in 'Snapshots of Practice', which provide examples of how concepts such as the internal diversity of a religious tradition can be taught, or how a teacher can help students to understand how a tradition has changed over time. Equally valuable are the 'Frequently Asked Questions' – hypothetical student questions with suggested answers. Difficult questions such as 'Is God real?' or 'Did the Jews kill Jesus?' or 'Is Islam a violent religion?' are given thoughtful responses appropriate for the classroom, in the hope of alleviating teachers' fears of sparking controversy by answering them. Finally, the report lists content knowledge and pedagogical competencies that are important for teachers preparing to teach about religion, and suggests that teachers participate in workshops or seminars, some of which are sponsored by the AAR, or take Religious Studies classes where available. The overall goal of the AAR *Guidelines* is to make the case to teachers and administrators that teaching about religion is both important and possible. Unfortunately, the AAR stopped short of creating a free-standing Religious Studies curriculum that could be used in schools, preferring instead to advocate for the inclusion of religion in existing Literature and Social Studies classes.

Building on the AAR *Guidelines* is the newly founded Religious Literacy Project (RLP). Based at Harvard Divinity School, the project is directed by Diane Moore, whose chapter in this volume sets out her analysis and approach, and who also chaired the AAR task force responsible for creating the *Guidelines*. The project is a web-based resource centre that both creates and curates curriculum supplements on the religious dimensions of topics already commonly taught in public schools. It is currently in the early stages of development; the website is scheduled to go live in February 2015. In addition to multimedia and curriculum supplements, the programme also conducts research into how religion is already being taught in public schools across the country, and maintains a blog about current events in religion that teachers can use in the classroom. The information and resources on the website are also intended to aid journalists, business leaders, politicians and policy-makers in developing their own religious literacy. The overall aim of the website, as stated in the Statement of Purpose in March 2013, is to enable all users to 'adopt a more sophisticated, educated and thought-provoking way of engaging with the various manifestations of religion on the ground' and 'make more informed decisions in whatever sphere of life they operate in.'

The programme's strategy for teaching about religion relies on a 'cultural studies' approach, which is built on three premises, as Chapter Two of this volume sets out: '(1) religions are internally diverse; (2) religions are dynamic and changing; and (3) religions are embedded in all spheres of human experience and not isolated in private expression or ritual practice'. Demonstrating these characteristics of religion through the resources they collect and create is a central concern of researchers. Videos designed for classroom use include a range of perspectives on the same issue from adherents of the same religion. Similarly, curriculum supplements are designed to show that religious traditions are not static, but change over time. Most importantly, the programme's resources are designed to help teachers integrate discussions of religion into existing curricula. Rather than creating stand-alone units or courses on religion, the programme offers short lesson plans and activities that will help teachers and students to understand the connections between religion and history or literature. Too many of today's textbooks, when they address religion at all, treat religious developments as something occurring without connection to politics or society; the programme curriculum supplements show how religion is culturally embedded, both shaping and being shaped by the surrounding culture.

The cultural studies approach, advocated by both the AAR and the Religious Literacy Project, has benefits and drawbacks. Advocates of the cultural studies approach (and its predecessor from the 1970s and 1980s, 'natural inclusion') argue that to separate religion out from the rest of the curriculum is to distort its natural connections to other spheres of life. Moreover, they argue, teachers of Literature and History are already teaching about religion by default, since religion is embedded in both subjects; what is needed is to make the religious content of the curriculum more explicit and to prepare teachers to discuss it openly rather than skipping past it to more familiar territory. However, Religious Studies scholars are divided on this issue, with some arguing that in today's already crowded curriculum, trying to squeeze religion into existing Literature or History courses is a recipe for either ignoring the topic or treating it superficially. To gain anything more than a superficial understanding of a religion requires a systematic effort, and there are simply not enough days in the school year to include religion among the countless other topics already deemed essential to a proper education in History or Literature. The solution for those on this side of the debate is to create a stand-alone Religion course, to be offered at the very least as an elective, if not as a required course. Such a course would be able to spend more than a day or two on Hinduism and Buddhism, and would be better suited to address the complex histories and internal diversity of the world's religions.

Stand-alone Religion courses are becoming more common in the US, but they remain few and far between, largely because of the limitations of school budgets and the already substantial demands on both teachers and students' time. However, as a 2007 study of a mandatory World Religions course for ninth graders in Modesto, California, showed, a stand-alone Religion course can go far in building both religious literacy and tolerance. The Modesto World Religions course was intended to make the city's many ethnic and religious minorities feel included in the community by representing their views and history in the curriculum; it also aimed to dispel the hostility the community's religious conservatives felt was directed at them and their beliefs (see Lester and Roberts, 2009). Under the leadership of Charles Haynes of the First Amendment Center, a team of teachers, college professors, outside consultants and administrators, with the help of an advisory council of local religious leaders, designed a nine-week course that would be required of all students in the district. Before the school year started, teachers of the new course underwent extensive training, attending seminars and lectures and reading books on both the content they would be teaching and the history and meaning of religious liberty. The goal was to simultaneously improve students' understanding of religious liberty and their religious literacy.

The history of religious freedom and freedom of conscience in America was the topic of the first two weeks of the course. These principles then served as a framework for students to approach the remainder of the course, which addressed Hinduism, Buddhism, Confucianism, Sikhism, Judaism, Christianity and Islam. To avoid controversy, teachers were instructed to be strictly descriptive, rather than comparative, focusing on dates, geography and historical and contemporary practices. Neutrality toward all religions studied was considered paramount. The result was what Emile Lester and Patrick Roberts, the authors of the Modesto study, describe as 'a Benetton world of many colors flavor to world religion' (Lester and Roberts, 2009, p 190). They note that this failure to address issues such as violence, attitudes toward women, or 'dangerous fanaticism and repression of vulnerable social groups' is a missed opportunity to give students a more balanced view of religions (Lester and Roberts, 2009, pp 190, 196). However, the approach did improve students' religious literacy as well as their religious tolerance. On a religious knowledge quiz, the average student score rose from 37 per cent before the course to 66 per cent afterwards (p 196). As for tolerance, before the course, the mean number of students who said they would 'defend a student whose religious beliefs were insulted by another student' was 55.6 per cent; after the course, this mean had risen to 65.1 per cent. Similarly, students who took the course demonstrated an increased willingness to extend political rights, such as free speech or holding public office, to a group they most disliked. And despite the fears of some critics, there was no statistically significant change in the number of students who said that one religion – theirs – was right and others were wrong. The combination of lessons about freedom of conscience and about other religions seems to have had a beneficial effect on student tolerance in Modesto, while causing little or no harm to the faith of individual students

Perhaps the most remarkable feature of the Modesto World Religions course is the lack of controversy it caused. Despite having what Lester and Roberts call 'all the elements of a perfect American cultural storm', at the time of their 2007 study, the course had not been challenged in court. Liberals and evangelicals found an overlapping consensus that pleased both sides. In Modesto, parents can choose to have their children opt out of the course, but this option is rarely exercised. Keeping all interested parties informed throughout the process of designing and implementing the course was essential to averting conflict; equally important was discerning, and then delivering, what liberals and conservatives each wanted from the course. Conservatives wanted to be able to talk about religion in schools instead of feeling that it was taboo, while liberals wanted students to learn and practice tolerance. The balance of religious knowledge and respect for religious freedom in the course met the needs of both groups and helped to ward off a potential culture war. Both the course itself and the process by which it was created and introduced provide excellent examples of how religious literacy can be successfully cultivated in American public schools, despite the many daunting challenges.

In addition to World Religions courses, the other major type of stand-alone Religion course is the Bible as Literature. Proponents of Religious Studies in schools have often argued that a working knowledge of the Bible is essential to understanding Western literature and Western politics. The National Council on Religion and Public Education produced handbooks and lesson plans for Bible as Literature courses beginning in the 1970s, but by 2005 a survey showed that only 8 per cent of high school students had access to an elective Bible course. Since it is unlikely that the remaining 92 per cent of students are receiving much instruction elsewhere in the Bible's content, history and contemporary influence, the need for Bible as Literature courses is clear. A variety of groups provide curricular materials for such courses, although fail to clear the constitutional bar. Those that lean toward a conservative Protestant reading of the Bible, such as that of the National Council on Bible Curriculum in Public Schools, have been repeatedly deemed unconstitutional by Bible scholars and the courts.

Other organisations are working to develop more appropriate materials to meet the needs of school districts that offer elective Bible courses. The most prominent of these is the Bible Literacy Project (BLP), founded by Chuck Stetson and Richard Scurry. In partnership with the First Amendment Center, the BLP published *The Bible in the public schools: A First Amendment guide* (First Amendment Center, 1999), which provided guidelines endorsed by a variety of liberal and conservative religious organisations. In addition, and with the support of Concordia University in Portland, Oregon, the BLP offers an online training programme for high school teachers who teach the Bible in public schools. The BLP also published – to mixed reviews – a textbook intended for use in public classrooms: *The Bible and its influence* (Schippe and Stetson, 2005). Some conservative religious groups have found it to be too liberal, while some liberal groups criticised Stetson's conservative religious and political affiliations. Yet the overlapping consensus between liberals and conservatives applies here just as it did in Modesto. Liberals find the BLP's textbook preferable to more overtly evangelical curricula, while conservatives prefer teaching the Bible in this way to not teaching it at all. An ideal Bible as Literature course has yet to be developed, but knowledge of the Bible is an essential part of religious literacy.

Current efforts to improve religious literacy in America revolve primarily around preparing teachers to teach about religion in the public schools so that the current generation of students grows up to be religiously literate citizens. Assistance is now available to teachers in two areas: *how* to teach about religion in a constitutionally sound way, as exemplified by the AAR's *Guidelines* and Chico State's RPEP; and *what* to teach about religion, as exemplified by Harvard's Religious Literacy Project and the Modesto World Religions course. There are also two models of how to integrate religion into public schools: through stand-alone courses or through supplements to existing courses. Each has its strengths, but for either to succeed, teachers must be adequately prepared to teach about religion in a way that passes constitutional muster, and there must be consistent communication with parents and the local community to avoid legal controversies. The task remaining is to convince school boards, administrators and teachers that it is worth their time to make use of these valuable resources.

Conclusion

In their 2010 study *American grace: How religion divides and unites us*, sociologists Robert Putnam and David Campbell found that 89 per cent of Americans believe that people of other faiths can still go to heaven. Even when asked the follow-up question of whether or not that is true if the other faith in question is not Christian, the percentage of respondents who answered yes remains high, with 89 per cent of Catholics, 82 per cent of mainline Protestants, and 98 per cent of Mormons saying 'yes'. The numbers drop slightly for more conservative groups, but 69 per cent of Black Protestants and 65 per cent of evangelicals agree that non-Christians can go to heaven (pp 535-6). Putnam and Campbell (2010) interpret this as a sort of American ecumenism in which social relationships with those of other faiths trump church teachings that would condemn those people to hell. Such disregard for doctrine, they argue, is precisely what allows America to be both religiously devout and religiously diverse. Is this a form of ecumenism? Perhaps it is, but it is also a manifestation of religious illiteracy. Even in the unlikely case that survey respondents were aware of traditional Christian teachings about who can enter heaven, they chose to ignore those teachings as unimportant. Their education, both in school and in church, has taught them that doctrinal and ritual particularities are insignificant and easily dismissed.

The lingering question is whether religious illiteracy is the price Americans are willing to pay for religious harmony. Religious knowledge does not automatically lead to religious tolerance; indeed, in some cases it has the potential to lead to intolerance and even violence. But religious literacy can also lead to a more robust tolerance, particularly for minority religious groups who do not fit into the Protestant model that has dominated American religious history. The organisations we have discussed show that it is not necessary to elide religious differences in order to peacefully coexist. Religious literacy has been sacrificed on the altar of tolerance for nearly two centuries in America, but one does not preclude the other. Ignorance is a cheap grace at best; the tolerance that comes with religious literacy comes at a higher price, but it is a far better investment.

References

AAR (American Academy of Religion) (2010) *The American Academy of Religion guidelines for teaching about religion in K-12 public schools in the United States*, Atlanta, GA: AAR.

Finke, R. and Stark, R. (2002) 'The coming of the Catholics, 1850-1926', in R. Finke and R. Stark, *The churching of America: Winners and losers in our religious economy*, New Brunswick, NJ: Rutgers University Press, pp 117-55.

First Amendment Center (1999) *The Bible and the public schools: A First Amendment guide*, Nashville, TN: First Amendment Center.

Hamburger, P. (2002) *The separation of church and state*, Cambridge, MA: Harvard University Press.

Hatch, N. (1989) *The democratization of American Christianity*, New Haven, CT: Yale University Press.

Haynes, C. and Thomas, O.(1988/2007) *Finding common ground: A guide to religious liberty in public schools. Nashville*, TN: First Amendment Center.

Hofstadter, R. (1969) *Anti-intellectualism in American life*, New York: Knopf.

Lasch, C. (1965) 'The anti-intellectualism of the intellectuals', in C. Lasch (ed) *The new radicalism in America, 1889-1963*, New York: Knopf, pp 286-349.

Lester, E. and Roberts, P.S. (2009) 'How teaching world religions brought a truce to the culture wars in Modesto, California', *British Journal of Religious Education*, vol 31, no 3, September, p 189.

Lofton, K. (2006) 'The methodology of the modernists: process in American Protestantism', *Church History*, vol 75, no 2, June, pp 390-1.

Pew Research (2010) *US Religious Knowledge Survey*, Washington, DC: Pew Research, Religion & Public Life (www.pewforum.org/2010/09/28/u-s-religious-knowledge-survey).

Prothero, S. (2002) *American Jesus: How the son of God became a national icon*, New York: Farrar, Straus, and Giroux.

Putnam, R. and Campbell, D. (2010) *American grace: How religion divides and unites us*, New York: Simon & Schuster.

Schippe, C. and Stetson, C. (2005) *The Bible and its influence*, New York, NY: BLP Publishing.

Vitz, P. (1986) *Censorship: Evidence of bias in our children's textbooks*, Ann Arbor, MI: Servant Press.

Wuthnow, R. (1988) *The restructuring of American religions: Society and faith since World War II*, Princeton, NJ: Princeton University Press.

FIVE

Religious literacy as *lokahi*: social harmony through diversity

Michael Barnes SJ and Jonathan D. Smith

Introduction

The concept of literacy has become a well-used term of late, applied to over 30 areas of study and practice, ranging from the functional (financial, digital) to the description of current trends (emotional, environmental) and the more abstract (philosophical, critical). Like many of these, religious literacy is an attempt to define and modernise a pursuit for understanding our world that is as ancient as creation stories. In this chapter we look at one such traditional model – at once ancient and yet new in the sense that it seeks to renew and re-energise one of the most important of contemporary debates.

The chapter is divided into three sections. The first articulates the ancient philosophical concept of *lokahi* from its Hawaiian roots to its post-modern relevance. The second engages with four key aspects of the definition of religious literacy as proposed by Dinham and Jones (2010), and proposes a contested definition of religious literacy as *lokahi*, in response. The third presents three case studies of religious literacy in practice in different professional contexts and continents. A brief conclusion brings us back to the 'new' contribution that an ancient tradition can offer to the contemporary world.

Concept of *lokahi*

The Lokahi Foundation, like many interreligious organisations that have sprung up in the UK in recent years, aims to deepen public understanding of religion and increase its sophistication. Most agencies recognise that the promotion of religious literacy as a civic practice, while neither simple nor straightforward, is primarily a matter of broadening the sense of human religiosity as a significant phenomenon for all spheres of modern society. *Lokahi*, however, is distinctive in seeing religious diversity not as a problem to be managed but as an inevitable and rich source of human diversity. In probing the foundations of religious beliefs and values of all kinds, *lokahi* begins with the conviction that diversity is inherent in individuals and communities of faith. The task is not to elide but to value difference and embrace it as part of working with others for the common good.

Simply put, the concept of *lokahi* means 'harmony through diversity'. It draws on and weaves together a number of ideas. The most remote, yet arguably the most important, is the religious culture of Hawaii and, quite literally, the Hawaiian geology and the volcanic landscape that supports it. The Lokahi Foundation's founding director, Gwen Griffith-Dickson, recalls her own experience of growing up there:

> There was a place we used to call Desolation Trail, cinders and ash and fragments of lava rock, with just a wooden walkway through it. When I was back there last year it had grown. Desolation had turned into rainforest. That principle – the reality that you see in nature and you see in environments, with different species coming together – is what the Hawaiians illustrated or labelled *lokahi*. (Griffith-Dickson, 2006, para 2)

The image of nature ever transforming itself, as tiny ferns and more substantial trees take root and flourish, acts as a sort of parable of the rich ecology of human living. It raises a new possibility, that different people, with different backgrounds, interests and concerns, can come together and create something new, even though they will never be the same, because the shared task of keeping the whole eco-system in being is itself creative and life-giving.

The *lokahi* idea that diversity is itself necessary for social harmony, and that people flourish when difference is acknowledged rather than suppressed, is supported by the recovery of philosophical and theological principles that pre-date debates about modernity, the secular and the autonomy of reason. This takes the *lokahi* account of diversity in a very different direction from the normative pluralism associated with John Hick. The philosophical grounding of Hick's (1973) vision of the 'universe of faiths', in which religions revolve planet-like around God or the Real, is worked out in terms of a Kantian distinction between the unknowable noumenon (that which cannot be grasped by the senses) and the phenomena of everyday experience (Hick, 2004). This makes for a plausible account of the plurality of religions, but depends on a liberal modern foundationalism that relies on the construction of some generic essence of religion. This generic essence not only obliterates important distinctions between the ways in which religions in all their fluidity have played out in real interactions; it also sets up an unhelpful dichotomy between traditional faith communities and the so-called secular and non-religious world of 'the West'. Religion is either reduced to a set of beliefs in other-worldly realities, or elided to 'mere' cultural activity, akin to a lifestyle choice. Too easily the inner complexity of religious communities, let alone the immense variety of responses that they generate with regard to outsiders, gets smoothed away by the overriding concern to achieve conceptual clarity.

The *lokahi* instinct is to treat such philosophical systematising with some suspicion. In order to preserve the rich ecology of human religiosity, the foundation works with a philosophy of relationality that places the social reality of persons-in-community at the centre of reflection. In dialogue with the critique of Kant by his major antagonist, Johann Georg Hamann, and with more contemporary personalist philosophies associated with the likes of Rosenzweig and Buber, the *lokahi* vision builds on an alternative reading of post-Enlightenment philosophy, one which refuses to dichotomise schools and positions, whether empiricist or rationalist, and commends instead a principled espousal of a cross-cultural and indeed cross-religious philosophical wisdom. This emphasis on the person as neither subject nor object but as the instantiation of virtues of mutual respect and disclosure builds the epistemological style and method that is typical of *lokahi*. People exist in relation – and the way to understand ourselves is not by avoiding but taking the risk of interpersonal engagement. For *lokahi* the problem that religious literacy seeks to address is not just ignorance but, more subtly, the suppression of 'the other', both in the stranger who appears in so many forms *and* in ourselves. Taking the line that if otherness is ignored or demeaned in some way it tends only to come back in another form, *lokahi* privileges a grammar of 'we' over 'us-them', or even 'I-thou', enabling attention not just to the diversity that exists *between* different religious communities but, more subtly, to that *within* them as well.

The person-centred approach makes religious literacy not a matter of bringing discrete sets of beliefs and practices into a correlation, but of working between individuals and communities of faith in conscious acknowledgement that their interlocking histories disclose contested canons of rationality. 'Reason' does not need to be imposed from without; all communities of faith have their own learned skills that enable them to interpret and communicate their vision of things. In this sense, the concept of *lokahi* fits within what Rowan Williams has spoken of as the 'work of religious intellect' (Williams, 2003). At stake is not the defence of a confessional position but the elucidation of the inner coherence of particular visions of things – visions which are, in principle, comprehensive. That they are, in practice, never finished only makes the task more significant, not just for the inner life of this or that community, but for the sake of sound and creative exterior relations with others. *Lokahi* thus attends to the interreligious element – not just learning *about* the other, but learning both *from* and *with* the other in a Hawaiian concept most closely related to the English word 'harmony'. What is required is a measure of reflection not just on the cultural and historical roots of difference, but on the processes internal to a community that enable the continuing translation of ancient practices into new forms. *Lokahi*'s sense of an ever-growing ecology of creative interactions suggests a model of dialogue as learning *and* teaching (Lash, 1996). Rather like a school, a religious community is not the passive protector of ancient wisdom; it also seeks to learn from that wisdom and to develop the skills that it can pass on to others. More than a passive exercise, this is literacy by writing, by engaging with difference in a way that transforms 'me' and 'you' to a richer, harmonious 'us'. The case studies that follow are transformative encounters through a process of learning-by-doing exercises.

Lokahi and religious literacy

In this section we create a dialogue with the concept of religious literacy in the UK (Dinham and Jones, 2010) and the concept of *lokahi* outlined above. We focus our discussion around four overlapping questions or challenges – about diversity, skills, context and aims – and then propose a definition for religious literacy as *lokahi*.

Why is religious literacy difficult?

Understood as the acquisition of knowledge about religious beliefs and practices, religious literacy is not a simple endeavour. Dinham and Jones acknowledge that 'building religious literacy is a challenge: partly because of disinterestedness, partly just because the world is increasingly diverse, people often find that religious traditions are poorly understood' (2010, p 6). Two elements of this complexity stand out: internal conflict within religious traditions and practices and the overlap at a variety of levels with other identity categories.

Religious movements are characterised by a struggle for legitimacy and authority within each tradition. While the major religions of the world have a number of accepted tenets that make them unique, there is a great deal of diversity within each faith tradition. Thus the most basic question, 'What do such-and-such believe?' will produce different answers depending not just on the particular stance of the respondent but on the presuppositions of the interlocutors. This is especially noticeable when it comes to religious positions on social issues – the issues most relevant to conversation in the public arena, for example, in the prominent debates on same-sex marriage, religious dress, the role of women and violence. Can single, or even dominant, positions be articulated in relation to each? The answer is almost certainly 'no'.

This diversity within religious traditions can be indicative of, as well as lead to, intrafaith conflict as members of a tradition vie with each other to speak on behalf of their co-religionists. Often this struggle is relegated to theological arguments waged by scholars, but it may spill over into often violent political struggles. The fall-out from the Protestant Reformation is only one of the most obvious examples. Although outbreaks of violence between Christian groups are fewer in number today than in 17th-century Europe, and the ecumenical movement has incorporated a sense of greater unity, the fact remains that Christianity is not a monolithic whole, and that definitions of belief and practice based on what are, in origin, historically instantiated denominational traditions, can raise more problems than they solve. Anyone wanting to develop religious literacy faces the challenge that religious beliefs are dynamic and varied.

A second formidable challenge is the innate diversity of the factors determining human identity. Religion is only one of many such identifiers, ranging from personality and ethnicity to marital status and type of employment (the University of Vienna, 2013, identifies 24 separate categories). Dinham and Jones note that the 'purpose [of religious literacy] is to avoid stereotypes, respect and learn from others, and build good relations across difference' (2010, p 6). An approach to religious literacy that fails to take account of the broader background of culture and custom runs the risk of reinforcing stereotypes that may not fit many of those who identify with that tradition. Building mutual respect and learning from others means treating each person as an individual rather than a representation of a group.

An example of the complex nature of religious diversity can be found in basic physical contact between men and women. If a man meets a Muslim woman for the first time, should he shake her hand? An understanding of common practice of Muslims reveals that physical contact between men and women who are not related is frowned upon. By not offering to shake the woman's hand, the man may feel he is showing respect for a religious belief. But if the woman in question believes that shaking hands does not violate this principle (as many do), it may well appear disrespectful to assume that she would not want to shake a man's hand. A religious literacy that reduces static 'religious practices' into behavioural norms carries the danger of dehumanisation and limiting understanding. The religious 'other' should not be viewed as a subject or object, but as a human instantiation of virtues of mutual respect and disclosure.

The *lokahi* approach to the challenge of religious diversity is to begin with an attitude of respect for the *diversity and complexity within ourselves* as much as in those around us, regardless of faith or belief identification. Effective acquisition of religious literacy thus requires an understanding of the common practices of a faith tradition, as well as respect for the diversity of practice as they may be manifested in this particular person or community. In addition to the acquisition of knowledge about the other, the *lokahi* approach proposes a process of critical *self*-reflection on the desire to learn, to respect and to adapt to diversity. The challenge is not to simplify or reduce religious beliefs into static components, but to appreciate the inherent complexity and dynamism of religion and how it contributes to our diverse society.

What are the attributes demanded by religious literacy?

If we understand religious literacy as part of a dynamic process of understanding and appreciating religious diversity, the process of acquiring cross-cultural and cross-religious philosophical wisdom demands a specific set of attributes to be effective. Dinham and Jones (2010, p 6) note the need for knowledge and skills, but they do not insist that they be clearly defined. Rather than attempting a generalised inventory of these attributes, it could be useful to elaborate on them through a specific context. This was also one of the outcomes of a recent foundation project.

The Good Campus Relations project aimed to build good relations between students and staff from different faiths, beliefs and cultures (Smith, 2012). Through a series of 50 semi-structured interviews conducted in 2010–12 at seven UK universities with student leaders, students' union officers and staff members involved in interfaith work, we identified a set of attributes that motivated participation and facilitated good relations on campus (see Figure 5.1). Some of the attributes were knowledge-based, such as awareness of the diversity and multiple perspectives within various faith traditions. Others were skill-based, including the ability to communicate in difficult situations, lead diverse teams and instil creativity and vision.

Figure 5.1: Attributes to foster good campus relations

Knowledge
- Traditions of one's own faith/belief group in its diversity and complexity
- Diverse perspectives of other faith and belief groups
- The concept of multiple identities
- University structures that affect collaboration
- Wider current affairs, political and social issues that affect collaboration
- Legal, ethical and personal boundaries and limits

Skills
- Communication in difficult situations: active listening and reflective reframing, chairing and representation, critical thinking and reflection
- Leadership and people skills: recruiting and motivating group members, mentoring and peer support for group members
- Organisation and administration with diverse groups: time management, organising and running successful events, administering meetings
- Creativity and vision: idea generation, multilateral thinking, group adoption of a vision, creating new events and activities to meet objectives

Attitudes
- Self-reflection and self-critique
- Openness to others' contribution to a shared vision
- Solidarity in a diverse campus community
- Confidence in relating to other groups and to university management

Aspirations
- Competence and resourcefulness
- Desire to contribute to positive change on campus
- Work in collaboration with diverse groups

In 2012, we developed a 10-hour Diversity Management course to facilitate acquisition of these knowledge and skill-based attributes, and piloted it with a group of students at Heythrop College, University of London. In order to ascertain whether there were any changes during the course, 16 course participants (undergraduate and graduate students from three faith and belief backgrounds) completed questionnaires at four points in time: before, during, immediately after and two months after. Twenty students who did not take the course also completed the questionnaire in order to compare results. The questionnaire measured participants' self-reported knowledge, skills, attitudes and aspirations on a five-point scale. Using a 2×3 mixed ANOVA to compare the results between course participants and non-participants over time, a significant difference ($p<0.05$) in interaction occurred in four out of six of the knowledge attributes (understanding traditions of your own group in its diversity and complexity; understanding the perspectives of other groups; university structures that affect collaboration; and legal, ethical and personal boundaries and limits), and two out of four of the skill attributes (communication in difficult situations; and organising and administration with diverse groups). The difference in these areas of knowledge and skill remained two months after the course was completed (Smith, 2014). The results point to the possibility of acquiring key knowledge and skills for religious literacy within a classroom setting.

Even with the acquisition of knowledge and skills, religious literacy must, to some extent, involve active engagement with difference. Why do people choose to engage with people from different backgrounds? This question drove the foundation's action-based research with university students. On highly diverse UK university campuses, students daily confront what is now commonly referred to as *superdiversity* (a concept with a growing field, including a research centre dedicated to its study at the University of Birmingham). Rather than viewing this diversity as an opportunity for learning, many students chose to spend their social time in groups with limited diversity, or did not engage in cross-cultural or cross-faith activities in a phenomenon that Dinham and Jones call 'disinterestedness' (2010, p 6). We found that the most difficult part of building good relations was to recruit and mobilise students to engage in interfaith activities, to prioritise them above the range of activities, both academic and non-academic, that students have before them.

Another striking finding of our research was that aspirations and attitudes were the attributes affected most significantly by students who chose to be involved in these collaborative projects. From the group of students who participated in our Good Campus Relations project from four universities in 2012–13, 14 undergraduate students (from five different faith and belief backgrounds) completed pre- and post- questionnaires measuring participants' self-reported knowledge, skills, attitudes and aspirations on a five-point scale. Analysis showed significant changes ($p<0.05$ using Wilcoxon matched pairs tests) in two areas: understanding and knowledge about students from different faiths and cultures ("I am able to put myself in their shoes"), and aspirations for working together ("I am devoted to working with societies of other faiths/beliefs and cultures"; "I want my society to influence other student societies positively"). In the aforementioned Diversity

Management course, where participants showed significant increases in areas of knowledge and skill, there were no significant changes in attitudes and aspirations compared to the group of non-participants (Smith, 2014). This data is based on a small sample, and it is not possible to generalise much beyond our specific context. It does, however, reinforce the idea that acquiring religious literacy requires a positive and relational encounter with people from different faiths and beliefs.

A well-known saying goes, 'You can lead a horse to water, but you can't make him drink'. A Hawaiian elder's twist to the saying is '… but you can make him thirsty'. The *lokahi* approach to religious literacy recognises the importance of individual motivation in learning about and working together with those whom society deems the 'other', and that institutions need to support opportunities for positive interaction in order to create an environment where knowledge and skills can be applied to building solidarity and understanding. The shared task of keeping the whole eco-system of our diverse society in being is itself creative and life-giving.

What is the context for religious literacy?

The acquisition of religious literacy takes place not in a laboratory, but in specific contexts that influence its attributes and challenges. A key challenge is posed by the space occupied. Dinham and Jones describe this as a 'civic' space where religions can be 'articulated publicly' (2010, p 6). The concept of religious literacy may conjure up images of a neutral space where secular institutions mediate a rational conversation in the framework of liberal democracy. From this perspective, the rational and objective learner can better understand the quaint beliefs and unusual practices of religious people in a world that is assumed to be neutral and secular. This is the vantage point tacitly assumed by a UK national government definition of religious literacy as 'the skills and knowledge required to engage in an informed and confident way with faith communities' (CLG, 2008, p 33). In other words, religious literacy is a tool for secular people to understand something called 'faith communities' which occupy a 'space' that is somehow fundamentally different from the standpoint occupied by the 'objective' enquirer. However, as Casanova (2006) reminds us, the secularisation thesis has not survived the 21st century particularly well, globally or even in the West. The assumption that faith communities are outsiders or part of a dying religious enclave creates a false dichotomy that is not borne out by the evidence of religious involvement in the public sphere.

If religion is not to be rendered somehow separate or irrelevant in this context, it is important that it not be regarded as a challenge to the authority of 'secular' conceptions of law and society. This concern is reflected in Dinham and Jones' suggestion that religious literacy should 'challenge any attempt to close down debates with "conversation-stopping" certainties and absolutes' (2010, p 6). Debates about expressions of personal identity in the public sphere – the wearing of the *niqab* (face covering) or Sikh turban by public officials – take on a different tenor when the issue stems from a religious belief that is perceived as obligatory and non-negotiable. Claims that are given an absolute or transcendent status are difficult to challenge, and attempts to engage with such claims theologically can create a situation where state institutions appear to be sanctioning some forms of religion above others, or even dictating what amounts to correct religious belief or practice. In other words, the 'neutral space thesis' does not so much free dialogue from the guarding of 'otherness', but compounds the issue with its own unchallengeable sense of certainty. At its most extreme this position posits the secular world as reasonable or rational, with those with religious beliefs as being somehow incapable of reasoned self-presentation.

The *lokahi* approach, recognising that diversity exists within all of humanity and is not to be limited to the absolutist claims of insiders and the supposed objectivity of outsiders, guards against 'othering' religious identification in an unhealthy manner. As Martin Luther King, Jr, famously stated, 'We are caught in an inescapable network of mutuality, tied in a single garment of destiny' (King, 1963, p 1). An awareness of our shared space encourages a measure of reflection, not just on the cultural and historical roots of difference, but on the processes internal to a community that enable the continuing translation of ancient practices into new forms. Within this framework of mutual respect, it becomes possible to engage in the most difficult of discussions about sensitive issues with an eye to working together within the framework of multiple differences rather than in spite of them.

What is the aim of religious literacy?

An awareness of our contentious public space can lead to a more nuanced appreciation about the aims of religious literacy. Dinham and Jones define the aim of religious literacy as 'seeking to inform intelligent, thoughtful and rooted approaches to religious faith that countervail unhelpful knee-jerk reactions based on fear and stereotype' (2010, p 6). The call to overcome knee-jerk reactions to religion with such a 'rooted' approach is in itself quite admirable, but raises a tricky question about the significance and value of 'rootedness'. It is commonly noted that religious groups are carriers of strong social capital and therefore have the potential to contribute to a better society. Building on Putnam's (2000) concept of bonding social capital, the South African sociologist of religion, Cochrane (2002), characterises the specific make-up of religious communities with a concept of 'lifeworlds', communities of lived values. Faith communities are special in this regard because of their attachment to a transcendent belief and a specific set of values. But they are not unique. The third sector also lives out of a set of analogous values, as, to some extent, do other spheres of influence in public life, the market and the institutions of the state itself. The rootedness we refer to is not rootedness in faith, but in a conceptualisation of faith as a category with which to engage.

The particular aims and concerns of religious groups and faith communities need to be understood within the wider framework of analogous concerns and interests that are to be detected at many levels of human interaction. For example, one concept that seemingly sets religious groups apart is proselytism – converting others to a different type of belief or sense of belonging. Arguably, however, this could be understood not as a 'special case' but within the broad contemporary culture of advertising and selling. Plenty of groups are 'out there', working to convert people to their way of thinking. In this climate, people of faith often feel as though they are targets of a sort of mass conversion rather than agents with their own particular brand to offer. Where does religious literacy fit into such a landscape? Might religious literacy itself be perceived as a missionary endeavour, with the goal of bringing an 'enlightened understanding' of and to faith communities? Alternatively, could it be seen as a further challenge to the authority of religious groups in the public sphere, encouraging not knowledge and understanding, but compliance in a secularist vision of how religion is to be understood and made acceptable in public life? If it is perceived or actually works according to these, or other, specific motifs, religious literacy could run the risk of being seen as part of the suppression of the other, a charge that is often levelled at religious groups themselves.

The *lokahi* approach aims to recognise and respect this scepticism about the aims of religious literacy. While concerned to achieve a better quality of conversation, the concept of *lokahi* as 'harmony through diversity' begins with difference, and aims to work against simplistic attempts to supress the otherness inherent in all members of a community. The salient principle is that harmony cannot be created without first achieving a deep respect for an *active* diversity.

Defining religious literacy as lokahi

Now that we have raised a few questions, we may attempt a definition of religious literacy as *lokahi*. This takes its stand not so much on religious as on *inter*religious literacy. The danger is that concepts of religious literacy that are not rooted in active encounter become so flexible that they end up meaning very little. *Lokahi* seeks to guard against this by deliberately avoiding any reductionist account of religion, instead seeing diversity as the fundamental 'DNA' of religious identity and religious communities. Dinham and Jones' (2010, p 6) definition – 'having the knowledge and skills to recognise religious faith as a legitimate and important area for public attention, a degree of general knowledge about at least some religious traditions and an awareness of and ability to find out about others' – helps people to engage with religion as a category in the first place. The *lokahi* approach is more focused on the face-to-face encounter of individuals and communities of all faiths and beliefs, their presence having been accepted. The conception of religious literacy as *lokahi* therefore rests firmly on an epistemology of knowledge as relational, as mutual disclosure – an epistemology that does not privilege a single faith tradition or cultural tradition in philosophy. Rather than knowing *about*, *lokahi* stresses knowing *with* and *from* positive interaction with religious diversity – both that discerned within myself and that disclosed in my respectful and honest endeavours to value and to promote a harmonious society.

Case studies: religious literacy as an encounter with diversity

The concept of *lokahi* as a variation within the project to promote religious literacy is best illustrated by recourse to a number of case studies, from different regions and professional contexts, which draw attention to its salient characteristics. The case studies that follow are transformative encounters with religious diversity through a process of learning-by-doing exercises.

Trauma therapy and religion in Uganda, Rwanda and South Africa

Based in the UK, Luna Children's Charity (LCC) is a mental health and human rights advocacy charity working with children suffering from post-traumatic stress disorder (PTSD) in the developing world. Luna trains mental health professionals in children's accelerated trauma therapy (CATT), which treats the symptoms of PTSD. Since 2010,

LCC has delivered training for local partners to deliver effective treatment of trauma in children in Rwanda, Uganda, Pakistan and South Africa (LCC, 2013). Many of the mental health professionals who train local partners in CATT are from the UK, and they encounter cultural and religious challenges that they do not usually encounter in their local practice. One common challenge posed by traditional beliefs attributes mental illness to spiritual possession and a preference for traditional methods of healing. Another challenge comes from the echoes of the history of colonialism's negative effects on local African communities. Although the approach of CATT is focused on addressing the needs of trauma sufferers rather than imposing a rigid system of treatment, the ethnic and national identity of the trainers sometimes raised suspicion.

One of the trainers was asked by a trainee in Uganda 'what it felt like to be a representation of colonial forces' (Weston, 2013, p 32). Even more difficult was the issue of religious belief and authority. One of the trainers encountered discrimination in Rwanda because of her atheist beliefs. On the first day of a week of training in Rwanda, one of the trainees, who was also a Christian pastor, questioned her legitimacy to teach the group, and actively encouraged other trainees to leave the training (Raby, 2012).

What does religious literacy mean for trainers in this contentious multicultural context? Certainly a knowledge of the traditional beliefs mentioned earlier is important. In this particular context, where external concepts are treated with suspicion, it is crucial to understand how the acceptance of beliefs stems, to some extent, from different ways of understanding legitimacy and authority. The Western secular approach may well view these religious and cultural beliefs as barriers that need to be torn down, or troublesome issues to be ignored. As noted earlier, this imposition of a 'neutral space' for dealing with religion fails to account for the historical context of Western engagement in post-colonial societies.

LCC trainers realised that they needed a deeper understanding of these dynamics of beliefs in order to successfully achieve their objectives. Working with LCC, The Lokahi Foundation developed a workshop for trainers in the management of conflicts of beliefs and values. The focus was not on specific religious beliefs, but concerned rather to address misconceptions about trainers and their world view in a way that demonstrated respect. Faced with a new method of treating trauma that conflicted with traditional approaches, trainees could either accept, reject or re-negotiate beliefs within their current framework. Rather than tear down a religious belief about the role of faith in psychotherapy, trainers reflected on how they could present the information in a way that helped local partners to incorporate CATT into their belief system.

One way to embed trauma therapy in the local context is to envisage treatment of trauma as compatible with traditional beliefs about healing. For example, the Rwandan belief in *lhahamuka* views the common post-traumatic stress symptom of shortness of breath as terror caused by the spirits of ancestors returning. By building on this link, trainers frame CATT as a way to help people deal with this recognised problem (Weston, 2013, p 31). In approaching the issue of endemic religious prejudice against atheism, trainers analyse the underlying beliefs that inform the suspicion of an atheist trainer, but also discover shared values to bridge the divide. Recognising that the trainer presents a challenge to the religious authority of the Christian minister, the trainer shows a respect for religious belief and demonstrates how CATT does not conflict with the Christian faith, but can be understood instead as a means for spiritual healing that can work not in distinction from, but in cooperation with, a Christian world view.

In addition to understanding conflicts of beliefs and values, the workshop included the skills needed to deal with difficult situations that trainers would face in the field. Participants created a list of personal emotional triggers that could derail their facilitation of a session. Examples included invoking God as a trump card to justify immoral behaviour, or women or children being treated in a patronising or unequal manner. One participant reflected, 'If disrespect [is] expressed to me through a verbal attack, I tend to freeze. If it [is] expressed to someone else, I tend to get aggressive and lose objectivity' (quoted in Smith, 2013). Participants then created a bank of techniques to help them manage difficult situations. These ranged from quick internal reminders such as 'take a deep breath' and 'create some emotional distance', as well as communication techniques using active listening by 'asking the other person to be clearer in order to help me understand better' and 'take a break and speak to person privately to better understand and address concerns' (quoted in Smith, 2013).

The most useful element of the training was a scenario-based exercise. Each trainer created a scenario that he or she would likely face in managing a conflict of beliefs. Working with colleagues, they acted out the scenario and rehearsed how they would manage the emotional triggers for themselves and for others in the group. In the example mentioned earlier, where the Christian pastor challenged the authority of the atheist trainer, participants acted out the roles -- the trainer, the pastor and another participant – allowing the trainer to practice in real time how to apply facilitation techniques, as well as develop a better understanding of the perspective of different people in the conflict. The trainers reported that they found these particularly useful tools while working with other trainers in the field, by creating a space for reflection and support in often uncomfortable environments (Raby, 2012).

The LCC case study illustrates two points made earlier about religious literacy as *lokahi*. By adopting a measure of reflection on the cultural and historical roots of conflict of beliefs, trainers begin to appreciate the internal processes of Rwandan and Ugandan communities in order to enable the continuing translation of ancient practices into new forms. With the *lokahi* focus on literacy as relationality, trainers can reflect on specific barriers to clear communication, both internal and external, and discover shared values to facilitate. The road to healing trauma in children runs through psychotherapeutic processes which are beyond labels of Western and traditional; they are diverse and relational.

Youth de-radicalisation in Pakistan

In 2009, the Pakistani army carried out a large-scale operation against the Pakistani Taliban in the Swat region. During the operation , up to 1,200 boys between the ages of 12 and 17 were captured and trained by the Taliban as foot soldiers and suicide bombers. They were 'recruited' with a range of tactics including kidnapping, buying them from families and offers of food and weapons. The majority reported physical or sexual abuse, and many came from families in abject poverty (Qazi, 2013, p 7). Many had only been taught the Taliban's version of Islam, and some expressed a belief that carrying out suicide attacks would help them to reach heaven, which was a better place than their current lives (Qazi, 2013, p 7). Rather than putting these severely traumatised young men in prison, the Pakistani army set up centres to help them. One of the most successful is the Sabaoon Centre for Rehabilitation, which is managed by the Hum Pakistani Foundation (HPF) at a facility maintained by the army in the Swat Valley (Qazi, 2013, p 7).

Where might religious literacy contribute to addressing violent behaviour in these victimised young men? A knowledge-based approach would most likely focus on religious education about Islam and violence, postulating that by correcting a limited interpretation of Islam, the desire to fight against the Pakistani army and the West could also be changed. Alternatively, a 'secular' focus might work with economic, psychological and social causes. Instead, Dr Feriha Perracha, the supervising psychiatrist at Sabaoon, and her team, adopted a broader approach, which includes the relational – *lokahi* – approach by addressing the diversity of causes to adopt violence by each individual through a holistic intervention. 'Sabaoon's eighteen-month program has four components: formal education, including corrective religious education; vocational training; counselling and therapy; and a social module to discuss social issues and hold sessions with the beneficiaries' families' (Qazi, 2013, p 7). This approach viewed the young people not as enemy combatants, but as people with dignity who could participate in the creation of a more just society. The young people were called beneficiaries and treated with a respect that sharply differed from how they had been treated by the Taliban (Seymour, 2011).

The key to Sabaoon's success is the focus on re-connecting the young people with their families and the communities where they had been marginalised. Young people are assessed as ready to be reintegrated based on their vocational skills, psychological wellbeing, educational performance and family support. Sabaoon then helps them to enter a school or job, and conducts a two-year follow-up process of support. This approach has proven highly successful – 143 of the 200 young people who have been beneficiaries of Sabaoon have since attended universities or colleges or have jobs (Qazi, 2013, pp 7-8).

The Sabaoon story illustrates the *lokahi* concept of embedding religious identity as only one of the multiple attributes that make up human identity. By valuing this innate diversity through addressing emotional, economic and spiritual needs, young men are treated with humanity in a way that could restore their own sense of belonging in communities that had previously marginalised them. With a new appreciation of their faith as well as their place in a diverse eco-system, they can escape the cycle of victimisation to become agents for creating a better society.

UK police and Muslim communities

In the wake of the attacks of 7/7, the UK government instituted a number of projects to counter further attacks under the banner of the Prevent Strategy. Due to the highly secretive nature of counter-terrorism operations and the impact of high-profile arrests on the treatment of local Muslim communities, there was a growing climate of suspicion between the police and Muslim communities that was feeding a widespread perception that Muslims were not welcome in British society. Recognising that intelligence from the Muslim community would be a key asset to preventing terrorist operations, in 2008, the Association of Chief Police Officers (ACPO) set up Operation Nicole to facilitate sessions for local police forces to engage with members of the Muslim community. Their aim was to dispel myths about counter-terrorism operations and enlist community cooperation (ACPO, 2010).

The sessions were envisaged as a briefing of police procedures, with the idea that it was possible to displace suspicion of the police through the provision of accurate information. Realising the benefit of outside facilitation, ACPO asked The Lokahi Foundation to facilitate the encounters. It became clear from the first event that the level of mistrust and suspicion was higher than anticipated, and that the information-based format of the encounter was not conducive to addressing this suspicion or dealing with the underlying problems. It was also clear that many local police involved in these encounters had a limited understanding of the diversity of Islam as practiced by British Muslims. Their basic knowledge was largely gleaned through intelligence briefings about extremist groups, with most seeing Muslim communities as either tacit supporters of extremists or politically uninvolved groups who were content with declaring that 'Islam is a religion of peace'.

The foundation transformed these sessions from an information exchange into an opportunity for envisioning the police and Muslims as partners in the community to solve the shared challenge of violent extremism. We named this type of encounter as Learning from Each Other's Stories (LEOS). Between 2008 and 2010, 50 weekend events were held and attended by 2,600 police officers, members of local Muslim communities and senior counter-terrorism officers. Participants sat around tables in small groups, working through a fictional storyboard about dilemmas faced by a Muslim youth worker and by counter-terrorism police around a potential violent community attack. The aim was to build trust, not by a perception that the police understand Islam, but by an encounter that demonstrates 'this police officer respects me as a person and as a Muslim'. By imagining what they would do in the situation, the result was a deeper appreciation of the barriers to sharing information with the police, and deeper appreciation of the challenges that counter-terrorism police face. As one community member said, 'I now appreciate the difficulties that exist in decision making by the police and the myriad of factors that have to be taken in to account'; the event also 'allowed us to challenge their beliefs about us' (quoted in Griffith-Dickson, 2015).

The results of this type of encounter were striking, especially considering that each event lasted only a day or a day-and-a-half. In research conducted with 100 participants one to two years after the events, 95 per cent said they had shared what they learned with others afterwards; 87 per cent reported that kept in contact with participants from the other group after the event; and 95 per cent said they were now able to explain to others the challenges faced by the police and the community (Griffith-Dickson, 2015).

Just two of the many stories emanating from these events give some indication of the positive impact of building trust. At the beginning of one event, a community participant found herself sharing dinner with a female police officer and describing the discrimination she faced on the high street as a woman wearing a headscarf. The police officer described the negative way she was treated as a woman and a police officer. In the final session, participants shared what their vision for a better future would look like, and what they would do to contribute to that vision. The participant volunteered that she was going to share a patrol with the local police officer to understand better how police were treated in her area. The female police officer also committed to wear a headscarf in the city centre in order to understand for herself the abuse that community members experienced on a daily basis (Griffith-Dickson, 2015).

In another example, trust built through this encounter helped to avert a suicide bombing in Bristol in March 2008. Shortly after an Operation Nicole event, community members who had suspicions about a young man who had been to a mosque with burns on his hands felt they could share this information with counter-terrorism officers. The police quickly moved in, finding explosives in the fridge, a detonator in the kitchen drawer and the suicide vest hanging in his wardrobe (Griffith-Dickson, 2015).

These LEOS events powerfully demonstrate the *lokahi* principle of knowledge as relational encounter. Rather than avoiding difficult issues of religion and violence in a climate of suspicion, participants have the opportunity to confront stereotypes about each other around a table. Instead of Muslim community members and the police learning separately about each other, they find ways to come to terms with matters of mutual importance *together*, creating bonds of trust that, in the last instance, quite literally saved lives.

Conclusions

The stories and examples of The Lokahi Foundation's experience cited in this chapter are all recent illustrations of a practical wisdom as old as Hawaii's ever-restless volcanoes. What they show is that change and transformation are possible when people grapple with the various levels of 'otherness' that exist both within and between them, through working together in community. For its practitioners, this is what makes the *lokahi* concept more than another useful idea in the task of addressing the neglected category of religion. Certainly The Lokahi Foundation agrees that religious literacy means paying careful attention to the presuppositions behind the received wisdom that religious chauvinism can be overcome by a more nuanced and informed mode of representation; that it is necessary to critique another not too hidden assumption – that left to themselves, religious groups will seek only to safeguard their particular vision of things, and therefore some 'third party' is always going to be necessary to mediate between 'the religious' and civil society; that religions as they exist are highly complex patterns of holiness which, if they are to be properly understood, must be set within appropriate historical, cultural and social parameters.

Where we feel the *lokahi* concept of 'harmony through difference' does offer something special, this lies with our insistence that people who identify with the great spiritual traditions of the world are themselves sources of renewal and new energy. This is not to ignore the propensity even in the best intentioned of people for self-deception and corruption. Nor does it propose some easy short-cut to the sometimes painful negotiations that have to take place if painful traumas and suspicions are to be overcome. On the contrary, it is to draw attention to the way modernity deals in abstractions, likes to tidy difference away into stereotypes, and tends to indulge in premature 'top-down' solutions. We have argued that it is precisely the tendency to construct binaries rather than embrace the messiness of human living that compounds the problem. Each one of our case studies draws attention to a strategy that broadens the context of engagement, deliberately including a number of different actors and seeking always to find sources of new energy in the interaction itself. The *lokahi* concept is a deliberate refusal to collude with the 'us' and 'them' logic that characterises so much contemporary community relations work. Put more positively, once people work together in human community, *lokahi* believes that the inner resources and deep virtues formed by culture, custom and religious tradition find space within which to 'write' religious literacy as a harmonious society.

Acknowledgement

We are particularly grateful to Gwen Griffith-Dickson for her inspiration and input into this chapter, and for exemplifying the concept of *lokahi* in her life and work.

References

ACPO (Association of Chief Police Officers) (2010) *Operation Nicole* (www.acpo.police.uk/documents/TAM/Op%20Nicole.pdf).

Casanova, J. (2006) 'Rethinking secularization: a global comparative perspective', *The Hedgehog Review*, Spring/Summer, pp 7-22 (http://iasc-culture.org/THR/archives/AfterSecularization/8.12CCasanova.pdf).

CLG (Department for Communities and Local Government) (2008) *Face-to-face and side-by-side: A framework for partnership in our multi-faith society*, London: CLG Publications (http://webarchive.nationalarchives.gov.uk/20120919132719/www.communities.gov.uk/publications/communities/facetofaceframework).

Cochrane, J.R. (2002) 'On religion and theology in a civil society', in L. Holness and R.K. Wustenberg (eds) *Theology in dialogue: The impact of the arts, humanities and science on contemporary religious thought: Essays in honour of John W. de Gruchy*, Grand Rapids, MI, London and Claremont, CA: Eerdmans, pp 116-32.

Dinham, A. and Jones, S.H. (2010) *Religious literacy leadership in higher education: An analysis* (http://religiousliteracyhe.org/wp-content/uploads/2010/11/Analysis-booklet.pdf).

Griffith-Dickson, G. (2006) 'Harmony from diversity', 9 March, Gresham College Lectures (www.gresham.ac.uk/lectures-and-events/harmony-from-diversity).

Griffith-Dickson, G. (2015: forthcoming) *Learning each other's stories*, London: Lokahi Press.

Hick, J. (1973) *God and the universe of faiths: Essays in the philosophy of religion*, London: Macmillan.

Hick, J. (2004) *An interpretation of religion* (2nd edn), Basingstoke: Palgrave.

King, M.L.K. (1963) 'Letter from Birmingham City jail', Martin Luther King, Jr Research and Education Institute (http://mlk-kpp01.stanford.edu/index.php/resources/article/annotated_letter_from_birmingham).

Lash, N. (1996) *The beginning and the end of 'religion'*, Cambridge: Cambridge University Press.

LCC (Luna Children's Charity) (2013) 'About us' (www.lunachildren.org.uk/aboutus.html).

Putnam, R. (2000) *Bowling alone: The collapse and revival of American community*, New York: Simon & Schuster.

Qazi, S.H. (2013) 'A war without bombs: civil society initiatives against radicalisation in Pakistan', *Policy Brief #60*, Institute for Social Policy and Understanding (www.ispu.org/pdfs/ISPU_Brief_CounterDeradicalization_2_14.pdf).

Raby, C. (2012) Discussion on materials creation and evaluation of Luna training, personal communication, 10 July.

Seymour, K. (2011) 'De-radicalisation: psychologists' war against militants', *International Express Tribune*, 17 July (http://tribune.com.pk/story/211479/de-radicalising-rehab-psychologists-war-against-militants).

Smith, J. (2012) *Good campus relations*, Lokahi University Research Briefing Paper 1, London: The Lokahi Foundation (http://lokahi.org.uk/analysis/resources/good_campus_relations_lokahi_university_research_b~127.html).

Smith, J. (2013) 'Facilitating conflicts of beliefs and values: Best practice guide for Luna Children's Charity trainers', Unpublished document, London: The Lokahi Foundation.

Smith, J. (2014) 'Developing good campus relations at UK universities', Unpublished paper.

University of Vienna (2013) *Dimensions of diversity*, Diversity Management (www.univie.ac.at/diversity/dimensions.html).

Weston, J. (2013) 'CATT: How does a child centred trauma therapy technique translate in a cross-cultural context?', Unpublished dissertation (www.lunachildren.org.uk/Research/Dissertation%20final.pdf).

Williams, R. (2003) 'Christian theology and other faiths', Lecture by the Archbishop of Canterbury at the University of Birmingham, 11 June (http://rowanwilliams.archbishopofcanterbury.org/articles.php/1825/christian-theology-and-other-faiths).

Section Two
Policy

SIX

Religious literacy and welfare

Adam Dinham

There is a strong argument for seeing welfare and education as the two spheres that have most driven modern religious change, and that have largely defined the contemporary religious landscape. More than that, I think together they have left contemporary societies across the West with a serious problem – and this is religious illiteracy.

While other chapters in this volume address education, both in schools and in universities, in this chapter I work towards an argument for religious literacy through the welfare lens, which recognises a new religious landscape, and is relevant to everyone, whatever one's own religious stance, or none. Although it is the first of the chapters in the 'policy' section in this book, it bridges, in fact, between theory and policy, by attempting to show both how policy has affected religious literacy, and how it presents a challenge to improve it.

The story I want to tell starts – in Britain at least – in the 1940s. It has other starts at other times and in other places, but it is this particular time that will be illuminating here. The welfare story is in three phases, the first of which concerns what I call a willing transfer of welfare from church to state. This is no simple moment in time. Welfare had already been a preoccupation of politicians and churchmen alike for decades – perhaps centuries – before the 1940s (see Prochaska, 2006). The UK's liberal governments of the first two decades of the early 20th century had already introduced a National Insurance scheme covering minimal payments during ill health and old age to prevent the poorest falling entirely into destitution (Pederson, 1993, p 125). A minimal safety net against poverty had already gradually emerged – but its strings were overly spaced apart, and the gaps were great and many.

The willing transfer

In my 'willing transfer' argument, I suggest that the Second World War had formed a cauldron for rethinking society in the most ambitious of terms, and I think the churches saw this too. In correspondence and discussion between two of the leading protagonists – William

Temple and William Beveridge – the idea of welfare took a much more focused shape in this context. So our first character in this story is William Temple, Bishop of Manchester, Archbishop of York (1929–42) and then of Canterbury (1942–44), when he died. Temple was an intelligent and imaginative Christian of considerable vision, and he shared this with a broadly interested nation, one which, by contrast with today, was absolutely 'all ears'. This marks a striking difference with the religious sensibility of the public realm today, as interventions by recent Archbishops suggest, which have tended to be either vilified or ignored.

Temple set out a manifesto for welfare, first in *Christianity and the state* (1928), in which he first coined the term 'welfare state'. He subsequently elaborated on this in *Citizen and churchman* in 1941, and then in *Christianity and the social order* (1942). This was published by the famous popular British publisher, Penguin, and immediately sold out, running for several reprints, into millions of sales – and I think this was a sign of the times as well as a mark of the man (Timmins, 2001, p 23). Can we imagine such a text selling out from a popular press nowadays? In it Temple asks such questions as 'What right has the church to interfere?'; 'How should the church interfere?'; 'What are Christian social principles?'; and 'What is the task before us?' Strikingly, these questions were familiar and recognisable to a popular audience. To the latter question he answers '... the national debt will be a heavy burden ... and there will be the need to reconstruct the devastated areas of many towns with all the adjustments of rights, vested interests and social welfare which any planning must involve' (p 84). He adds, 'The structure of life as we knew it ... has already been profoundly modified.... How far do we want to restore it if we can?' (p 84).

He then explores what Christian thought might have to say on these matters. He concludes that what must be rebuilt is 'the family as the primary social unit' (p 85) – for which he identifies houses as a key issue; the 'sanctity of personality' (p 87) – for which he prescribes good health and education; and 'the principle of fellowship' (p 90) – for which he turns to the end of educational division and the maintenance of a Christian character in state education for all.

The book goes on to use a combination of theology and common sense to argue for employment for all – 'every citizen should be in secure possession of such an income as will enable him to maintain a home ...' (p 99) he says, as well as liberty and leisure. In short, he says 'the aim of a Christian social order is the fullest possible development of individual personality in the widest and deepest possible fellowship' (p 100). I think in this way Temple sets out a blueprint for both the approach and content of the welfare state, which subsequently captures the public imagination, right up to the present day.

This is big thinking at a big time in history. Temple drew on the Christian faith to argue that the country as a whole had an opportunity to rethink the entire politics and practice of care. What is really amazing is that people listened. This was an Archbishop who had a broad and willing audience.

The other part of this 'willing transfer' story lies not with a churchman, but with a politician – another William, William Beveridge – and this was no accident. The relationship between Beveridge and Temple had begun 40 years before, when they first met at Balliol College, University of Oxford. Between them (and with Richard Tawney), they were to develop and realise the welfare vision for Britain. While at Oxford these young men were challenged to go to Toynbee Hall in the Settlement Movement in the East End of London, to 'find friends among the poor, as well as finding out what poverty is and what can be done about it.'[1]

The reforms that Temple and Beveridge achieved in the 1940s represented the heights of a shared 'big vision' for Britain in the last century. This was a case of intellectuals, church leaders and government agreeing, both on the big vision and on the ways in which it could be delivered.

Beveridge was considered an authority on unemployment insurance from early in his career, serving under Winston Churchill on the Board of Trade as Director of the newly created Labour Exchanges and later as Permanent Secretary of the Ministry of Food. He was Director of the London School of Economics and Political Science (LSE) from 1919 until 1937, when he was elected Master of University College, Oxford, so he was also an established academic. In May 1941, the Minister of Health, the Liberal MP Ernest Brown, announced the formation of a committee of officials to survey existing social insurance and allied services, and to make recommendations. Beveridge was asked to chair this committee, and it is often said that this was expected to be an insignificant body designed to distract him from his attempts to influence the development of new manpower policy, a subject on which he had reportedly made himself something of a 'bore'.

However, Beveridge used the committee to think big, drawing at least in part on the vision he had discussed and developed over many years with Temple, and the committee published *Social insurance and allied services*, which proposed that all people of working age should pay a weekly National Insurance contribution (Beveridge, 1942, p 11). In return, universal benefits would be paid as entitlements to people who were sick, unemployed, retired or widowed. Beveridge argued that this system would provide a minimum standard of living 'below which no one should be allowed to fall'. It also recommended that the government should find ways of fighting what he called the five 'Giant Evils of Want, Disease, Ignorance, Squalor and Idleness'.

Beveridge also assumed in the report that there would be a National Health Service (NHS) of some sort, and much has been said (although little written) about the NHS as somehow occupying a religious space in the British imagination – a new national religion (Beveridge, 1942, p 11).

The impact was huge, and this was another report that sold in large numbers. Beveridge's arguments were widely accepted. When Attlee won the 1945 General Election for the Labour Party, he announced that he would introduce the welfare state first described by Temple in *Christianity and the social order* (1941), and fleshed out in the 1942 Beveridge report. This was seen as nothing less than, having won the war, now 'winning the peace'. Temple said of this that it was 'the first time anyone had set out to embody the whole spirit of the Christian ethic in an Act of Parliament' (quoted in Barnett, 2001, pp 26-7).

This was quite a moment. Before 1948 welfare was almost entirely the provenance of the churches, and huge amounts of social work, community work and charity were done by parishes and congregations up and down the land. After the war, it was done – or at least seen to be done – by the state. And remarkably this shift was undertaken with the full support and collaboration of the Church of England. What I think this shows is that church and state were then so closely related that it was of no concern to the church that one might be taking over the functions of the other, at the other's expense. There was apparently no question that church could diminish as a result. The welfare state was the very embodiment of the Christian church. But in fact, it was a very profound turning point for religion in the public realm.

On the upside, the transfer of welfare from church to state undid centuries of paternalism, sexism and top-down philanthropy that the war had done so much to undermine. It also challenged the random nature of welfare provision that had emerged when it was left to the so-called well-meaning amateurs. Church-based welfare had been the biggest postcode lottery of all, in which the parish you found yourself in would largely determine the quality and availability of services you could draw on.

On the downside, the welfare transfer loosened the connection between people and parish that had so effectively engaged people, not just in individual concerns, but also through the family, to communities.

The language of religion was no longer the leading language of the public sphere of care.

Nobody should romanticise the pre-1940s church-oriented community, nor see it through rose-tinted glasses, but the connections that were lost have been agonised over by policy-makers ever since. There have been regular waves of anxiety about a crisis of community since 1948, and countless government initiatives have sought to address it in the UK, often using the word 'community' – from the Community Development Projects of the 1960s, to the New Deal for Communities in the 2000s. All have depended heavily on a rhetoric of 'restoring community', and all have relied on the participation of churches and other faiths that they see as being somehow good at community. They have all tended to dictate the goals in political terms, however, such as increased employment, reduced crime and a better built environment. They have also all seemed incapable of encapsulating those alternative preoccupations with which faiths are also concerned, such as love, hospitality, generosity, and so on, and this is a key challenge for our times: how to articulate the values found in a Christian West in a newly post-religious, post-secular, plural context in which Christianity would probably not be appropriate – at least, not on its own – and in which the majority of people have largely lost the language to articulate it anyway.

I explored this in 2006 in a particular way when I was part of a research team on a project called 'Faith as social capital: connecting or dividing?' (Furbey et al, 2006). This used the idea of social capital to explore what faiths contribute in the public realm. It concluded that faith communities contribute substantial and distinctive bridging and linking social capital in at least six key ways: through co-presence in urban areas; by generating and providing connecting frameworks (infrastructure); through the wider communities' use of faith buildings; as spaces that their associational networks open up between people; by engagement in various forms of governance; and through work across boundaries with others in the public domain, for example, voluntary and community sector bodies and local authorities (Furbey et al, 2006).

The study also found that there are difficulties and obstacles, including: misunderstanding and suspicion of faiths among external partners such as local authorities; financial barriers, for example, in faith groups being eligible to access funding; inappropriate buildings that are difficult to use for what is needed, or which are a liability because of their age and their heritage status; actual or perceived state managerialism and regulation, which was seen as cumbersome or inhibiting; bridging and linking that is undertaken only by a small minority of members of faith communities, with the majority having little or no involvement or awareness; and specifically, according to our analysis at the time, women and young people participating less in bridging and linking forms of social capital and more in bonding, probably because of issues of power and the role of women and children (Furbey et al, 2006).

The point is that all of these observations were rooted in an analysis of what they contributed to the public sphere as policy-makers see it. I have since come to argue that this over-emphasises those aspects that are seen as valuable within existing policy logics, and over-burdens faith groups with an inchoate policy hope that they will somehow restore community. Yet those aspects that might have some chance of doing so – relationality, hope, love, generosity – remain largely outside the public discourse, and off the public radar. They exemplify a muddle in the relationship between state and faith-based languages and logics of care.

In the case of community politics, all the political projects have essentially failed – the latest being the Conservative-Liberal Democrat Coalition's notion of the 'Big Society'. The idea of community remains stubbornly difficult to define, articulate and reproduce (Stacey, 1969; Mayo, 2000). It is ephemeral, although no less sought after for being so.

That said, the reality of the welfare state has always been more mixed than it looked. Faith groups have maintained a constant and consistent presence, often working in the most disadvantaged areas where all other agencies have withdrawn. And this brings us to the second phase in my three-part evolution. I call this 'invisible presence'.

Invisible presence

This is a period in which the transfer from church to state is *assumed* to have resulted in the wholesale nationalisation, professionalisation and therefore secularisation of welfare. Public professionals such as the new NHS doctors, social workers and state-employed teachers had taken on the care functions of the churches. These were now the people to whom publics turned. Yet the point is that, despite the shift away from a religious articulation of welfare, faiths continued to play a crucially important role, although one that was far less visible.

This was possible because the leading politicians of the welfare age very quickly came to realise that the welfare state was not resulting in the eradication of society's 'five great evils'. There was neither sufficient money nor political agreement to launch the welfare state in its entirety, or in some perfect condition of wholeness. Choices and priorities had to be made right from the beginning, and even before the NHS was established in 1948, it was realised that the balance of contributions and the benefits they yielded would always be unstable. Even though the welfare state was able to prevent a fall below a certain level of poverty and exclusion for the first time, it was, nevertheless, piecemeal, not total, and in the estimation of many, this has been its undoing ever since.

During the 1950s this led to renewed enthusiasm for community-based policies rooted in neighbourhood and self-help – precisely the sorts of work faith-based providers have always been so good at. In particular, it was apparent that architectural renewal was insufficient to the building of communities. The Gulbenkian report (Younghusband, 1968) took this crisis of community up in the 1960s, envisaging new kinds of work in communities ('concerned with affecting the course of social change through the two processes of analysing social situations and forming relationships with different groups to bring about desirable change' – see Younghusband, 1968, p 22). It identified a set of values that should underpin community that reflect those of many faith-based endeavours, although it did so in avowedly non-religious language.

First, it said that people matter, and policies and public administration should be judged by their effects on people. Second, participation in every aspect of life is of fundamental importance. Third, work in communities should be concerned with the distribution of resources towards people who are socially disadvantaged.

Much of this newly imagined community work was conducted in neighbourhood-level projects, and many of those were initiated by faiths. This was in part a result of the Church of England's parish system that ensured that there were staff, buildings and resources in every area of the country (Dinham, 2009, p 124). Bodies like the Churches Community Workers' Alliance sprang up to support the work. These were new ways of being present – although prolific, they were far less visible and far less recognisable than the old parish-based welfare.

So while it rings of the old manifesto set out by William Temple in *Christianity and the social order*, and it represented a new context in which faith actors could engage, it was very differently visible. Welfare would not, after all, be done by the state. But state – secular – forms and language were now in the ascendant when people thought and talked about welfare.

Nevertheless, it was a context that faiths could identify with in terms of the insistence on human worth and value, and on critiques of the shape of politics and society. Faiths were indeed prolific in providing interventions in communities at this time, and were able to thrive in a context that was friendly to them.

So the story of this second phase – the period of invisible presence – is that secular welfare had quietened faith-based care, but it hadn't stopped it happening. People weren't talking about it, or using religious language, like Temple's. But it was still happening. Note, however, that this non-religious articulation of welfare contributes to the loss of the ability to talk well about religion now.

Anxious re-visibility

So now to my third phase in the evolution. This I call 'anxious re-visibility', and this part of the story starts in 1979, when the first Thatcher Conservative government achieved power in the UK. By now welfarism had come to be seen, by Thatcher's party at least, as part of the problem, not the solution, and this was, of course, being mirrored by Reagan in the US. There was a shift in the UK and the US to 'market led approaches in the 1980s and early 1990s' (Mayo et al, 2003, p 28). The role of the state was minimised throughout the 1980s in favour of the handing over of service provision once again to non-government providers. This mixed economy of welfare had the effect of readmitting faith providers into welfare spaces, this time in a very visible way. This has allowed faiths to practice visibly once again in at least four spheres of activity.

First, they provide services through community development projects, as laid out above. These services are very local and respond to locally identified need, often with locally resident staff and volunteers. Second, they provide services on a larger scale through public sector tendering for large-scale services such as housing and major social care initiatives. Third, they have increasingly provided strategic services as partners and networks. This has found faiths setting up bodies such as the Faith-based Regeneration Network (FBRN), with government funding, designed to connect faith groups with each other, and with secular bodies, and to communicate with national and regional government. For example, in Britain, a former FBRN chief executive officer (CEO) was also an adviser to the Secretary of State for Communities and Local Government. Fourth, they have increasingly provided services as social enterprises – making a profit from a service (sometimes a completely unconnected service) that is used to pay for welfare services that are then free at the point of delivery.

This all chimes with the neoliberalism of the contemporary West. Various reports by faith groups themselves claim a crucial contribution right across the UK in this period, often articulated in financial terms (see further Dinham, 2007). In the South East, *Beyond belief* (March 2004) identifies at least two community action projects for each faith centre in the region. *Faith in the East of England* (July 2005) finds that there are 180,000 beneficiaries of faith-based community development in the region. In London, *Neighbourhood renewal in London: The role of faith communities* (May 2002) identified 7,000 projects in 2,200 faith buildings. In the West Midlands, *Believing in the region* (May 2006) reported that 80 per cent of faith groups deliver some kind of service to the wider community. In the North West, *Faith in England's North West* (November 2003) shows that faith communities were running more than 5,000 social action projects generating income of £69 million to £94 million per annum. In Yorkshire and the Humber, *Count us in* (2000) showed that in Hull, 90 per cent of churches were involved in social action, and *Angels and advocates* (November 2002) reported that there were 6,500 social action projects in churches. In the South West, *Faith in action* (June 2006) demonstrated that 165,000 people were supported by faith groups in the region, by 4,762 activities. In the East Midlands, *Faith in Derbyshire* (May 2006) claims that, on average, churches run nine community activities each.

But it's not just how much they do that matters; it is also what they do. Crucially we find that faith groups are doing the care work others don't or won't – with the homeless, addicted and sex workers, for example (Dinham, 2009).

As I have argued in my analysis of policy (see Dinham, 2009), the point is that, altogether, faith-based welfare turns out to be widely present at the margins of visible welfare, a sort of buttress for state welfare. It is possible that without it, the architecture of state welfare would collapse. And crucially, the mixed economy of welfare has made such faith-based activities highly visible again.

So this is the welfare story – church hands welfare over to the state. Everybody quickly realises that the state is not solving all the problems everywhere after all. In particular, rebuilt communities find themselves struggling, and churches prove highly active in addressing their needs. Finally, a neoliberal critique has the effect of re-mixing the welfare economy, and faith groups are suddenly very visible again after a period when nobody had talked about them, or about religion, for years.

Here we come to the crux of the problem. The really important thing to note is that two significant changes accompanied all this, and together they impose a whole new dimension – anxiety.

First is the fact that things have changed since the Church of England last called itself the national church. This is true of Anglican and established churches across the West. In general terms, the evidence suggests that religion and belief are both much less formal and significantly less creedal than they were 50 years ago (see Woodhead and Catto, 2012).

The second change occurred due to 9/11, and in London, 7/7 (although this was, of course, a global concern, with many local incidents). This tended to broadly distort perceptions of religion and belief (as suggested in Chapter Seven), and is criticised for having done so especially in relation to Islam. Stereotypes of religion and belief based on anxiety about extremism and violence are not conducive to the better quality of conversation that religious literacy seeks.

So we find ourselves in a very strange period. The relationship between religion and the secular has not gone as expected, and religion has changed dramatically, precisely in the period when secular theory was at its height and we were therefore thinking about it least. It turns out that society is neither simply secular nor simply religious, but complexly both. But the period in which we didn't talk well – or much – about religion – the 20th century, the period of secular dominance – leaves us precarious on the subject now, in practically every walk of life. The welfare state first accidentally silenced religion and the religious sensibility as the primary language of care. Then the increasingly mixed economy of welfare has accidentally readmitted religiously based actors at the heart of the public sphere in a context of far greater diversity and plurality, alongside far less capacity for addressing it. This is the conundrum of religious literacy as it presents through the welfare lens. It confronts the public sphere with the urgent need to re-skill its public professionals and citizens for the daily encounter with the full range of religious plurality. This is a challenge that will be picked up in subsequent chapters.

Note
[1] See www.toynbeehall.org.uk for more information about this service that still runs today.

References
Barnett, C. (2001) *The audit of war*, London: Pan.
Beveridge, W. (1942) *Social insurance and allied services*, London: HMSO.
Dinham A (2007) *Priceless, unmeasureable? Faiths and communuty development in 21st century England*, London: FbRN.
Dinham, A. (2009) *Faiths, public policy and civil society: Problems, policies, controversies*, Basingstoke: Palgrave Macmillan.

Furbey, R., Dinham, A., Farnell, R., Finneron, D., and Wilkinson, G. (2006) *Faith as social capital: Connecting or dividing?*, Bristol: Policy Press.

Mayo, M. (2000) *Cultures, communities, identities: Cultural strategies for participation and empowerment*, Basingstoke: Palgrave Macmillan.

Mayo, M., Mendiwelso-Nendek, Z. and Packham, C. (eds) (2013) *Community research for community development*, Basingstoke: Palgrave Macmillan.

Pederson, S. (1993) *Family, dependence and the origins of the welfare state: Britain and France, 1914-1945*, Cambridge: CUP.

Prochaska, F. (2006) *Christianity and social service in modern Britain: The disinherited spirit*, Oxford: OUP.

Stacey, M. (1969) 'The myth of community studies', *British Journal of Sociology*, vol 20, no 2, pp 134-47.

Temple, W. (1928) *Christianity and the state*, London: Macmillan & Co

Temple, W. (1941) *Christianity and the social order*, Penguin Special.

Timmins, N. (2001) *The five giants: A biography of the welfare state*, New York: HarperCollins.

Woodhead, L. and Catto, R. (eds) (2012) *Religion and change in modern Britain*, Abingdon: Routledge.

Younghusband, E. (1968) *Community work and social change*, Report of a Study Group on Training, set up by the Calouste Gulbenkian Foundation, London and Harlow: Longmans.

SEVEN

Religious literacy, radicalisation and extremism

Matthew Francis and Amanda van Eck Duymaer van Twist

Policy-makers frequently conceive of religion in three ways (often at the same time): as an *opportunity* (for delivering welfare programmes); as a *resource* (for community cohesion); and as a *threat* (to community cohesion and security) (Dinham et al, 2009, pp 5-6). This last aspect is often seen as reflecting a 'sinister side' of religion. Government policies in many countries have been developed to address the disturbing perception of religious ideology's apparent ability to motivate violent action. Likewise, the media has often focused on ways in which religion has been a threat to society, often at the expense of the positive and constructive contributions of faith-based communities and organisations, and episodes of religious violence frequently form the basis of (anecdotally based) evidence for public conversations about the dangers and ills of religion in the 21st century. This is also strongly reinforced by the reporting and quality of discourse after terror attacks; someone like Anders Breivik was dealt with as 'crazed' and the recent Washington DC shooter Aaron Alexis was described more as 'traumatised by 9/11' than as a Buddhist – it was mentioned in passing that he chanted. Had either frequently attended a mosque, the reporting would probably have been different. These examples serve to highlight that these acts were political as well as religious, but in certain cases the discourse afterwards focuses on the religious more than on the political.

There should be no surprise about this. Events such as 9/11 and 7/7 were atrocities by all bar a minority of understandings, and the posthumous attributions by their perpetrators of religious motivations has ensured that they will always be seen primarily as examples of religious violence. While these events may receive the majority of attention in Anglo-American discussions of religious terror, attacks around the world, from Madrid to Bali, Baghdad to Kabul, Bosnia to Palestine, are also primarily constructed as religiously driven, although the role of who is perpetrator and who is victim may shift according to the audience. In such conversations, supposedly divisive and even violent aspects of religions are frequently expanded in scope and time, to reach back to the religious wars of mediaeval Europe, the Crusades, and in more contemporary discussions of religiously motivated homophobia, sexism and sexual abuse.

In the UK, awareness of this 'sinister side' of religion may be seen to have come back to the fore in 1979 with the Iranian Revolution and in 1989, during the episodes of book-burning following the publication of *The Satanic Verses*, as both Grace Davie and Diane Moore have already suggested. Most especially, since an outbreak of 'disturbances' in 2001 in some religiously and ethnically diverse northern cities in the UK, religion has been conceived of as constituting a special threat to community cohesion, although some argued that these were the same old ethnic/anti-immigrant tensions that had been redefined when some communities began self-defining by religion rather than ethnicity (see Malik, 2009).

In many sectors (for example, higher education [HE] and justice), spaces (universities, prisons and mosques) and communities, religion, and in particular, Islam, all have played a prominent role in the considerations of politicians and policy-makers in how they counter extremist or even terrorist threats and build cohesive communities. Initiatives to achieve this have ranged from those received as openly divisive (CCTV monitoring of Muslim-majority neighbourhoods) to those more broadly accepted (interfaith programmes). But often the assumptions that underpin these initiatives, both in situating the threat and in framing the response, are overly simplistic. For example, following the 9/11 attacks, the then UK Prime Minister, Tony Blair, stated that he had read the Qur'an so that he could understand Islam (Deane, 2001). This kind of approach, while presumably well-meaning, reveals a simplistic understanding of a religion which has many other sources of textual authority, even more variations of belief and practice and millions of believers spread across hundreds of communities and cultures across the globe. Using the Qur'an to understand the actions of Mohamed Atta and his co-conspirators is as limited in scope as using the Bible to understand George W. Bush's response to the attacks. Both may have cited their respective religious faiths as motivations or justifications for action, but to assume that these provide the sole or even main means of explanation demonstrates a lack of religious literacy that crucially undermines policy-makers' ability to respond well or even appropriately.

In this chapter we demonstrate how religious literacy can contribute to a better understanding of the contexts, challenges and questions to ask about religion and belief. It explores how this might help policy-makers to make better policy about religion and belief. It focuses on policy as it has appeared, while acknowledging that the aspirations of policy are frequently lost in translation in the chain of delivery.

Such a religiously literate approach takes as its starting place an understanding that religion is lived and real for many people. Understanding holy texts and learning 'facts' about religion only takes politicians and practitioners so far, and assuming that getting different communities to talk together will bring them together misses the possibility that, as Lord Parekh has said, people can 'just learn how to kill each other better' (quoted in Dinham, 2011, p 3). Understanding that religion is flavoured by local community dynamics, that believers often choose what to believe, how to practice it and where – and whether – to belong, are all required to deliver a religiously literate response to these kinds of policy concerns. We also demonstrate that actions seen to be motivated solely by religion are often equally driven by these same local dynamics, personal experiences and broader power dynamics, in the same way as the actions of people committed to non-religious ideologies. We do so through a discussion of not just recent concerns over religious behaviour, but looking back to past concerns about religions – such as scare stories about new religious movements, or 'cults', for example, as well as how a religiously literate, sociological approach to studying religion can lead to positive policy outcomes.

Tackling the threat through policy

Government policy has targeted the divisive aspects of religion both directly and indirectly. Following terror attacks in the US, Spain and the UK, laws across Europe targeting immigration were dramatically re-written and accompanied by laws targeting the security of the state and the prevention of terrorism, both nationally and internationally (Cesari, 2009). In the UK, for example, the Anti-Terrorism, Crime and Security Act 2001 allowed for the detention of foreign nationals deemed a threat to security, and it has been suggested that this, and similar legislation, has disproportionately affected Muslims (Kundnani, 2003). Recently released Home Office figures show that, under terrorism legislation, 2,297 people were arrested from August 2001 to August 2012 (BBC, 2013b), 46 per cent of whom were Muslim, despite Muslims making up only 4.8 per cent of the UK population (ONS, 2012).

Beyond the criminalisation of acts glorifying terrorism, other policy approaches also directly or indirectly focused on the role religion (sometimes explicitly Islam) could play in building cohesive and safe communities. The *National Policing Plan 2005–08* (Home Office,

2004) highlighted the need to increase trust and resilience within 'minority faith communities' to underpin the government's counter-terrorism strategies. Muslims were actively recruited to play a part in the implementation of the counter-terrorism 'Prevent' policy, which included initiatives to train Imams and to empower Muslim women to play a positive role in society, including that of tackling extremism (Home Office, 2005; CLG, 2007). While an increased focus on religion in policing pre-dated the counter-terrorism Prevent agenda (McFayden and Prideaux, 2013), the conflation of this with counter-terrorism strategies undoubtedly demonstrated the threat that certain religious communities were deemed to pose.

The effect of this legal apparatus against terrorism was to securitise the UK Muslim population (Cesari, 2009), and to recast it as a 'suspect community' (Hickman et al, 2011). This isn't the first time in recent UK history that religion has played a role in stigmatising a community in the light of terrorism, as has been shown in an analysis of the impact of terrorism laws on the Irish community (Hillyard and Liberty, 1993). However, as Hickman et al (2011) have shown, the way that religion has been portrayed in more recent legislation is significantly different, and they write: 'only in the case of Islam is religion identified as the source of a potential ideological threat' (p 4), and they further note that due to the incorporation of religion into counter-terrorist initiatives, Islam and Muslims have increasingly become coterminous with terrorism in public discussions (see also Moore et al, 2008, p 3). Studies of the media have shown the common interweaving of Muslim identities with terrorist actions, demonstrating that Islam is the most talked about religion in the UK media, for example, and most commonly in a negative light (Baker, 2010; Knott et al, 2013). In the US, Pew Research recently released figures demonstrating that the majority of Muslims (over 11 surveyed countries) were against suicide bombings and violence (Pew Research, 2013). The findings themselves are not extraordinary, but the idea of asking such a question of Christians, or Buddhists, would be. Despite increasing Buddhist violence in Sri Lanka and Burma, and a long history of Christian violence in many locales, it is Islam that is fixed in the public imagination as at best troublesome and at worst violent.

Government responses to Islamic violence have frequently tended to portray the actions of a few terrorists claiming Islamic justifications as representative of a 'bad Islam'. The government, in response, seeks to engage with 'good Muslims', a discourse that further hardens the public recognition of a good/bad distinction within Islam and of religion more broadly (Geaves, 2004; Haddad and Golson, 2007). Played out beyond discussions of Islam, writers such as Dawkins (2006) and Harris (2004), among others, point to the violence and harm that religion in general has caused around the world, suggesting that religion is incapable of being anything other than violent (Harris, 2004, p 225).

The creation of these binaries – good/bad religion (and for some, bad religion/good secularism) – all suffer from a lack of religious literacy at the level of understanding the categories themselves. In addition to being unhelpful generalisations in themselves, they flatten the religious landscape under homogeneous headings that do little justice to the rich variety of contemporary belief and practice.

Of course, both policy-makers and practitioners are aware that there is more variation to religions and to particular communities than is set out in simple binaries of good/bad, moderate/extremist, and so on. But as more detailed analysis of their impact has shown, too often this knowledge is not apparent in the experiences of religious communities (Spalek, 2008; Cesari, 2009; Hickman et al, 2011). This disconnection between policy intention and impact is likely due in no small part to a failure to understand the complexity of the religious landscape. The variety of beliefs, communities and practices varies from country to country – the US has a markedly different historical, legal and popular context to the UK, and the same can be said for countries around the European Union (EU). However, it is to the UK context that we now turn, and, as we outline, some of the broad lessons learned from the UK can be applied elsewhere.

From many gods to more

As set out in Chapter One, the introductory chapter, and in the Foreword to this volume, the relationship between religious and secular ideals in the UK is complex; to argue that the country is simply becoming more secular glosses over a much messier picture. The same is equally true when talking about the diversity of religions. Often, when talking about the recent plurality of religions in postwar Britain there is an assumption that the spiritual life of the country has devolved somehow, from one God to many. But while the Church of England had, and continues to enjoy, a position of privilege in regards to the state, the assumption that the country was previously just 'Christian' or 'Anglican' forgets the extensive variety of alternatives. Setting to one side the fact of many competing Christian denominations since the Reformation (some of which were so marginalised and persecuted they set out to found new colonies), the UK has long been home to prominent atheists, Theosophists, Spiritualists, Jehovah's Witnesses,

Jews, Muslims, Buddhists, Zoroastrians, Jains, many kinds of Pagans, and a variety of sects, among others. Since the Second World War the sizes, varieties and numbers of non-Christian (as well as Christian) communities have grown, but this diversity only complicates the picture further. Some communities self-identify as a syncretism of religious traditions which had previously been seen as separate (such as the Ravidassia, where some identify as Hindus, others as Sikhs, and some as both or neither), whereas others may identify with only a small aspect of a wider tradition (such as Vaishnavas, who worship Vishnu over and above other gods in the Hindu pantheon). Sticking with Southeast Asian religions, there are monotheist Hindus, polytheist Hindus, atheist Hindus, a plethora of schools of Buddhism, those who follow particular Sants (living saints) and, for many of these, their Western hybrids. This hybridity is a further feature of these religious communities, both in 'sending' and 'receiving' countries, and is reflected in the explosion of new religious movements, particularly noticeable in the postwar period. These new religious movements can be new in the sense that they are newly established in the West (but old in their native environment), recently established, re-interpreted, re-imagined, or recently syncretised with other convictions (be they environmental, political, psychological or other).

This diversity stretched any pre-existing ideas of what religion is, and many countries struggled to accommodate the new diversity in a consistent and fair way – with varying results. Despite many human rights instruments guaranteeing rights related to freedom and belief, there is no internationally recognised definition of religion, and it remains undefined as a matter of international law (Gunn, 2003). The UK's approach has been a broadly hospitable one, allowing religions to enter and operate within the laws of the land, and to register as a religious charity in order to practice advancement of religion, education, or be otherwise of benefit to the community. However, this illuminates aspects with which the UK public sphere has also struggled: in order to register as a religious charity in the past, a religious organisation had to be theistic and have an element of worship. Consequently, some applications of organisations that self-defined as religious were rejected because they did not have these features. In a later review of charity law, the requirement of a supreme being and worship made way for a focus on public benefit in an effort to make charity law more inclusive, and perhaps more relevant in a diverse society. Yet, public benefit proved a challenge as well, as shown in the case of the Exclusive Brethren, who follow a doctrine of moral and physical separation, and have struggled to get registered as a religious charity as a result of this doctrine (and the practice of withdrawing from those who are considered to have strayed off the 'right path'). This exclusiveness clashes with the UK Charity Commission's concept of public benefit, which states that benefit should extend to those who are not adherents. Nonetheless, the Exclusive Brethren have appealed, and in 2014 the Charity Commission accepted an application for registration on the condition that the Exclusive Brethren revise a governing document to make the organisation more compliant with the Commission's standards of public benefit. Although the concept of public benefit bypassed many complicated and fraught debates about defining aspects of religion (and whether it must include a supreme being and acts of worship), public benefit has not yet made the registration of religious charities void of controversy.

Increasing diversity has also led to tensions within existing communities, and within faith traditions, as the idea of what makes up a particular religious tradition is contestable. For example, Sunni Muslims are generally happy to consider Shi'as as Muslim brethren, but both would dispute that the Ahmadiyyas are Muslim brethren within their fold. The latter are persecuted in Pakistan and have set up their headquarters in the UK. They are often considered a challenge at interfaith meetings (when invited), and many Sunni and Shi'a Muslims would argue they are 'not really Muslims', referring to them as 'Qadianis', a derogatory term used by their opponents. Likewise, Sikhs have a variety of Gurdwaras throughout the UK, but some associated with particular Sants (holy men) are generally avoided by the majority of Sikhs. Such a case came to a head a few years ago when one Sikh referred to a particular Sant as a cult leader, and criticised the way a Gurdwara associated with this person was run. The Sant sued for libel, the case took four years, and was ultimately unsuccessful (Singh, 2012).

Many of these tensions and frictions are played out within specific communities, and the rest of society is often mainly oblivious to this. It happens on a relatively small scale, and interfaith and intrafaith work often resolves many of these disputes. However, in other cases tensions can increase and lead to conflict.

Of course these are not always new tensions; there are also pre-existing ill feelings that reappear in a new cultural context. Tensions between religious traditions that have their roots in conflict and the displacement of communities can suddenly reappear as new folk devils based on old stereotypes, for example, and fears can rapidly be rekindled. Stories of Muslim men seducing the daughters of Sikh and/or Hindu families so that they will convert to Islam have been quite persistent. In the UK there have been recent allegations of Muslim men grooming vulnerable 'English' girls to exploit them. In the Netherlands similar stories were found with the so-called 'loverboys', who were reported to be mainly young Moroccans who would groom girls, ply them with gifts and promises, only to later prostitute them. Although such grooming and/or abuse does occur, it is not necessarily tied with religion. Being Muslim does not automatically make a person's crimes 'Muslim crimes'. In some cases, the accusations and stories were rooted in old tensions between communities stemming from historical battles in other parts of the world (Sian, 2011; van San and Bovenkerk, 2013), but once folk devils have been created, it is difficult to dissolve them (Cohen, 1987).

Division from cohesion

These divisions, within and between religious movements, have many and complex causes, and remaining attentive to them is important. Why this is so can be seen in some of the assumptions made in government policy to improve community cohesion. Defined as a policy objective, this grew out of the response to the riots in 2001 in a number of northern towns and cities in England resulting in an inquiry and the Cantle report (2001), which identified communities in the affected cities as living 'parallel lives'. Several religious factors were highlighted among the findings, such as extremists exploiting intercommunal ignorance and the role of faith schools as strengthening divisions. The government's response, the Denham report (2001), likewise highlighted the need for interfaith dialogue, and debate about shared values and religion became an explicit element of these discussions. Policy developments on this theme continued throughout the decade, including increased support for bodies like the Inter Faith Network, the creation of a Prime Minister's special envoy to all faith communities (John Battle, MP) and perhaps most significantly, the *Face to face* report (CLG, 2008), which promoted a framework for increased interfaith dialogue.

The growing focus on faith-related policy, faith and interfaith forums as places for discussion, and faith being on the national agenda more broadly, represented not just a policy shift, but also an increased awareness of an underlying Balkanisation of what had broadly been seen as a homogeneous 'Other'. Whereas UK multicultural policy had initially been focused on bridging between a white majority and black minority, over time, the latter was increasingly shown to contain greater layers and multiplicity of identities, from black to also Asian, which itself subsequently further devolved to Indian, Pakistani and

Bangladeshi, and so on. However, as Cantle has observed, in providing clearer and more accurate pictures of distinct communities, this process has increased the level of difference and exclusion (Ahmed et al, 2009, pp 86-7).

This is because identity formations naturally exclude, as well as include – identity is defined as much by what binds a group together as what separates it from others. Even though government policies were generally targeted at interfaith and multifaith projects (Dinham, 2012, pp 62-3), these could also still be exclusive. For example, questions about who has access to power and funding are important issues, as has been argued by Druids who have been refused membership of the Inter Faith Network, excluding them from local and national networks, discussions and other resources (Gledhill, 2012).

Definitions of 'religion' are slippery and often contradictory in academic discussions as well as legal and policy debates. They change over time and have real consequences, as shown in the recent (2013) legal decision to accord a Scientology chapel religious status in relation to marriage, a decision which reversed an earlier judgment that Scientology could not be a religion because it lacked belief in a 'supreme being'. Whereas the earlier judgment had carried, in its interpretation of 'religious worship', an implicit theistic definition of religion, the appeal concluded that there has never been a universal legal definition of religion in English law (*Hodkin v Registrar General* [2013] UKSC 77 at 32-34). The new ruling maintained that, for the purposes of registering a place of worship, religion should not be confined to faiths involving a supreme deity (since to do so would exclude Buddhism, Jainism and others), but also allow for non–theistic worship (*Hodkin v Registrar General* [2013] UKSC 77 at 51-52).

These definitions are important where policy attempts to negotiate with religious groups, and where assumptions of interreligious harmony, institutional comparability and common structures of representation are made. For example, promoting interreligious networks as places of common encounter assumes that all groups are equally welcome, that organisations have the means to send participants, and that there are easily identifiable representatives.

This latter point has been shown to be problematic where assumptions based on a history of dealing with the Church of England have meant that local and national governments frequently look for similar hierarchical arrangements in other religious groups, arrangements that often simply do not exist. Further complicating matters is the fact that representatives may be self-nominated or nominated by a small portion of 'their' community, such that the voices of women, young people and many considered to be on the margins of movements are often not heard, while the voices of some can be amplified beyond the influence or respect they actually command. (For the impact of this on policing Muslim communities, for example, see Spalek and Lambert, 2008, p 264.)

Governments' focus on faith communities also runs the risk of alienating non-religious ideological and belief movements, the British Humanist Association being a prime and vocal example. While equalities law recognises non-religious systems of belief, government policy has frequently been felt to exclude such groups, both through interfaith forums and through policies around faith schools.

So while seeking to promote community cohesion, policy can be seen to damage these aims through assumptions about which religious groups have been included; parity of resources allowing engagement; representativeness of spokespeople; and exclusion of comparable non-religious movements. A more religiously literate iteration of these policies would understand these realities, recognising, for example, that 'representatives' of religious communities are rarely that. For instance, while the Roman Catholic Church has a very clear and hierarchical representative structure, recent research shows that there is a wide disparity between the Pope's teachings on the use of prophylactics and the practices of those who call themselves Catholic – with only 9 per cent of professed British Catholics suggesting that using a condom is problematic (Woodhead, 2013).

So while members of religious communities may share common identities, or aspects of identity, they do not necessarily share all of the beliefs and values that inform those identities. In contemporary Britain, where cultural and religious pluralism has led to far greater variety, and where consumer culture is increasingly echoed in religious choices too, it is important not to assume hegemony of belief, and to allow for marginalised and often counter-intuitive voices to also be heard.

Intracommunal as well as intercommunal difference will always be part of a pluralistic society. Any definition of a cohesive community of believers is pitched against those who do not cohere (which is essentially and by definition divisive). Such distinctions can lead to tension, friction and even violence in cases when a certain mix of cultural and political conditions coincides. In supporting religious communities, policy-makers need to understand that division is the other side of the coin from cohesion. Whenever an attempt is made to make a community unified, this involves creating community identity – which risks pitching it against another identity. Boundaries are always set, and while difference can normally be (and is normally) celebrated, nevertheless discord can arise, which in its extremes can lead to violence.

Case study in complexity: Buddhism in the UK

The proposition of this chapter is that religious literacy is important for good policy-making about religion and belief, especially as it relates to radicalisation. It is also important in helping people to talk about differences as well as similarities in an informed manner in general. This requires access to reliable information, which can avoid or at least respond to media and moral panics, especially when they concern violence and extremism. But this is difficult when groups are unpopular, have a bad reputation, and reliable information is difficult to collect. Some communities do keep to themselves, they may have what appears to be a separatist attitude, or keep those who they perceive as intruders out in order to keep the faithful safe. Some isolated groups can be problematic, while others just prefer to keep to themselves – yet this distinction can be difficult to make for an outsider.

This recalls aspects of the so-called cult wars of the 1970s, where some new religions were demonised, and from these, generalisations were made about all new religions. In reality, the problematic groups were a very small minority, and the remainder a largely harmless diversity of new and minority religions and spiritualities – a diversity which, as we have noted, has grown further since. Most people have heard about Waco (the Branch Davidians) and Jonestown (The Peoples Temple). Yet their reputation rubbed off on countless minority groups who happened to be new in town, notwithstanding their beliefs, practices, or even religious tradition.

It is perhaps difficult to talk about the complexity of religious communities in the UK without giving a complex example. For many people, Buddhism is an example of a peaceful religion, popularly involving meditation and yoga. As we show here, even in the UK, where Buddhism is a relative newcomer, there is a great depth of complexity to the different Buddhist communities and strands of belief, and some controversy too.

The introduction of Buddhism to the West came initially through intellectual routes (through scholars, writers and artists), many of them officials who were posted to different parts of Asia during the colonial period, and who also happened to be amateur scholars. Many of the first centres founded in the West focused on Buddhist text, teachings and philosophy, mainly from a scholarly perspective, and were founded by Western scholars and writers. Buddhism became a popular subject of study and discussion, through organisations such as the Theosophical Society and later, several travelling Englishmen returned to the UK as ordained Buddhists. Eventually a number of people got together and formed the Buddhist Society of Great Britain and Ireland in 1907, which was succeeded in 1924 by the London Buddhist Society. The latter provided a platform for all schools and traditions of Buddhism.

In Britain in the 1960s, Eastern religions became fashionable, and lamas (Tibetan Dharma teachers) and other Asian gurus began travelling to the West. By 2001 there were over 30 different traditions or sub-traditions of Buddhism in Britain, with almost 1,000 Buddhist groups and centres in all. By 2011 the Buddhist population had grown as a result of immigration. In England and Wales, according to the 2011 Census, the largest proportion of Buddhists (247,743) was Asian or Asian British (147,796) and of these, the largest proportions identified as Chinese (49,344) and 'Other Asian' (93,581), whereas Caucasian Buddhists amounted to 83,635. This may, of course, not include those who practice meditation and visit Buddhist temples but who also identify with another religion, or who are not formally affiliated to a *sangha* (commonly meaning a community of Buddhists). Western Buddhists tend to be lay Buddhists – there are far more monastic orders in the East.

Although the early Buddhists in Britain were mainly from Theravadin groups (Burma, Thailand and Sri Lanka), followed by Zen and Tibetan Buddhism, by 2014 almost every Buddhist tradition is represented in Britain. Furthermore, some Buddhist traditions have been syncretised and adapted to contemporary society. British-founded Buddhist movements include Sangharakshita's (aka Dennis Lingwood) Friends of the Western Buddhist Order (FWBO, now the Triratna Buddhist Community) founded in 1967, and the New Kadampa Tradition (NKT), founded in 1991. Triratna is an interdenominational Buddhist group dedicated to communicating Buddhist teachings in ways it deems appropriate to the modern Western world; it was developed from the Gelug school of Tibetan Buddhism.

Both groups have been controversial both within and outside of the traditions in which they placed themselves. Sangharakshita sought to include sexually inclusive teachings into the Buddhist practice, but some argued that this created an atmosphere where some felt coerced into gay relationships as part of their Buddhist lifestyles at the FWBO. Others felt he was indulging his own sexuality within a religious context where sexuality should not be directing the dynamics of the community. (For more information on this issue, see www.ex-cult.org/fwbo/fwbofiles. htm#sidesteps and a response by the then FWBO can be read at http://response.fwbo.org/guardian-article/guardian.html). The NKT courted controversy for practices (including meditation and prayers) linked to the Protector Deity Dorje Shugden. The NKT has pointed to support of Dorje Shugden shown by important figures in Tibetan Buddhism including the Fifth Dalai Lama. However, the current (Fourteenth) Dalai Lama renounced the practice of Dorje Shugden in 1975, explaining that the practice has a history of contributing to a climate of sectarian disharmony in various parts of Tibet, and between various Tibetan communities. The disagreement has led to members of the NKT to stage protests against the Dalai Lama.

These disputes may seem esoteric and specific to their particular groups, which are small and statistically insignificant. However, these issues, among others, have created disputes within the Network of Buddhist Organisations, and so many groups have now left this umbrella group that it can no longer be considered representative of Buddhists in Britain. Furthermore, both groups have sought to integrate into the wider community, and consequently, these allegations and issues occasionally rear their heads again. The FWBO, now known as the Triratna Buddhist Order, has become a leading promoter of meditation as a technique for promoting mental health. They have started a separate website and service called 'Breathing Space', which was set up at the London centre by Dr Paramabandhu Groves, an NHS consultant psychiatrist and Buddhist practitioner, in 2004. Their courses take place in a 'secular space' at the London Buddhist Centre. They have received £260,659 of government funding from Futurebuilders for offering free meditation courses and retreats for those on a low income. The NKT offers meditation classes at bookshops and university campuses, among other places, but does not explain from the start that their form of Tibetan Buddhism is considered sectarian by many other Tibetan organisations.

There are many such disputes within religious traditions in Britain that go unnoticed by the mainstream media and the general public. This is partly because such disputes are often difficult to understand, and the groups involved are considered more mainstream than 'cults'. Of course the idea of what makes a cult is subjective and different for every individual – for many, it is a stereotyped visual image of 'Moonies' (mass weddings) and Rajneeshies (orange robes and a charismatic leader with Rolexes and Rolls-Royces), and for some it is the theologically non-Trinitarian Watchtower Society, while for others it is the politicised Hizb-ut-Tahrir. Much of the assumed knowledge about 'cults' is picked up from the media, where the focus is on those atrocity tales that are more likely to sell newspapers. Yet the media are influential, in shaping both knowledge and policy (Beckford, 1985).

The point of all this is that we need to know what we are talking about, but of course obtaining knowledge at the level of detail shown here is difficult and realistically restricted to specialists. Being religiously literate does not require in-depth knowledge of the kind we have outlined here, but it does require an understanding that these kinds of complexities exist. It is essential to be ready and open to ask questions and pursue more detail where necessary.

'Brainwashing' and 'radicalisation': we've been here before

One of the significant concerns to come out of the case of one of the more famous 'cults', Aum Shinrikyo (the group responsible for releasing sarin gas on the Tokyo underground rail system in March 1995), was how so many young and apparently intelligent people came to be 'brainwashed' into following its guru, Asahara. This concern about brainwashing has been a real concern in the UK too, and shares some characteristics with what is commonly thought of as 'radicalisation'.

In the UK brainwashing became national news when, in 1981, the *Daily Mail* (a popular tabloid newspaper) published an in-depth article on the Unification Church (UC), whose adherents were then often referred to as 'Moonies' (followers of its leader, Sun Myung Moon), and accusing it of brainwashing its members. The church sued the *Daily Mail* for libel, but lost in what was then the biggest libel pay-out. The paper subsequently also won a British Press Award for the story (Borders, 1981). This happened at a time when the concept of brainwashing was common currency for explaining why young people would throw away their promising lives and join unsavoury religious cults. In the *Daily Mail* case, the court used expert testimony of Margaret Singer, an adjunct Professor of Psychiatry in the US, who explained how individuals could be brainwashed against their will.

The term 'brainwashing' had its origins in the writings of Robert Jay Lifton and Edgar Schein, who wrote about the effects of physical and social deprivation on American prisoners of war after the Korean war, which had led to some making anti-American statements. Lifton referred to the process as 'thought reform', while Schein used 'coercive persuasion'; both agreed that it had a temporary effect, that any thought reform or coercive persuasion that had occurred was not irreversible. But these general concepts were later used in theories to explain why young people joined so-called 'cults'. Singer, in particular, became a popular expert witness in court cases, arguing what became known as the 'brainwashing defence' – individuals should not be held responsible for crimes committed while under 'mind control'.

Other scholars (mainly sociologists) questioned the validity of her theories, and argued that the new religious movements generally accused did not have the kind of retention rates of followers that would suggest they had mastered irreversible mind-control techniques, and that there existed no generally accepted scientific theory that supported brainwashing theories. Eileen Barker's (1984) research on the UC in particular established that the church had no access to irresistible and irreversible techniques of brainwashing. The American Psychological Association (APA) asked Singer to chair a task force to investigate the validity of brainwashing as a theory, but later this report was rejected by the Board of Social and Ethical Responsibility for lack of scientific rigour (APA, 1987; Cesnur, 1999).

Despite finding no scientific evidence to support the term, 'brainwashing' continues to cause controversy (Zablocki and Robbins, 2001). The fears of mass brainwashing by 'Moonies' in the 1970s were still repeated, if less breathlessly, at the death of Reverend Moon in 2012, and the weird sexual practices, murder and abuse of supposed cults still make good newspaper headlines (see, for example, Jones, 2013; Shears, 2013; Steward, 2013). While there have been persuasive and conclusive experiments that show people can be persuaded by authority, peer pressure and group pressure, it is not possible to predict conclusively, however, exactly how someone will react, to what extent, and for how long (for example, see Phillip Zimbardo's Stanford Prison Experiment, Solomon Asch's conformity experiments and Stanley Milgram's experiments testing obedience to authority).

Hence, as Professor Eileen Barker often says, the brainwashing debate was a critique of style and content – cults are bad, religion is good. Echoes of this debate continue to this day with 'extremists' replacing 'cults' and 'brainwashing' being replaced with 'radicalisation'. Just like arguments a few decades ago that brainwashing could be countered by deprogramming, there are now de-radicalisation programmes. The overlap between the concepts are displayed in the case of John Walker Lindh (the 'American Taliban'), an American citizen, baptised Catholic, who was captured as an enemy combatant in Afghanistan in 2001 and whose parents believed he had been brainwashed into fighting against his country (BBC, 2002).

Like brainwashing, the concept of radicalisation can also lead to ill-informed debate and comment; one of the issues with both concepts is that they tend to argue from the exception. While millions of followers were claimed to be brainwashed by the Moonies in the 1970s, Barker

(1984, p 65) has shown that in 1981 there were likely only 1,800 full-time members in the US, and perhaps 50,000 worldwide. Likewise, theories of radicalisation have been based on low numbers of people in comparison to the broader populations the examples were drawn from (for example, young and Muslim). The problem with building arguments based on few examples is that the data are inevitably skewed. Arguments highlight the psychopathology of the individuals, or the economic deprivation of their upbringing, the unsettled nature of their families or their anger at foreign policy. Yet for each of these compelling conclusions there are, of course, plenty of other individuals in similar situations who have not acted violently, and who do not hold extreme beliefs.

Conclusions

In the high stakes games of preventing violent radicalisation, these 'arguments from exception' have had disproportionate policy results. For example, the top 19 UK areas in receipt of community cohesion funding from 2008 to 2011 also happen to be the areas with the 19 largest Muslim populations (Kundnani, 2009, pp 13-14). As Kundnani (2009, p 12) points out, this suggests that decisions as to which areas provide the biggest risk of terrorism were made on the basis that Muslims are a risk. Therefore the implication is that more Muslims equals more risk. This analysis did not appear to take account of local concerns or analysis of potential risks. Kundnani argues that in allowing funding to be linked to the size of what was seen as one particular religious community, it led to the securitising of all Muslims.

This draws attention to the religiously illiterate assumption that all Muslims belong to a single community. While a few Muslims do talk of belonging to, or needing to create, a global community or state (an *Umma*), this is not a universal aim, and indeed many Muslims come from groups that would be persecuted under such a state.

However, because Muslims hear the talk of the threat of Islam and how politicians will prevent it (regardless of their nationality, sect or beliefs), this can also have the unintended consequence of making some Muslims feel threatened, which may itself result in 'radicalising' them (Cesari, 2009). This is an example of a religiously illiterate policy approach having precisely the opposite effect to that intended.

While much of the focus of counter-terrorism efforts continue to be targeted at Muslim groups, the religious roots of violent action have been downplayed in the most recent iteration of government policy (HM Government, 2011). This reflects the reality that religious beliefs are only one of a number of causes of violent action, and that the move to violent action can be seen to be motivated by a number of factors, including situational factors that can include socioeconomic deprivation and specific triggers like wars, as well as rational strategic decisions (Francis, 2012). Put simply, there is no straightforward conveyor belt of radicalisation, religious or otherwise. It does not have common ingredients; it cannot easily be predicted.

A more useful policy focus therefore would be on individual beliefs, and in the case of violence, on those sacred or non-negotiable beliefs that can motivate or justify violent action (Francis and Knott, 2011; Francis, 2015). This makes writing policy (and media headlines) more complicated, of course, but policy would be improved where it recognised that it is not Islam, or Sunni Islam, or even Salafi Islam – or for that matter, Christian, or Jain, or any other tradition – which makes someone violent, but a belief that violence is legitimate in response to certain events. Focusing on these beliefs, religious or non-religious, also encourages a realisation of the need for understanding the great complexity of beliefs that exist within religious communities in the UK.

A future for religiously literate policy?

We have suggested that government policy on community cohesion, where it has supported single and multifaith initiatives, has also tended to reinforce the fences between differing movements. We have also argued for a need to look beyond the homogenised labels of religious groups and their representatives, to allow for the huge variety of individual beliefs within these communities. This religiously literate approach allows people to see the gates in the fences, so to speak, where shared values may create shared sites for cohesion.

In respect to radicalisation, as with community cohesion and other aims of government policy, this much broader scope of engagement with religious beliefs could further complicate and potentially diminish the ability of government to meaningfully engage with religious believers. After all, it can be hard enough getting representatives of religious communities to sit around the same table without also including every sub-group, dissident faction, campaign and so on. But plurality, diversity and multiplicity are the reality. In practice, a degree of pragmatism is likely to be necessary, although where possible, robust information and data on groups and potentially excluded voices should always be considered, and more decisions on inclusion and funding devolved to local settings where they can be more meaningfully applied to the local context. Indeed, this focus on local context has been found to be a positive element of some police forces' interaction with a complex mix of local actors, for example, where research has also called for context-specific religious literacy in community policing (McFadyen and Prideaux, 2011).

Here, good academic research can play a role. The gathering of objective, reliable quantitative and qualitative data that provides valuable nuance and detail on religious groups is something that many academics and organisations have undertaken for some time, in some cases making special efforts to connect this to government and policy-making. Whether it is providing detail about Buddhist groups that challenges assumptions of intergroup harmony or data about what Anglicans think about same-sex marriage that contradict the views of former archbishops, such information has a valuable role to play in policy decisions.

This information can also play a role in understanding and positively responding to concerns about radicalisation and a perceived 'sinister side' of religion. It can reveal how divisive aspects of religious groups are sometimes the flip side of those same aspects that can promote cohesion. At the same time, it is important to note that cases where this division leads to discord are in the minority, and should not detract from what appear to be the overwhelmingly positive benefits of engaging with faith communities (Dinham, 2007). Research on religion in universities (Dinham and Jones, 2010) and in the police (McFadyen and Prideaux, 2013) have shown how religious communities are often helpful, practically identifiable groups that represent a community of values which can sometimes be otherwise difficult to reach. Radicalisation, extremism and cultism are best understood when they are placed in the context of complexity, understood as reflecting identity, rather than tradition, and it is recognised that they constitute a tiny minority, rather than representing most of the story of public religion and belief.

References

Ahmed, M., Cantle, T. and Hussain, D. (2009) 'Faith, multiculturalism and community cohesion: a policy conversation', in A. Dinham, R. Furbey, and V. Lowndes (eds), *Faith in the public realm: controversies, policies and practices*, Bristol: Policy Press, pp 83–103.

APA (American Psychological Association) (1987) Memorandum to Members of the Task Force on Deceptive and Indirect Methods of Persuasion and Control (DIMPAC) (www.cesnur.org/testi/APA.htm).

Baker, P. (2010) 'Representations of Islam in British broadsheet and tabloid newspapers 1999–2005', *Language and Politics*, vol 9, no 2, pp 310–38.

Barker, E. (1984) *The making of a Moonie: Choice or brainwashing?*, Oxford: Basil Blackwell.

BBC (2002) 'Profile: John Walker Lindh', *BBC News* (http://news.bbc.co.uk/1/hi/world/americas/1779455.stm).

BBC (2013) 'Terror-arrest charges reach highest level', *BBC News* (www.bbc.co.uk/news/uk-24059944).

Borders, W. (1981) 'Moon's sect loses libel suit in London', *The New York Times* (www.nytimes.com/1981/04/01/world/moon-s-sect-loses-libel-suit-in-london.html).

Bowcott, O. (2014) 'Afghan atheist granted UK asylum', *The Guardian*, (www.theguardian.com/uk-news/2014/jan/14/afghan-atheist-uk-asylum).

Bowers, P. (2011) *Review of Prevent strategy*, London: House of Commons Library (www.parliament.uk/briefing-papers/SN05993).

Bunting, M. (1997) 'The dark side of enlightenment', *The FWBO Files* (www.fwbo-files.com/guardian_article_v2.htm).

Cantle, T. (2001) *Community cohesion*, London: Home Office.

Cesari, J. (2009) *The securitisation of Islam in Europe*, Brussels: Centre for European Policy Studies.

Cesnur (1999) CESNUR - APA Documents on Brainwashing. Cesnur. (www.cesnur.org/testi/APA_Documents.htm).

CLG (Department for Communities and Local Government) (2007) 'Muslim women to advise Government on preventing violent extremism' (http://webarchive.nationalarchives.gov.uk/20080205233224/http://www.communities.gov.uk/news/corporate/554064).

CLG (2008) *Face to face and side by side: A framework for partnership in our multi faith society*, London: Department for Communities and Local Government.

Cohen, S. (1987) *Folk devils and moral panics: The creation of the mods and rockers*, 2nd edn, Oxford: Basil Blackwell.

Dawkins, R. (2007) *The God delusion*, London: Black Swan.

Deane, J. (2001) 'War on terror: PM strides globe in bid to defeat terrorists', *Birmingham Post*, p 5.

Denham, J. (2001) *Building cohesive communities: A report of the Ministerial Group on Public Order and Community Cohesion*, London: Home Office.

Dinham, A. (2007) *Priceless, unmeasureable? Faiths and community development in 21st century England*, London: Faith Based Regeneration Network UK.

Dinham, A. (2011) 'What is Theology and Religious Studies for?', *Discourse*, vol 10, no 3, pp 1–7.

Dinham, A. (2012) *Faith and social capital after the debt crisis: The laughter of bishops*, Basingstoke: Palgrave Macmillan.

Dinham, A. and Jones, S.H. (2010) *An analysis of challenges of religious faith, and resources for meeting them, for university leaders*, York: Religious Literacy Leadership in Higher Education Programme.

Francis, M.D. (2012) 'What causes radicalisation? Main lines of consensus in recent research' (www.radicalisationresearch.org/features/Francis-2012-causes/).

Francis, M.D.M. (2015) 'Why the "sacred" is a better resource than "religion" for understanding terrorism', *Terrorism and Political Violence* (http://www.tandfonline.com/doi/full/10.1080/09546553.2014.976625).

Francis, M.D. and Knott, K. (2011) 'Return? It never left. Exploring the "sacred" as a resource for bridging the gap between the religious and the secular, in *Islam and religious norms in the public sphere*, Berkeley, CA (http://igovberkeley.com/content/return-it-never-left-exploring-%E2%80%98sacred%E2%80%99-resource-bridging-gap-between-religious-and-secular).

The Friends of the Western Buddhist Order (FWBO) (1999) 'The Guardian's article on the FWBO' (http://response.fwbo.org/guardian-article/guardian.html).

Geaves, R. (2004) 'Who defines moderate Islam "post"-September 11?', in R. Geaves et al (eds), *Islam and the West post 9/11*, Aldershot: Ashgate, pp 62–74.

Gledhill, R. (2012) 'Interfaith group's refusal to admit Druids sparks row', *The Times* (London) (www.thetimes.co.uk/tto/faith/article3617192.ece).

Haddad, Y.Y. and Golson, T. (2007) 'Overhauling Islam: Representation, construction, and cooption of moderate Islam in Western Europe', *Journal of Church and State*, vol 49, pp 487–516.

Harris, S. (2006) *The end of faith: Religion, terror, and the future of reason*, London: Free.

Hickman, M.J., Thomas, L., Silvestri, S. and Nickels, H. (2011) *'Suspect Communities'? Counter-terrorism policy, the press, and the impact on Irish and Muslim communities in Britain*, London: London Metropolitan University.

Hillyard, P. (1993) *Suspect community : People's experience of the Prevention of Terrorism Acts in Britain*, London: Pluto Press.

HM Government (2011) *Prevent Strategy*, London: HM Government.

Hodkin and Anor, R (on the application of) v Registrar-General of Births, Deaths and Marriages [2013] UKSC 77 (http://www.bailii.org/uk/cases/UKSC/2013/77.html).

Home Office (2004) *National Policing Plan 2005–08: Safer, Stronger Communities*, London: Home Office (http://webarchive. nationalarchives.gov.uk/20100303141507/http://police.homeoffice. gov.uk/publications/national-policing-plan/national_policing_plan. html).

Home Office (2005) *Preventing Extremism Together: Working Groups August to October 2005*, London: Her Majesty's Stationery Office.

Jones, D. (2013) 'The Devon cult that canes tiny children to "cleanse their sins": As social services launches investigation, a mother's shocking testimony lifts the lid on the mysterious commune squatting on a Devon Farm', *Mail Online* (www.dailymail.co.uk/news/ article-2444736/Devon-cult-canes-children-cleanse-sins-Mothers-testimony-lifts-lid-mysterious-commune.html).

Juergensmeyer, M. (2003) *Terror in the mind of God: The global rise of religious violence*, 3rd edn, Berkeley, CA: University of California Press.

Knott, K., Poole, E. and Taira, T. (2013) *Media portrayals of religion and the secular sacred: Representation and change*, Farnham: Ashgate.

Kundnani, A. (2003) 'Stop and search: police step up targetting of Blacks and Asians', Institute of Race Relations (www.irr.org.uk/ news/stop-and-search-police-step-up-targetting-of-blacks-and-asians/).

Kundnani, A. (2009) *Spooked! How not to prevent violent extremism*, London: Institute of Race Relations.

Lynch, C. (2000) 'Dogma, praxis, and religious perspectives on multiculturalism', *Millennium – Journal of International Studies*, vol 29, no 3, pp 741–59.

Malik, K. (2009) *From fatwa to jihad: The Rushdie affair and its legacy*, London: Atlantic.

McFadyen, A. and Prideaux, M. (2011) *Effective community policing: Negotiating changing religious identities*, Cambridge: Cambridge Interfaith Programme(www.interfaith.cam.ac.uk/en/resources/ papers/ecp).

McFadyen, A. and Prideaux, M. (2013) 'The placing of religion in policing and policing studies', *Policing and Society*, vol 24, no 5, pp 1–18.

Moore, K., Mason, P. and Lewis, J. (2008) *Images of Islam in the UK: The representation of British Muslims in the national print news media 2000–2008,* Cardiff: Cardiff School of Journalism, Media and Cultural Studies.

Office for National Statistics (2012) *Religion in England and Wales 2011*, London: Office for National Statistics (www.ons.gov.uk/ons/rel/ census/2011-census/key-statistics-for-local-authorities-in-england-and-wales/rpt-religion.html).

Pew Forum (2011) *Religion in the news: Islam and politics dominate religion coverage in 2011*, Washington DC: Pew Research Center (www.pewforum.org/Government/Religion-in-the-News--Islam-and-Politics-Dominate-Religion-Coverage-in-2011.aspx).

Pew Forum (2013) *Muslim publics share concerns about extremist groups*, Washington DC: Pew Research Center (www.pewglobal.org/2013/09/10/muslim-publics-share-concerns-about-extremist-groups).

Reader, I. (2000) *Religious violence in contemporary Japan: The case of Aum Shinrikyo*, Richmond, Surrey: Curzon.

San, M. van and Bovenkerk, F. (2013) 'Secret seducers', *Crime, Law and Social Change*, vol 60, no 1, pp 67–80.

Shears, R. (2013) 'Cannibal cult leader who drank girls' blood is hacked to death by villagers after escaping from a Papua New Guinea jail and murdering another woman', *Mail Online* (www.dailymail.co.uk/news/article-2406624/Cannibal-cult-leader-Stephen-Tari-hacked-death-villagers-Papua-New-Guinea.html).

Sian, K.P. (2011) '"Forced" conversions in the British Sikh diaspora', *South Asian Popular Culture*, vol 9, no 2, pp 115–30.

Singh, H (2012) 'The libel survivor', Legal Week, Spring, pp 59-60.

Spalek, B. (2008) 'Muslim communities post-9/11 – Citizenship, security and social justice', *International Journal of Law, Crime and Justice*, vol 36, no 4, pp 211–14.

Spalek, B. and Lambert, R. (2008) 'Muslim communities, counter-terrorism and counter-radicalisation: a critically reflective approach to engagement', *International Journal of Law, Crime and Justice*, vol 36, no 4, pp 257–70.

Stewart, W. (2013) 'Siberian cult leader who claimed he was alien god from the star Sirius jailed for ritual rape of dozens of disciples', *Mail Online* (www.dailymail.co.uk/news/article-2274974/Siberian-cult-leader-claimed-alien-god-star-Sirius-jailed-ritual-rape-dozens-disciples.html).

Woodhead, L. (2013) 'YouGov surveys reveal widening gulf between Catholics and Church teaching' (http://faithdebates.org.uk/research/).

Woodhead, L. and Catto, R. (2009) *'Religion or belief': Identifying issues and priorities*, London: Equality and Human Rights Commission(www.equalityhumanrights.com/advice-and-guidance/your-rights/religion-and-belief/).

Zablocki, B.D. and Robbins, T. (eds) (2001) *Misunderstanding cults: Searching for objectivity in a controversial field*, Toronto: University of Toronto Press.

EIGHT

Religious literacy, equalities and human rights

Rebecca Catto and David Perfect

Introduction

This chapter examines six recent legal cases in England on religion or belief, to explore whether greater religious literacy on behalf of the employer or service provider, or employee or job applicant, might have resulted in solutions that would have avoided litigation.[1]

Recent legal developments in relation to religion or belief have emerged in a context influenced by a tangled, historic and evolving relationship between church and state. Since the late 1970s, religious groups in England and Wales have been able to seek rights and protections if they could be identified with a racial or ethnic group. The Human Rights Act 1998 then enshrined the European Convention on Human Rights (ECHR) into domestic law. Article 9 of the Convention protects freedom of thought, conscience and religion and their individual or communal manifestation (within limits). Consequently, religion or belief then became explicitly protected in England and Wales. Since 1998, domestic human rights and equality legislation has further developed, with religion or belief becoming recognised as an equality strand. The Equality Act 2006 brought into being the Equality and Human Rights Commission (EHRC) in 2007 to be responsible for monitoring and promoting human rights and equality in Great Britain.

Following the enactment of the Equality Act 2010, religion or belief is protected specifically in employment and the provision of goods and services in England and Wales, alongside eight other protected grounds, including gender, marriage and civil partnership, and sexual orientation. There is also a duty on public sector organisations to foster equality and good relations. Certain exemptions from employment equality law are in place for employment for religious purposes.

Religion or belief cases are usually, although not invariably, taken first to an Employment Tribunal, then to an Employment Appeal Tribunal, then to the Court of Appeal, and finally to the Supreme Court. If unsuccessful through the domestic court system, claimants may apply for their case to be considered by the European Court of Human Rights (ECtHR) in Strasbourg. Equalities law distinguishes between direct and indirect discrimination. Direct religious discrimination occurs when an individual is treated less favourably than someone else because of their religious or philosophical beliefs. Indirect religious discrimination occurs when an individual is put at a disadvantage compared with others because of their religious or philosophical beliefs and this cannot be objectively justified.

The 'or belief' in the protected ground indicates that it is not only religious beliefs that are now protected in England and Wales. Belief in the importance of public broadcasting, against foxhunting, and in man-made climate change have all been considered qualifying beliefs in domestic cases, while political party membership has not (Sandberg, 2011a). Such cases are indicative of the complex and fast-changing nature of the legal and social landscape in relation to religion or belief. As such, it is important to take into consideration beliefs and identities that are not religious when engaging in and/or discussing religious literacy (a 'lack of belief' is also now part of the religion or belief protected ground in England and Wales). Yet, this growing recognition of non-religious and other stances alongside religious ones is a massive topic in itself (Winter and Catto, 2012). Hence, in this chapter we focus specifically on religion-related employment cases.

Here religious literacy is conceived in terms of employers or service providers being open to having a dialogue about the positions of their employees, and to consider seriously any requests they may receive for their beliefs and practices to be accommodated. Religious literacy also involves a willingness on behalf of employees to recognise that others (including colleagues and customers) may not share their particular beliefs, and that they do not have the right to impose these views unilaterally. More broadly, the chapter also explores academic, media and other coverage of the cases selected, considering what difference improved knowledge, understanding and empathy could have made to how they have been presented and debated publicly. While our review of such coverage is not exhaustive, we believe that bringing together and comparing different sources is in itself a new and helpful contribution.

The cases

The six cases are: *Eweida v British Airways*; *Ladele v Islington Borough Council*; *McFarlane v Relate Avon*; *Noah v Desrosiers*; *Amachree v Wandsworth Borough Council*; and *Fugler v MacMillan*. The first three cases are well known as they are long-running disputes that were only finally concluded at the ECtHR in Strasbourg in 2013. Moreover, research for the EHRC by London Metropolitan University found that, in a small workplace survey of employers, they were the first, third and fifth best-known religion or belief cases (Donald, 2012, p 145). The latter three cases we have selected have not received the same extent of national media or academic coverage, but nonetheless highlight significant points.

To put the cases in context, it should be noted that there are relatively few religion or belief-related Employment Tribunal cases compared with other equality strands. Thus in 2013–14, 584 claims of discrimination on grounds of religion or belief were accepted by Employment Tribunals compared with 13,722 claims for sex discrimination, 5,196 for disability discrimination and 3,064 for race discrimination.[2] In keeping with the success rate for all types of Employment Tribunal cases (most are dropped or settled before coming before a tribunal), very few religion or belief claims are successful: of 818 religion or belief discrimination cases processed in 2013–14, only 3 per cent were successful at hearing, while in a further 31 per cent of cases, an ACAS (Advisory, Conciliation and Arbitration Service) conciliated settlement was reached (Ministry of Justice, 2014, Tables 1.2, 2.2 and 2.3).[3]

We begin by providing a description of each case in turn, before examining their academic, media and other coverage and their religious literacy implications.

Eweida v British Airways[4]

Nadia Eweida joined the check-in staff of British Airways (BA) in 1999. A Coptic Christian from London, she regularly attended work wearing a silver cross on a chain. In 2004, a new BA uniform policy required its female staff to wear an open-necked blouse and a cravat. Certain items of clothing considered mandatory to a religion, such as the Muslim *hijab* or the Sikh *kara*, were permitted, but all other items of jewellery were prohibited.

After previously concealing it under her clothing, Eweida began wearing a cross openly in May 2006 to show her religious commitment.

After initially agreeing to remove it, she refused to do so, and in September 2006 was sent home on unpaid leave, later refusing an offer of an alternative administrative position without customer contact (but with no loss of pay). Following highly critical newspaper articles (discussed below), BA reviewed and then amended its uniform policy from February 2007 to allow staff to display a faith or charity symbol while wearing the uniform (Hill, 2013). Eweida returned to work, but BA refused to compensate her for the earnings she had lost since the previous September.

In December 2006, Eweida lodged a claim at the Employment Tribunal for direct and indirect discrimination and harassment under the Employment Equality (Religion and Belief) Regulations 2003 (now part of the Equality Act 2010). After she had turned down an out-of-court settlement of £8,500 offered by BA, the tribunal dismissed all her claims in January 2008, as did the Employment Appeal Tribunal the following April. In February 2010, the Court of Appeal rejected her argument that the Employment Appeal Tribunal had wrongly held that, for her indirect discrimination claim to succeed, she was required to show that the uniform policy put, or would put, Christians at a particular disadvantage.[5] Instead, the Court of Appeal considered that BA's actions had been a proportionate means of achieving a legitimate aim. Prior to the decision, BA's actions had been strongly criticised by John Reid, a former Labour Home Secretary, and other leading politicians; Reid claimed that the action taken against Eweida 'will play into the hands of extremists' (Cockcroft, 2010; see also Donald, 2012, p 69).

Refused leave to appeal to the Supreme Court, Eweida lodged an appeal in August 2010 to the ECtHR, which joined her case in April 2011 with that of Shirley Chaplin, an NHS nurse who also wished to wear a small visible cross at work contrary to her employer's uniform policy. In January 2013, the ECtHR majority ruled that Eweida's Article 9 right to manifest her belief had unjustifiably been breached. It stated that domestic courts had given too much weight to the employer's legitimate need to project a corporate image and not enough to the employee's right to wear a visible cross, which did not adversely affect that corporate image. Two judges, including the UK's judge, Nicolas Bratza, disagreed, but the UK government did not submit a request for a rehearing from the ECtHR's Grand Chamber. At the same time, the ECtHR ruled against Chaplin, arguing that health and safety considerations were paramount, and justified her employer's actions. Chaplin requested a rehearing, but the Grand Chamber refused leave to do so in May 2013.

Academic coverage

Academic discussion of *Eweida* centres on the related issues of demonstrating group disadvantage, the question of whether a manifestation of religion or belief is mandatory or not, and the nature of religion or belief relative to other equality strands. The Employment Appeal Tribunal and Court of Appeal decisions in *Eweida* are criticised for placing too much emphasis on the number of people likely to be affected by the employer's policy, when Eweida herself stressed that wearing a cross was an expression of her personal faith rather than a religious requirement. Vickers (2009, 2010), Sandberg (2011a) and Pitt (2011) all argue that Article 9 of the ECHR protects individual as well as collective religion or belief. Hill (2013) points out that in light of the Strasbourg ruling in January 2013, obliging an applicant to demonstrate that a practice is mandated by their religion in order for Article 9 to be engaged is now outlawed. The tension between a test for general recognition (respectability and compatibility with human dignity) and protection for minority and unusual religion or belief is also raised by Vickers (2009, 2010), Pitt (2011), Whistler and Hill (2012) and Cranmer (2013).

The 2013 judgment in *Eweida et al* and its implications is examined by Gibson (2013), Hill and Whistler (2013), Pitt (2013), Leigh and Hambler (2014) and McCrea (2014). While Leigh and Hambler (2014) welcome, and Pitt (2013) and McCrea (2014) recognise, the move to protecting individual belief as well as religious prescription under Article 9 of the ECHR in the Strasbourg judgment, Hill and Whistler (2013) are of the opinion that it is confused and regressive in terms of assessing manifestation of religion or belief. A practice may no longer have to be prescribed by a group in order to qualify for protection, but it must directly express or be closely connected to an underlying belief, and/or be a generally recognised form of practice, and the judgment provides little guidance in terms of how to assess actions against these criteria.

The case is cited as an example of the courts adjudicating on questions of faith and doctrine (Sandberg, 2011a; Trigg, 2012). Pitt (2011) regards the courts' intervention in matters of religion as now unavoidable, following the Equality Act 2010. Vickers (2010) considers the courts more willing to judge questions of religious doctrine in relation to Christianity than other faiths, and suggests that this is a problem.

Eweida was strongly supported from 2006 by certain high-profile Christian leaders, including Dr John Sentamu, Archbishop of York (Stuart and Ahmed, 2012, p 145) and a former Archbishop of Canterbury,

Lord Carey (Whistler and Hill, 2012, p 11). Whistler and Hill (2012) also report that the Roman Catholic Church, the Christians in Parliament All-Party Parliamentary Group, London Mayor Boris Johnson and Prime Minister David Cameron were all critical of the domestic judgments in *Eweida*. The case is seen to have fed into a sense of unfair treatment among some Christians (Woodhead with Catto, 2009; Donald, 2012).

In contrast, Donald's research found that employers generally felt that the domestic courts had reached the correct conclusion in relation to *Eweida* (and *Chaplin*) and feared greater regulatory burdens. There was also little sympathy for Eweida from trade union representatives, but concern was expressed that the domestic judgments could create the erroneous impression that Muslims who wear headscarves are privileged over Christians (Donald, 2012).[6]

Gibson (2013) examines *Eweida et al* to explore whether an employer duty of reasonable accommodation for religion or belief, similar to that in place in Canada, should be introduced in the UK. He argues that in this case accommodation would have been permitted under the Canadian model (Gibson, 2013, pp 613-14). Pitt (2013) also examines whether the outcome of the four cases will lead to employers effectively having a duty of reasonable accommodation. In contrast to Gibson, she concludes that such a duty is not necessary and should be resisted.

Media and other coverage

Stuart and Ahmed (2012) carried out a quantitative analysis of reported instances in *The Guardian*, the *Daily Mail* and *The Daily Telegraph* between 2000 and 2010 of calls for, and responses to, action from public institutions, as well as religion-related legal claims brought by Christians, Hindus, Jews, Muslims or Sikhs. The *Daily Mail* published 50 per cent of these claims, *The Telegraph* 33 per cent and *The Guardian* 17 per cent (Stuart and Ahmed, 2012, p 183). Largely thanks to the *Daily Mail*'s coverage, especially in 2006, Eweida accounted for 14 per cent (n=361) of all reported instances in the study (Stuart and Ahmed, 2012, p 35).

Stuart and Ahmed (2012, p 178) document only one reference to opposition to Eweida's claim in their three sources. But there have been other examples: thus *The Freethinker* (one of the main journals of atheism in Britain) welcomed the Employment Tribunal's decision in January 2008 under an emotive headline (Duke, 2008).[7]

On the day of the ECtHR combined judgment, the Secretary of State for Communities and Local Government, Eric Pickles, was reported to be delivering a speech to the think tanks British Future and Policy Exchange 'vowing to change UK law to support the right of people to discreetly display a symbol of faith in their workplace if their case [*Eweida* and *Chaplin*] is rejected' (Chapman, 2013). Given that *Eweida* and *Chaplin* were decided differently on the facts of the cases, Cranmer (2013) wonders which law Pickles intends to change.

Religious literacy

BA could have avoided many of the problems that it subsequently faced through realising at the outset that although the wearing of particular religious dress or symbols is not mandatory for all Christians, as it is for adherents of some other religions, it is still very important to some. BA compounded this by placing too much emphasis on the fact that only Eweida among its employees complained. Other employers should note that the issue of religious symbols will not fade away. Weller et al (2013, p 332) note that: 'High profile controversies and legal cases reflect continued experience of what is felt to be unfair treatment with regard to employer dress codes in relation particularly to Muslim women using head coverings and to Christians wearing crosses.' This observation indicates a general need for greater knowledge and understanding of religious symbols among employers.

A greater willingness from Eweida to accept a compromise would have made a difference – a point also noted by trade union respondents to the London Metropolitan University research (Donald, 2012, p 68). Had she accepted an alternative position initially, Eweida could have continued to wear a cross openly, or she could have withdrawn her claim once BA changed its uniform policy in 2007, but she chose not to do so.

Ladele v London Borough of Islington[8]

Lillian Ladele began working for Islington Borough Council in 1992, becoming a registrar of births, deaths and marriages in 2002. Although not employed by Islington, she was paid by the local authority and had to follow its policies. The Civil Partnership Act 2004 gave same-sex couples the rights and responsibilities comparable to civil marriage from December 2005; in the same month, Islington designated all its registrars as civil partnership registrars. A member of an Evangelical Anglican church in South London, Ladele considered that civil partnerships conflicted with her Christian beliefs, and refused to perform ceremonies. Initially she made informal arrangements with colleagues to avoid doing so, but when two of them accused her of homophobia in March 2006, Islington launched a disciplinary investigation. In August 2007, Islington insisted that she must undertake at least some civil partnership registrar duties, although she did not have to conduct ceremonies. When she refused to do so, she was dismissed in March 2008.[9]

Ladele's application to the Employment Tribunal claimed direct and indirect discrimination on grounds of religion or belief and harassment, which was accepted by the tribunal in July 2008. It argued that Islington's policy of requiring all registrars to perform civil partnership duties put individuals who held an orthodox Christian belief (that marriage was a union between one man and one woman for life) at a disadvantage when compared with others who did not hold that belief. However, in December 2008, the Employment Appeal Tribunal overturned this ruling, arguing that the council's actions had been a proportionate means to achieve a legitimate aim, the provision of the registrar service on a non-discriminatory basis, a decision upheld by the Court of Appeal in December 2009. The Court of Appeal accepted that Ladele was in breach of the council's 'Dignity for All' equality and diversity policy. Moreover, she was employed in a public role by a public authority, and her refusal to perform what was 'a purely secular task ... involved discriminating against gay people in the course of that job.' The Court of Appeal also discounted the fact that other local authorities had decided not to designate all its registrars as civil partnership registrars.

Refused leave to appeal to the Supreme Court, Ladele lodged an appeal in September 2010 to the ECtHR that joined her case with that of Gary McFarlane (discussed later) in April 2011. In January 2013, the ECtHR majority found that Islington's application of its policy to refuse to exempt an employee from particular duties was within the range of permissible choices available to the employer. It also found that the domestic courts had not exceeded the wide discretion given to them when determining this case that involved striking a balance between competing Convention rights. The Court majority also rejected Ladele's argument that the employer should have accommodated her conscientious objection.

Two judges disagreed and supported Ladele's claim, a decision endorsed by Addison (2013), who argues that the dissenting opinion raised a real principle deserving re-examination; Leigh and Hambler (2014, p 19) also find their views 'persuasive'. In contrast, McCrea (2014, p 283) considers that the dissent was 'misconceived'. Nevertheless, the ECtHR Grand Chamber announced on 27 May 2013 that it had refused to allow Ladele a rehearing in the Grand Chamber, and the case therefore concluded.

Academic coverage

Hill (2013, p 6) describes Ladele as the 'real loser' in the January 2013 ECtHR judgment, and Cranmer (2013) considers her 'unlucky'. There are differing opinions on the case. *Ladele* was apparently one of the most polarising cases for Donald's participants, and trade union and equality non-governmental organisational representatives tended to endorse the domestic decision in *Ladele* (Donald, 2012). Malik (2012) asserts that the Court of Appeal's decision was legally and politically correct. Nonetheless, overall, a sense that insufficient consideration was given to Ladele's freedom of religion and Islington's capacity to accommodate it emerges.

Trigg (2012) views *Ladele* as symbolic, capturing the contemporary clash between a right to equal treatment and not to be discriminated against, and a right to religious freedom. He argues that the Court of Appeal failed to recognise that 'although rights to equal treatment are important, respect for religious freedom goes to the heart of human rights' (Trigg, 2012, p 96). Sandberg (2011a) considers the Court of Appeal's ruling that Ladele's belief did not constitute a reason for her treatment to be misleading. He argues that the case was indicative of a trend to downplay discrimination on the grounds of religion or belief, compared with discrimination on grounds of sexual orientation, and also of judges' discomfort in dealing with cases related to religious rights. Religion or belief is also to be protected under Islington's equality policy (Sandberg, 2011a). Yet Ladele's Christian belief was unquestionably counted as a protected belief, whereas less widely held and less established beliefs are subject to greater scrutiny (Pitt, 2011).

According to Vickers (2010), insufficient attention was paid in the domestic judgments to the fact that the Civil Partnership Act 2004 does not require all registrars to be automatically designated for civil partnerships, and that other local authorities had been able to deliver equal access to registration for gay and lesbian couples without designating all registrars. She takes the case as indicative of less strict scrutiny of employers' justifications in relation to religion or belief cases than in relation to other protected characteristics, while Hambler (2010) bemoans the Employment Appeal Tribunal's lack of a critical assessment of the employer's justification. Parkinson (2011, p 293), while also emphasising that other local authorities had acted differently, argues that Islington had 'created a conflict that could have been avoided if the Council had shown proper respect for Ms Ladele's genuinely-held religious beliefs'. Pitt (2011, p 400) concludes from *Ladele* (and *McFarlane*) that 'employers with equality and diversity policies (which should be all of them) should find it relatively easy to deal with' such clashes of rights.

For Hambler (2010), *Ladele* shows that religious public officials are left with a stark choice when faced with an employer such as Islington that will not compromise: go against their conscience or leave the role, whether through resignation or dismissal. He sees this as a 'deeply unsatisfactory state of affairs' (Hambler, 2010, p 16), leading to negative consequences for society as religious voices are marginalised. In a later article, Hambler (2012) concludes that registrars should have the conditional right to opt out of performing civil partnerships on grounds of religious conscience, dependent on the practicability of accommodation for the employer. In a House of Commons debate on the Marriage (Same Sex Couples) Bill in May 2013, a new clause allowing registrars to opt out of conducting marriages of same-sex couples on the grounds of conscientious objection was rejected by 340 votes to 150 (Pocklington, 2013).

Leigh and Hambler (2014) argue that the harm to others in *Ladele* was purely notional, and propose a 'reversibility test'. This would require the courts to identify which other individuals' rights would be violated if the religious claimant was accommodated. They argue that Strasbourg jurisprudence has established that same-sex civil partnership is not a Convention right. Hence, in the particular context, Ladele's Article 9 right to dissent should have taken precedence. McCrea (2014, p 282) also regrets that the judgment failed to specify which 'rights of others were being protected' in the case. Yet, he goes on to argue that protecting a right to discriminate is deeply problematic, and the Court could have gone further in its rejection of Ladele's claim.

Pitt (2013, pp 407-8) reminds us that Ladele and McFarlane (see below) 'were seeking permission to discriminate directly on grounds of sexual orientation', and sees resolution in the 'application of the usual principles of direct and indirect discrimination, not by preferring one protected characteristic to another.' However, Gibson (2013, p 612) concludes that 'Canadian reasonable accommodation may have enabled accommodation to have been reached in *Ladele*.'

Media and other coverage

Stuart and Ahmed (2012, p 130) note that 6 per cent ($n=24$) of employment-related claims in their three newspaper sources between

2000 and 2010 were about *Ladele*. In *Marginalising Christians*, The Christian Institute (2009) cited this case, as well as *Eweida*, as evidence that Christianity is being marginalised by the drive for equality and diversity in Britain. In contrast, Symon Hill of the think tank, Ekklesia, and a Christian, went further in welcoming the Court of Appeal's decision in 2009 and severely criticising Ladele by bluntly stating that: 'There was nothing Christian about her actions' (Hill, 2009). The EHRC (2011) also endorsed the domestic courts' decision in *Ladele*.

John Scriven (2012), a former chair of the Lawyer's Christian Fellowship, argues that Ladele should have been accommodated, primarily because her beliefs were not irrational and were based in a traditional faith system.

Religious literacy

The differing academic and professional opinions, as well as the volatility of the ensuing public debate around this case, indicate its challenging nature. Islington Council should have shown greater religious literacy through acknowledging that some Christians would have strongly held and sincere views on same-sex relationships. Like other local authorities, it could have taken this into account when deciding whether or not to make all its registrars civil partnership registrars; its failure to do so was characterised by Parkinson (2011, pp 292-3) as an example of a missed pathway to peace. The extent to which Islington consulted its employees and took other steps to prepare the way before introducing the policy change in December 2005 is unclear, but arguably the council could have done more in this respect.

Ladele could have shown greater religious literacy by a fuller appreciation that some of her colleagues with differing views or beliefs (including some other Christians, as well as those with secular viewpoints) might be offended by her uncompromising attitude towards same-sex relationships. Similarly to Eweida, she could have accepted the compromise that Islington offered that she would not have to conduct civil partnership ceremonies.

McFarlane v Relate Avon Ltd[10]

Gary McFarlane, a member of a Pentecostal Church in Bristol, was employed as a counsellor by Relate Avon, a firm that provides relationship counselling services, from 2003. Believing that homosexual activity was sinful, McFarlane did not wish to work with same-sex couples where sexual issues arose. After he had voluntarily signed up for Relate's postgraduate psychosexual counselling course, he agreed to undertake psychosexual therapy with same-sex couples if asked. However, after complaints from other therapists and following an investigation, his employer found him reluctant to do so, and he was summarily dismissed by Relate Avon in March 2008 for gross misconduct.

McFarlane lodged a claim for unfair dismissal, wrongful dismissal and indirect discrimination. The Employment Tribunal dismissed his claim of direct discrimination in January 2009, and found that the indirect discrimination had been proportionate to the aim of 'ensuring that no person received less favourable treatment on the basis of personal or group characteristics'. The Employment Appeal Tribunal upheld this decision in November 2009. The Court of Appeal, following the precedent in *Ladele*, refused McFarlane's leave to appeal in January 2010 and again in April 2010. The renewed application for a hearing in April was notable for a witness statement by a former Archbishop of Canterbury, Lord Carey, who also called for religious cases to be heard separately by judges sensitive to religious issues (Donald, 2012, p 61). However, in response, Lord Justice Laws concluded that to give legal protection or preference to a particular moral position because it was faith-based would be 'deeply unprincipled'.

Refused leave to appeal to the Supreme Court, McFarlane lodged an appeal to the ECtHR in June 2010 that subsequently joined his case with that of *Ladele* (as previously discussed). In January 2013, the ECtHR unanimously found that a fair balance was struck between the competing interests at stake, the key factor being that the employer had sought to secure the implementation of its policy of providing a service without discrimination. Accordingly, although recognising that the loss of a job was a severe sanction with grave consequences, the Court again ruled that domestic courts had not exceeded the wide discretion available to them.

McFarlane, who later worked for the West of England Baptist Association before resuming counselling and therapy work, requested a rehearing from the Grand Chamber, but this was rejected in May 2013.[11] Inevitably, given the close association of *Ladele* and *McFarlane*, coverage of *McFarlane* has already been addressed to an extent, but we move on now to consider it specifically.

Academic coverage

Pitt (2011) thinks that counsel's argument in the Employment Appeal Tribunal case that discrimination against McFarlane's manifestation of belief equalled discrimination against his belief was given insufficient consideration. Trigg (2012, p 142) takes Lord Justice Laws' words in the case as indicating a basic message that Christian principles no longer even deserve public respect. He is critical of Laws for raising concerns about the dangers of 'theocracy' and labelling religion subjective: for 'making assertions that are totally unsupported by argument' (Trigg, 2012, p 145).

Donald (2012, p 87), in contrast, quotes from the same section of the Court of Appeal judgment, but as recognition of respondent Simon Barrow from Ekklesia's point that 'rooting conscientious objection in religious credentials does not automatically confer greater legitimacy'.

Sandberg (2010, p 367) finds Laws' general underlying point that 'we do not live in a theocracy' sound, but queries his implication that values are protected only on their own merits rather than because they may be religious. He argues that religion does continue to receive special protections and to be valued for its own sake in English law. Like Trigg, Sandberg is also critical of Laws' assertion that it would be irrational to protect a position purely on religious grounds, yet grounds his criticism in the assertion by Lord Nicholls in *Williamson*[12] that freedom of religion does protect the subjective belief of an individual. Parkinson (2011, pp 288-90) goes further in his criticism of Laws' assessment of Lord Carey's intervention that he discusses in detail; he concludes that 'Lord Justice Laws, in a forthright judgment condemning an argument that had never been advanced, spectacularly missed the point.'

Sandberg (2010, p 370) is also very critical of Lord Carey's wish for religious cases to be heard separately by judges sensitive to religious issues, a call he considers to show a complete lack of understanding of the judicial process and nuance. Although otherwise sympathetic to Carey's perspective, Parkinson (2011, p 288, note 31) agrees that this approach is not acceptable.

Gibson (2013, p 613) concludes that accommodation was less likely in *McFarlane* than in *Ladele*, an important difference between the two cases being that employee reallocation would not have been practicable in the former. Leigh and Hambler (2014, p 12) also distinguish between the two cases, arguing that McFarlane's decision to seek a position 'which would conflict with his religious beliefs ... rightly weighs against him to a certain extent.'

Media and other coverage

Stuart and Ahmed (2012, p 130) reported that McFarlane's case accounted for 5 per cent (*n*=20) of employment claims in their three sources between 2000 and 2010. Lord Carey's involvement in this case received particular public attention.

Religious literacy

Arguably, greater religious literacy would have made less difference in this case than in the others discussed here. However, Relate could have thought in advance how its policy on same-sex therapy might cause difficulties for Christian therapists (and perhaps also for Muslims and others) with strong views on same-sex relationships. Like Islington, it could have planned accordingly. Parkinson (2011) goes the furthest by suggesting that McFarlane might have been permitted to return to counselling general couples only, rather than taking on psychosexual therapy cases.

Like Ladele, McFarlane could have appreciated that others would not share his beliefs. He could also have shown a much greater willingness to engage in constructive discussions with his employer to see if a solution acceptable to all parties could be found. Perhaps above all, he could have decided not to undertake the postgraduate psychosexual therapy training and instead remained in general counselling.

Lord Carey could perhaps have been more sensitive to the legal and religious situation in contemporary Britain before intervening. The differing opinions expressed by Trigg, Donald and Sandberg on the Court of Appeal ruling suggest that judges also ought to take great care when pronouncing more broadly on the nature of society and religion (Cranmer, 2011).

Noah v Desrosiers[13]

Sarah Desrosiers, a Canadian, set up what she called a 'funky, urban' hairdressing salon in King's Cross, London, called Wedge, in 2006. When she advertised for new stylists, Bushra Noah, a young Muslim woman, applied and attended the interview in March 2007 wearing a headscarf, which she habitually wore. During the interview, Desrosiers stated that she would have to remove her headscarf to work at the salon, because it was an 'absolute basic' requirement of the job that stylists had their own hair on show (and their hairstyles had to be 'contemporary'). Noah was not offered employment (nor was anyone else).

Noah lodged a claim of direct and indirect discrimination at the Employment Tribunal under the Employment Equality (Religion or Belief) Regulations 2006 (now incorporated into the Equality Act 2010), with Desrosiers' case being funded by the National Secular

Society (2008). The Employment Tribunal ruled in June 2008 that the regulations applied to job applicants, as well as to those in employment, and that Desrosiers' requirement for her staff to have their own hair visible was not a proportionate means of achieving a legitimate aim. The employer had placed too much weight on the need to display modern hairstyles, and not wearing a headscarf did not constitute a requirement for the job. Noah was awarded £4,000 for injury to feelings in connection with her successful indirect discrimination claim. However, the claim of direct discrimination was rejected.

Desrosiers did not appeal the judgment, although she did complain bitterly to the *Daily Mail* (which supported her) that the outcome could ruin her business (Courtenay-Smith, 2008).[14] In fact, Wedge continued to operate until 2014 when Desrosiers returned to Canada.[15] Meanwhile, Noah found a part-time job in another sector.

Academic coverage

Donald (2012, p 48) offers this case as an example of how Employment Tribunals may appear to show that restriction of wearing a cross is proportionate, but restriction of wearing a headscarf is not, the proportionality decision having been weighed differently in the different contexts. Howard (2011, p 90) comments that the employer could have examined the situation in more detail, and through exploring other options 'might have found other ways of pursuing her aim with a less discriminatory impact.'

Noah arguably suffered less than Eweida (and others), because the job did not actually exist: there was no real disadvantage (Sandberg, 2011b). Nonetheless, Sandberg (2011a) welcomes the attention to justification rather than disadvantage in Noah's case, providing a more nuanced, context-specific decision. Some respondents to EHRC-commissioned research felt that the Employment Tribunal had asked the employer to bear the cost to too great an extent in this case (Woodhead with Catto, 2009). Hill (2013) cites this case as an example of Muslims earning the right to wear the veil because it is doctrinally mandated (an argument that will no longer be applicable following the Strasbourg decision in *Eweida*).

Media and other coverage

Three references to Noah (0.7 per cent of employment claim-related references) were found in Stuart and Ahmed's (2012, p 180) media analysis. One of Desrosiers' clients who works in the media expressed her concern in *The Guardian* about how the Employment Tribunal decision might be seized on by 'middle England' (also referencing *Eweida* and *Ladele*), and the potential future consequence of employers being less honest in their reasons for failed applications (Rutherford, 2008).

In an article for a free, online magazine seemingly with a conservative and anti-Islamic agenda, Jackson (2008) asserts that an immigrant could learn from this case that 'there is money in outrage'. A *Freethinker* article on the case took a similar line (Duke, 2007). These two examples show how a specific case can be interpreted in light of a pre-existing agenda and ideology.

In *Equal Opportunities Review*, Johnstone (2009) comments that the case shows the importance of employers demonstrating a proportionate pursuit of a legitimate aim in religion or belief cases.

Religious literacy

Greater religious literacy by Desrosiers – who appears to have had little or no understanding about the importance that some Muslim women attach to wearing the *hijab* – might have led her to handle the situation very differently. She could have reviewed her perception of the absolute necessity for stylists to wear their hair uncovered and, even if she then considered this essential, could have explored with Noah in advance both the latter's requirements and her own expectations.

Noah should perhaps have informed Desrosiers in advance about her beliefs, although the onus was not on her to do so, but rather on Desrosiers as the employer, and she might reasonably have concluded that to have done so would have prejudiced her chances of getting the job.

Amachree v Wandsworth Borough Council[16]

Duke Amachree, a member of the Nigerian-based UK World Evangelism Church, was employed by Wandsworth Borough Council between 1991 and 2009 latterly as a Homelessness Prevention Officer. This involved interviewing applicants at risk of homelessness. When interviewed in January 2009, Ms X, a potential housing client, stated that she was suffering from an incurable disease. Amachree then outlined his religious views and suggested, according to Ms X, that her 'problem was that I did not have God or faith in my life and was therefore ill as a result'; Amachree's own recollection of the discussion differed. Immediately afterwards, Ms X complained in writing to

Wandsworth Council. Amachree was suspended on full pay pending a disciplinary investigation. He was told to seek legal advice, but to treat the matter as confidential.

Amachree was interviewed several times during the investigation and disputed Ms X's account. He also gained the support of the Christian Legal Centre (CLC), which issued a press release on his behalf in March 2009, and gave an interview to the *Daily Mail* the following day. As a result of the national press coverage, it became possible for others to be able to identify Ms X. Consequently, following its investigation, Wandsworth determined that Amachree was guilty of gross misconduct for having made 'offensive and inappropriate comments' to Ms X, and for releasing her personal details to the media, and dismissed him in July 2009. Backed by the CLC, which launched a 'Justice for Duke' campaign in December 2009, stating that he had been dismissed for 'mentioning God in the workplace', he issued a claim for unfair dismissal and wrongful dismissal, arguing that his religion was the reason.

In August 2010, the Employment Tribunal dismissed all of Amachree's claims, arguing that he had been dismissed for misconduct, and not because of his religious beliefs, and that Wandsworth's decision was within the range of reasonable responses. The tribunal added that if the misconduct had been limited to the inappropriate interview comments, those allegations alone might not have been sufficient to justify dismissal, but noted that the decision was taken against the background of a serious breach of confidentiality. Although initially stating that he intended to appeal the decision, Amachree did not in fact do so, and subsequently became a director of a property development company in South London.[17]

Academic coverage

This case is briefly discussed in Donald (2012, 2013) and in Hambler's doctoral thesis (Hambler, 2013), but apparently not, as yet, in other academic sources. One of Donald's respondents, Andrea Williams of Christian Concern, denied that Amachree's case had been damaged by the press release issued by the CLC, arguing that 'he would have been fired anyway', and that the publicity ensured that Wandsworth Council could not 'get rid of [him] quietly' (Donald, 2012, p 121). In contrast, there is a great deal of online coverage of the case available.

Media and other coverage

Stuart and Ahmed (2012, pp 179, 291) found three references to this case, and also noted that the *Daily Mail* supported Amachree. For Donald (2012, p 114), 'The *Amachree* case illustrates the perils of quoting selectively from complex legal judgments, especially when those partial accounts achieve media prominence.' She cites an article by Melanie Phillips (2009) in *Daily Mail Online* as an example of such misreporting. The article is entitled 'Just for once, the Archbishop is right ... treating Christians as cranks is an act of cultural suicide', and is a response to the then Anglican Archbishop Rowan Williams' criticisms of government approaches to religion. In the article, Phillips cites *Amachree* as an example of persecution of British Christians, writing: 'In July, Duke Amachree, a Christian who for 18 years had been a Homelessness Prevention Officer for Wandsworth Council, encouraged a client with an incurable medical condition to believe in God. As a result, Mr Amachree was marched off the premises, suspended and then dismissed from his job.'

An influential blogger on UK religious issues, 'Archbishop Cranmer' posted that Amachree was fired for mentioning God in the workplace (*Cranmer*, 2009).[18] In contrast, an article posted on the National Secular Society's website two days later approved the fact that Wandsworth had upheld its decision to dismiss Amachree (Evans, 2009).

Religious literacy

Amachree could have shown greater religious literacy by recognising that his comments and actions were likely to cause distress to anyone who held different views about religion and illness, particularly those from a secular perspective.[19] The CLC could have avoided compounding the problem by launching its media campaign as it did, and thereby inadvertently causing a chain of events that contributed to Amachree's dismissal.

Wandsworth could have thought more in advance about how it should deal with a situation of an employee's religion or belief affecting service delivery, although it is hard to criticise its decision to dismiss Amachree in the circumstances.

Fugler v MacMillan-London Hair Studios Limited[20]

Jake Fugler, who was Jewish, was employed by Macmillan Hair Studios in London as a technician from November 2001. On 25 September 2004, Yom Kippur, the most important festival in Judaism, when many secular, as well as religious, Jews fast, refrain from work and attend a synagogue, fell on a Saturday. Fugler requested a day's holiday, but this was refused as his employer had discouraged holiday requests on Saturdays, the salon's busiest day, and several other staff had already booked the day off. After arguing with the salon owner, Fugler walked out.

Fugler lodged a claim for religious discrimination, as well as race discrimination, constructive unfair dismissal and other claims under the Employment Equality (Religion and Belief) Regulations 2003. In June 2005, the Employment Tribunal found that the employer's provision indirectly discriminated against Jews, and was not justified since the employer had failed to consider whether its staffing needs could have been accommodated in some other way. It therefore ruled that Fugler had been unfairly constructively dismissed, and upheld his claim of indirect religious discrimination. Fugler was awarded compensation, and by March 2005, had found employment in another hair salon, Taylor Taylor London.[21]

Academic coverage

This case is briefly discussed in Sandberg (2011a, p 109) and by Donald (2012, 2013). The former argues that *Fugler* is an example of how new religious discrimination law goes beyond the Human Rights Act 1998 and the 'specific situation rule', an employee's freedom to resign.[22] Donald (2013) notes that it is one of the few indirect religious discrimination claims that have succeeded at Employment Tribunal.

Media and other coverage

This case has received little public coverage, but it is included in a summary of key cases in relation to working hours and religion or belief on the 'Employers Forum on Belief'. The summary concludes with the importance of employers demonstrating other possible solutions were considered rather than working hours unilaterally imposed.[23]

Religious literacy

London Hair Studios could have shown much more awareness of the potential importance of particular religious festivals to their adherents, including the significance of Yom Kippur to both religious and secular Jews.

Knowing the day of the week on which the festival would fall, Fugler could have planned ahead, anticipating when he would require time off for a religious holiday, and explaining clearly to his employers the reason when making the request. The employer, once it had been explained, should have given this more consideration than others' reasons for leave requests.

Discussion and conclusions

The point of greater religious literacy giving employers and service providers greater confidence and openness to dialogue was raised during an EHRC-commissioned 'dialogue event'.[24] It was felt that government, non-statutory bodies such as the EHRC, and religion or belief and civil society groups could all play a role in supporting the development of such confidence. The EHRC's release in February 2013 of new guidance on religion or belief in the workplace is an example of such support (EHRC, 2013). It might also be helpful for the growth of religious literacy if Employment Tribunal judgments could routinely be made freely available online so that lessons can be drawn from them.

The diversity of academic and non-academic views and interpretations presented in this chapter serves as a reminder of the importance of reflexivity concerning the position from which we all come, and the interests we all bring into debate, discussion, dialogue and negotiation. As noted, the subtleties of legal reasoning in specific cases often get lost in the translation. The relationship between freedom of religion and anti-discrimination legislation is complicated (Pitt, 2011), and the case law on the latter can no longer be understood without knowledge of human rights law (Sandberg, 2011a). Perhaps then lawyers and legal scholars need to do more to get their messages across, and, given the extensive coverage particular judgments have received, particularly in *McFarlane*, perhaps judges could be more sensitive and circumspect in their rulings in high-profile cases. Indeed, Sandberg (2014) suggests that judges could benefit from more sociological as well as legal training.

Research and learning from research are important aspects of religious literacy. Donald (2013, p 7) points out that 'legal cases are not necessarily representative of common experience or a reliable indicator of the place of religion or belief (or specific religions or beliefs) in society'. Religious and legal literacy can inform the gap between perception and practice.

Given that Christianity remains the largest religious group in Britain (almost 60 per cent, according to the 2011 Census), it is perhaps unsurprising that the majority of cases in this chapter have involved Christians. As discussed, four of these cases, *Eweida*, *Ladele*, *McFarlane* and *Amachree* (as well as other cases such as *Chaplin*) have been used as evidence of increasing Christian marginalisation and even persecution in the country. For Easter 2013, Lord Carey published an article in the *Daily Mail* accusing Prime Minister David Cameron of aiding and abetting 'aggressive secularisation', and quoting the results of a ComRes poll showing that 'more than two-thirds of Christians feel that they are part of a "persecuted minority"' (Carey, 2013).

Such discourse gained sufficient traction to prompt the Christians in Parliament All-Party Parliamentary Group to conduct an investigation (Christians in Parliament, 2012), but, the inquiry found no evidence of Christian persecution in the UK. In August 2013, another former Archbishop of Canterbury, Rowan Williams, stated that he was:

> ... always very uneasy when people sometimes in this country or the United States talk about persecution of Christians or rather believers. I think we are made to feel uncomfortable at times.... But don't confuse it with the systematic brutality and often murderous hostility which means that every morning you get up wondering if you and your children are going to make it through the day.... It's not quite what we are facing in Western society. (Furness, 2013)

Discerning what constitutes persecution and what is loss of privilege in a changing and now simultaneously Christian, secular and religiously plural society (Weller, 2005) requires religious literacy. Results from the 2013 Lancaster/YouGov poll 'Faith Matters' indicate the varieties of Christianity and other religions present in UK today: the attitudes of particular, vociferous, religious senior figures on a range of moral issues cannot be assumed to represent those of the majority of people who identify with that religion (Woodhead, 2013.

Religion is multidimensional and, as seen, different from other characteristics now protected by UK equalities legislation (Vickers, 2010; Woodhead with Catto, 2009). A tension emerges in the case law and commentary between the subjective and objective. Nevertheless, the assumption that behaviour follows belief – whether individual and subjective or mandated – generally goes unchallenged (Vickers, 2010, and Whistler and Hill, 2012 being exceptions). This is despite emerging empirical research that a direct, causal relationship between propositional religious belief and behaviour cannot be assumed (Riis and Woodhead, 2010; Day, 2011). Greater understanding of the lived complexity of religion in Britain today (Woodhead and Catto, 2012) may facilitate greater mutual acceptance, between and within religious groups, and between non-religious or religiously indifferent and religious individuals, including in the courts and in the media. Greater discussion and debate regarding the values operating in the modern secular state and how secularism is lived might also encourage such acceptance (Asad, 2009).

The small proportion of tribunal cases brought on the grounds of religion or belief suggests that media, think tank and pressure group coverage and concern may be disproportionate, and there is a growing consensus that litigation ought to be a last resort in resolving religion or belief-related disputes. Weller et al (2013) have found a general reduction in the incidence of reported unfair treatment since 2001 in England and Wales, and a sense of improved relations between religious groups: there are therefore grounds for optimism regarding the future relationship between religion or belief, equalities and human rights in England and Wales (Donald, 2013), which improved religious literacy can further strengthen.

Notes

[1] The authors are grateful to Alice Donald, Andrew Hambler, Francine Morris, Russell Sandberg, Lucy Vickers and Daniel Whistler for their expert advice and comments on a draft of this chapter.

[2] The number of accepted claims for religion or belief discrimination fell from 939 in 2011–12 and 979 in 2012–13 to 584 in 2013–14.

[3] Of the remaining cases, 27 per cent were withdrawn, 12 per cent were struck out (not at a hearing), around 11 per cent were dismissed at a preliminary hearing or upon withdrawal, and 15 per cent were unsuccessful at hearing.

[4] This summary is based largely on ECtHR (2013). The judgments in the three earlier domestic cases and the ECtHR decision are available on the Law and Religion Scholars Network (LARSN) website: see www.law.cf.ac.uk/clr/networks/lrsncd.html

[5] See Sandberg (2011a) for a full explanation of the legal test for direct discrimination and indirect discrimination in the context of religion or belief.

[6] Some of the coverage of *Noah* discussed later suggests such a concern has good grounds.

[7] The same author wrote a similarly emotively titled piece in response to *Noah* (see later).

[8] The summary of the case is based largely on ECtHR (2013). The judgments in the three domestic tribunals can be found on the LARSN website.

[9] The Statistics and Registration Act came into force in December 2007. Consequently, Ladele was reclassified as an employee of Islington, and thus could be dismissed from her job.

[10] The summary of the case is based largely on ECtHR (2013). The Employment Appeal Tribunal judgment (and a summary of the Court of Appeal judgment) can be found on the LARSN website.

[11] See www.webassoc.org.uk/office.aspx and www.garymcfarlane.com/addiction/

[12] *R v Secretary of State for Education and Employment, ex parte Williamson* [2005] UKHL 15.

[13] The full Employment Tribunal judgment does not appear to have been made available online. The most detailed summary is in Sandberg (2009), and a short summary is available on the LARSN website.

[14] The case thus provides a rare religion or belief example when the *Daily Mail* and the National Secular Society were on the same side.

[15] See www.wedgehair.co.uk/

[16] The full Employment Tribunal judgment does not appear to be available online. The most detailed summaries available are in Hambler (2013) and Henson (2010).

[17] See www.dellam.com/07488469-REX%20ESTATES%20LTD.html

[18] Not to be confused with law and religion specialist and fellow blogger Frank Cranmer.

[19] Two differing examples in the EHRC's 2013 guide for employers indicate when praying for other people may, and may not, be appropriate.

[20] The full judgment is available on the Practical Law Company website: http://plc.practicallaw.com/6-381-7680

[21] See www.prweb.com/releases/2005/03/prweb213729.htm

[22] The 'specific situation' rule applies where someone has voluntarily submitted themselves to a system of norms, for example, by entering into a contract (see Donald, 2012, p 43).

[23] See www.efbelief.org.uk/pages/summary-of-key-cases-working-hours.html

[24] Details of this initiative can be accessed at https://sites.google.com/site/religiousliteracy2/ehrc-dialogues

References

Addison, N. (2013) 'Eweida and others – first views', *Religion Law Blog*, 15 January (http://religionlaw.blogspot.co.uk/2013/01/eweida-and-others-first-views.html).

Asad, T. (2009) 'Free speech, blasphemy, and secular criticism', in T. Asad, W. Brown, J. Butler and S. Mahmood (eds) *Is critique secular? Blasphemy, injury, and free speech*, Townsend Papers in the Humanities no 2, Berkeley, CA: University of California Press, pp 20-63.

Carey, Lord (2013) 'The PM's done more than any leader to make Christians feel they're persecuted', *Mail Online*, 29 March (www.dailymail.co.uk/debate/article-2301314/Lord-Carey-David-Camerons-leader-make-Christians-feel-theyre-persecuted.html).

Chapman, J. (2013) 'I'll protect faith from attack by militants who hate religion, says Eric Pickles', *Mail Online*, 15 January (www.dailymail.co.uk/news/article-2262472/Ill-protect-faith-attack-militants-hate-religion-says-Eric-Pickles.html).

Christian Institute, The (2009) *Marginalising Christians: Instances of Christians being sidelined in modern Britain*, Newcastle upon Tyne: The Christian Institute.

Christians in Parliament (2012) *Clearing the ground inquiry: Preliminary report into the freedom of Christians in the UK* (www.eauk.org/current-affairs/publications/clearing-the-ground.cfm).

Cockcroft, L. (2010) 'BA "wrong" to ban Christian from wearing cross because it "plays into extremist hands"', *The Telegraph*, 19 January (www.telegraph.co.uk/news/7028261/BA-wrong-to-ban-Christian-from-wearing-cross-because-it-plays-into-extremists-hands.html).

Courtenay-Smith, N. (2008) 'How I nearly lost my business after refusing to hire a Muslim hair stylist who wouldn't show her hair', *Mail Online*, 18 June (www.dailymail.co.uk/femail/article-1027300/How-I-nearly-lost-business-refusing-hire-Muslim-hair-stylist-wouldnt-hair.html).

Cranmer (2009) 'Duke Amachree – sacked by Wandsworth Council just for mentioning God', *Cranmer*, 16 December (http://archbishop-cranmer.blogspot.co.uk/2009/12/duke-amachree-sacked-by-wandsworth.html).

Cranmer, F. (2011) 'Beating people is wrong: Campbell and Cosans, Williamson and their aftermath', in M. Hunter-Hénin (ed) *Law, religious freedoms and education in Europe*, Farnham: Ashgate, pp 283-304.

Cranmer, F. (2013) '*Chaplin, Eweida, Ladele* and *McFarlane*: the judgment', *Law & Religion UK*, 17 January (www.lawandreligionuk.com/2013/01/17/chaplin-eweida-ladele-and-mcfarlane-the-judgment/).

Day, A. (2011) *Believing in belonging: belief and social identity in the modern world*, Oxford: Oxford University Press.

Donald, A. (2012) *Religion or belief, equality and human rights in England and Wales*, Equality and Human Rights Commission Research Report no 84, Manchester: Equality and Human Rights Commission (www.equalityhumanrights.com/uploaded_files/research/rr84_final_opt.pdf).

Donald, A. (2013) 'Advancing debate about religion or belief, equality and human rights: grounds for optimism?', *Oxford Journal of Law and Religion*, vol 2, no 1, pp 50-71.

Duke, B. (2007) 'Boo-hoo, another Muslim's feelings are hurt – and only cash will ease the pain', *The Freethinker*, 8 November (http://freethinker.co.uk/2007/11/08/boo-hoo-another-muslim%E2%80%99s-feelings-are-hurt-%E2%80%93-and-only-cash-will-ease-the-pain/).

Duke, B. (2008) 'Hallalujah! (sic) Cross-wielding zealot's case comes unstuck', *The Freethinker*, 29 January (http://freethinker.co.uk/2008/01/29/hallalujah-cross-wielding-zealots-case-comes-unstuck/).

ECtHR (European of Court of Human Rights) (2013) *Case of Eweida and others v United Kingdom*, Judgment, Strasbourg, 15 January (www.bailii.org/eu/cases/ECHR/2013/37.html).

EHRC (Equality and Human Rights Commission) (2011) *Eweida and Chaplin v United Kingdom and Ladele and McFarlane v United Kingdom*, Submission of the Equality and Human Rights Commission to the European Court of Human Rights (www.equalityhumanrights.com/uploaded_files/legal/ehrc_submission_to_ecthr_sep_2011.pdf).

EHRC (2013) *Religion or belief in the workplace: A guide for employers following recent European Court of Human Rights judgments* (www.equalityhumanrights.com/publication/religion-or-belief-workplace-guide-employers-following-recent-european-court-human-rights-judgments

Evans, S. (2009) 'Wandsworth Council uphold decision to sack evangelical housing officer', *National Secular Society*, 18 December (www.secularism.org.uk/wandsworth-council-uphold-decisi.html).

Furness, H. (2013) '"Persecuted" British Christians need to "grow up", says former Archbishop Rowan Williams', *The Telegraph*, 15 August (www.telegraph.co.uk/news/religion/10244716/Persecuted-British-Christians-need-to-grow-up-says-former-Archbishop-Rowan-Williams.html).

Gibson, M. (2013) 'The God "dilution"? Religion, discrimination and the case for reasonable accommodation', *Cambridge Law Journal*, vol 72, no 3, pp 578-616.

Hambler, A. (2010) 'A no-win situation for public officials with faith convictions', *Ecclesiastical Law Journal*, vol 12, no 1, pp 3-16.

Hambler, A. (2012) 'Recognising a right to "conscientiously object" for registrars whose religious beliefs are incompatible with their duty to conduct same-sex civil partnerships', *Religion & Human Rights*, vol 7, no 3, pp 157-81.

Hambler, A. (2013) 'Legal responses to the individual manifestation and expression of religion in the workplace in England and Wales: a conceptual framework', Unpublished PhD thesis, Durham University.

Henson, P. (2010) 'Religious discrimination – Amachree v Wandsworth Borough Council', *Employment Law Update*, 19 December (http://employmentlawupdate.wordpress.com/2010/12/19/religious-discrimination-%E2%80%93-amachree-v-wandsworth-borough-council/).

Hill, D. and Whistler, D. (2013) *The right to wear religious symbols*, Basingstoke: Palgrave Macmillan.

Hill, M. (2013) 'Religious symbolism and conscientious objection in the workplace: an evaluation of Strasbourg's judgment in Eweida and others v United Kingdom', *Ecclesiastical Law Journal*, vol 15, no 2, pp 191-203.

Hill, S. (2009) 'A judgment Christians should celebrate', *The Guardian*, 15 December (www.guardian.co.uk/commentisfree/belief/2009/dec/15/christian-registrar-civil-partnership-case).

Howard, E. (2011) *Law and the wearing of religious symbols: European bans on the wearing of symbols in education*, Abingdon: Routledge.

Jackson, M. (2008) 'Crying all the way to the bank', *New English Review*, August (www.newenglishreview.org/Mary_Jackson/Crying_All_the_Way_to_the_Bank/).

Johnstone, S. (2009) 'Headscarf requirement was discriminatory', *Equal Opportunities Review Online*, 1 April (www.eordirect.co.uk/default.aspx?id=1099048).

Leigh, I. and Hambler, A. (2014) 'Religious symbols, conscience and the rights of others', *Oxford Journal of Law and Religion*, vol 31, no 1, pp 2-24.

McCrea, R. (2014) 'Religion in the workplace: *Eweida and Others v United Kingdom*', *Modern Law Review*, vol 77, no 2, pp 277-307.

Malik, M. (2012) 'Religious freedom in the 21st century', *Westminster Faith Debates*, 18 April (http://faithdebates.org.uk/wp-content/uploads/2013/09/1352122648_MALIK-Westminster-Faith-Debates-RELIGIOUS-FREEDOM-IN-THE-21ST-CENTURY-Maleiha-Malik2.pdf).

Ministry of Justice (2014) *Tribunal Statistics Tables: April to June 2014* (https://www.gov.uk/government/statistics/tribunal-statistics-quarterly-april-to-june-2014).

National Secular Society (2008) 'Hairdresser cleared of discrimination, but £4,000 awarded for "hurt feelings"' (www.secularism.org.uk/hairdresserclearedofdiscriminati.html).

Parkinson, P. (2011) 'Accommodating religious belief in a secular age: the issue of conscientious objection in the workplace', *UNSW Law Journal*, vol 34, no 1, pp 281-99.

Phillips, M. (2009) 'Just for once, the Archbishop is right.... treating Christians as cranks is an act of cultural suicide', *Mail Online*, 14 December (www.dailymail.co.uk/debate/article-1235638/MELANIE-PHILLIPS-Just-Archbishop-right-Treating-Christians-cranks-act-cultural-suicide.html).

Pitt, G. (2011) 'Keeping the faith: trends and tensions in religion or belief discrimination', *Industrial Law Journal*, vol 40, no 4, pp 384-404.

Pitt, G. (2013) 'Taking religion seriously', *Industrial Law Journal*, vol 42, no 4, pp 398-408.

Pocklington, D. (2013) 'Marriage (Same Sex Couples) Bill: report and third reading', *Law & Religion UK*, 22 May (www.lawandreligionuk.com/2013/05/22/marriage-same-sex-couples-bill-report-and-third-reading/).

Riis, O. and Woodhead, L. (2010) *A sociology of religious emotion*, Oxford: Oxford University Press.

Rutherford, A. (2008) 'Barnet unfair?', *The Guardian Online,* 17 June (www.guardian.co.uk/commentisfree/2008/jun/17/religion.discriminationatwork).

Sandberg, R. (2009) 'Noah v Desrosiers t/a Wedge', *Law and Justice,* no 163, pp 191-2.

Sandberg, R. (2010) 'Laws and religion: unravelling *McFarlane v Relate Avon Limited*', *Ecclesiastical Law Journal,* vol 12, no 3, pp 361-70.

Sandberg, R. (2011a) *Law and religion,* Cambridge: Cambridge University Press.

Sandberg, R. (2011b) 'A uniform approach to religious discrimination? The position of teachers and other school staff in the UK', in M. Hunter-Hénin (ed) *Law, religious freedoms and education in Europe,* Farnham: Ashgate, pp 327-46.

Sandberg, R. (2014) *Religion, law and society,* Cambridge: Cambridge University Press.

Scriven, J. (2012) 'Human rights, conscience and the public good', in N. Spencer (ed) *Religion and law,* London: Theos, pp 117-24.

Stuart, H. and Ahmed, H. (2012) *Faith in the public sphere: A study of media reporting of faith-based claims,* London: Henry Jackson Society (http://henryjacksonsociety.org/wp-content/uploads/2012/12/HJS-Faith-in-the-Public-Sphere-Report.pdf).

Trigg, R. (2012) *Equality, freedom, and religion,* Oxford: Oxford University Press.

Vickers, L. (2009) 'Indirect discrimination and individual belief: *Eweida v British Airways plc*', *Ecclesiastical Law Journal,* vol 11, no 2, pp 197-203.

Vickers, L. (2010) 'Religious discrimination in the workplace: an emerging hierarchy?', *Ecclesiastical Law Journal,* vol 12, no 3, pp 280-303.

Weller, P. (2005) *Time for a change: Reconfiguring religion, state, and society,* London: New York, T & T Clark International.

Weller, P., Purdam, K., Ghanea, N. and Cheruvallil-Contractor, S. (2013) *Religion and belief, discrimination and equality,* London: Bloomsbury.

Whistler, D. and Hill, D.J. (2012) *Religious discrimination and symbolism – A philosophical perspective,* Liverpool: University of Liverpool (http://philpapers.org/rec/WHIRDA).

Winter, N. and Catto, R. (2012) *Non-religious identities in policy and practice,* Workshop Report, London, 20 April. Lancaster: Lancaster University (www.religionandsociety.org.uk/events/programme_events/show/non_religious_identities_in_policy_and_practice).

Woodhead, L. (2013) 'Religious leaders don't represent religious people', Public Spirit, 20 August (http://www.publicspirit.org.uk/religious-leaders-dont-represent-religious-people/). Woodhead, L. and Catto, R. (2012) *Religion and change in modern Britain*, London: New York, Routledge.

Woodhead, L. with Catto, R. (2009) *Religion or belief: Identifying issues and priorities*, Equality and Human Rights Commission Research Report no 48, Manchester: Equality and Human Rights Commission.

Section Three
Practice

NINE

Religious illiteracy in school Religious Education*

James C. Conroy

Introduction

This chapter attempts to explore two central concerns in and for Religious Education (RE) in a liberal democratic society. The first is a marked decline in functional religious literacy, and the second, that such functional illiteracy both feeds off and nurtures a kind of pathology in the practices of RE that militate against the seriousness of claims to the theological. The discussion here is informed by, but not confined to, the findings of a major three-year ethnographic study of RE practices in 24 schools across the UK (Conroy et al, 2013). The study comprised a series of interlocking steps, beginning with a two-day expert Delphi seminar (Baumfield et al, 2012), out of which emerged a professional focus on the particular shape and challenges of RE. The next step in this multidimensional exploration was to send five ethnographers into the schools over a two-year period for a minimum of 10 days in each location. The observation schedule included the description and analysis of the geographical location, physical and pedagogical/material resources, curriculum documents, informal settings and class lessons (largely focused on Key Stage 4/Year 11 – the final year of compulsory RE). Additionally we conducted interviews, focus groups and coffee conversations, and a student attitude survey. In a preliminary analysis of the data, we deployed a heuristic based on Kerry's (1982) work on a tripartite hierarchical structure of teacher–student linguistic interactions: *data, concept, abstract*. In a penultimate iteration, a number of drama specialist teacher education students were invited to analyse the data for four emerging themes and to create five-minute dramatic vignettes (adapting insights from Boal's Forum Theatre workshops; see Boal, 1979; Lundie and Conroy, 2012). During a launch of

* This paper is based on the 'Does Religious Education Work?' project funded by the AHRC/ESRC Religion and Society programme.

findings conference in 2011, the students performed the vignettes in front of high school students who, in turn, acted as a further focus group. Finally, we conducted a series of workshop conversations with an audience of teachers, advisers and academics. This extensive and complex data set has enabled us to burrow into the *nested* (Conroy and Lundie, 2015: forthcoming) interior of RE practices. In doing so we are acutely aware that the ensuing descriptions of RE and its impact on religious literacy and illiteracy are not, in any straightforward sense, representative. Like many social practices, RE embodies significant and substantial variation and, of course, 24 schools are, in absolute terms, a small number. Nevertheless, we are confident that our study is robustly indicative of major themes and trends in practice and, allied to our choice of schools that were identified (both by self-nomination and by Ofsted reports) as sites of good practice, it exposes some of the structural, epistemological and theological deficiencies of contemporary practice.

In our deliberations, and as far as possible, we allowed the analysis to follow the shape of the material, and this led us into some unexpected spaces, most notably into the use of textual and related resources, and the relationship between text and examination. As we shall see, the relationship between examinations and religious literacy is as significant as it is complex. Other emerging themes included the confusion between epistemic claims and personal value attachments as well as the absence of any historic-theological understanding. In all of this I would wish to distinguish religious literacy from religious practice, which can too often (especially by religious communities themselves) be construed as a proxy for literacy. There is, arguably, no reason why religious literacy should collapse in the way in which religious practice in Europe has (for a full discussion, see Herbert, 2003). Importantly, this is not a chapter primarily concerned with secularisation, but with the capacity to cultivate a discourse in the civil polity about religion, most especially in and through education.

Sum and the parts

The notion of religious *literacy* has received significant and substantial treatment in RE in recent years, significantly in the work of Andrew Wright (1993, 2001; see also Conroy and Davis, 2007), and, of course, denotes not an attachment to any particular religious formulary or doctrine per se, but an acquaintance with, an understanding of, the nature of religious language, religious concepts and practices, and some grasp of the complexities, contradictions and challenges of at least one religious tradition. Perhaps more than any of these, religious literacy is an engagement with religious language and its import (which again, is not, of course, to imply offering some kind of assent or credence to any particular religious or theological claims). It also embodies the capacity to locate particular ideas within their historical, ethical, epistemological and social context. Given that in the UK there is compulsory schooling it would not be unreasonable to consider such capacities as the mark of a religiously educated person. Religious illiteracy, on the other hand, is founded, not only on the absence of these elements that comprise religious literacy; in addition, it is grounded on the confusion of parts and wholes, where partial understanding or explanation inclines to mis-representation and mis-understanding. Let me explore this a little further. In his discussion of the relationship between the whole and its parts in *Cratylus*, Plato indicates that the two require some kind of congruity with respect to their claims to verisimilitude:

> Socrates: But is a proposition true as a whole only, and are the parts untrue?

> Hermogenes: No; the parts are true as well as the whole.

> Socrates: Would you say the large parts and not the smaller ones, or every part?

> Hermogenes: I should say that every part is true. (Plato, *The Cratylus: A dialogue*, 2008)

A similar concern is to be found in the Buddhist text, *The questions of King Milinda*:

> Nagsena: Then is it the combination of poke, axle, wheels, framework, flag-staff, yoke, reins, and goad which is the "chariot"?

> Milinda: No, Reverend Sir!

> Nagsena: Then, is this "chariot" outside the combination of poke, axle, wheels, framework, flag-staff, yoke, reins and goad?

> Milinda: No, Reverend Sir!... It is in dependence on the pole, the axle, the wheels, the framework, the

flag-staff, etc, there takes place this denomination "chariot", this designation, this conceptual term, a current appellation and a mere name.

The consequence of singling out only the parts is that they can be made to look partial, ridiculous or inflated. It is, after all, not difficult to extrapolate a social or liturgical practice from its historical or theological context and point to its apparent absurdity. So it was that advice to teachers from one South East England Standing Advisory Council for Religious Education (subsequently removed after succumbing to substantial criticism) included the suggestion that they should avoid using such terms as 'the Wailing Wall' when referring to the Western Wall of the temple in Jerusalem on the grounds that this might suggest to students that Jews 'moaned' a lot. Nor, in speaking about Christian Eucharistic celebration, should they refer to 'the body and blood' of Christ on the grounds that this carried the connotation that Christians were cannibals. The fallacy of inappropriate extrapolation is not reserved solely for those wishing to avoid given offence, opponents of religion such as Richard Dawkins (2007) have almost turned it into an art form.

In our own study examples included, in church schools, an invitation to 'feel' the suffering of Jesus without any discussion of the theology of sacrifice, or where religious propositions serve as forms of proof texting intended to secure particular behavioural outcomes in the classroom. On other occasions it was clear that the shape of the curriculum and examinations were intended to elicit very specific answers (but I shall return to this). Such questions and answers refer to part of a thing rather than to the thing. For example, in the 2012 Assessment and Qualifications Alliance (AQA) Religion and Morality examination,[1] students were asked (for three marks) to distinguish between a hospice and a hospital! While it is no doubt a good thing to know some vocabulary, it hardly amounts to a theological or religious insight unless it is located in a historical theology of hospitality.

What these examples, and the very many similarly perfunctory questions that are increasingly common in public examinations, evidence is a penchant for disaggregating synoptic questions that appear to have grown as the performative impulses of education have grown. These impulses often takes the shape of examination questions that invite students to, for example, offer two reasons why a Jew might believe X, as if believing X was somehow merely propositional. Moreover, this practice has tended to ignore, or at best significantly downplay, the complex and integrative relationship between religious propositions and moral and emotional attachments, between narrative and event, and between what *is* and what *might be*. Yet, as I shall illustrate later, personal preference plays a substantial role in the RE classroom. It is, of course, the case that education has always embodied degrees of performativity – after all, medieval schools were instituted to prepare clerks and clergymen for their professional calling. Yet the shape of performativity has changed markedly in the wake of the public examination. More specifically, in the course of our ethnography, the growing dominance of the examination has arguably had a corrosive effect on the claim that a particular set of religious beliefs might offer an integrated account of being, and, in its turn, be offered to students as a synoptic account of a belief system. Of course, all education involves some disaggregation. Analysis is predicated on an exploration of parts, but not only the parts per se. Rather, it is concerned to reassemble the disaggregated or constituent parts into something like a coherent whole that carries not only descriptive, but explanatory, force.

These, and other related examples point to the failure to understand the nature of religious language and its commitments. The educational response to the conundrum of how to treat religion in a culture that feels some discomfort with the religious has often been to naturalise it, that is, to ensure that it referred to something that could, in Voegelin's (1952 and 1965) sense, be made or construed as immanent. Sometimes this emerges in oblique ways wherein what appears to be an invitation to enter into a dialogue with religious stories and religious meaning tends to occlude the particularity of theological language in favour of personal interpretation. Hence in one (fairly typical) example from Dundon School, the teacher engages a class of 12- to 13-year-olds as follows:

> "... I want you to go out of this class knowing how to read stories, how to read myths, how to read religious stories, and *decide what they mean for yourselves*." Mr Dylan says that, when they listen to the stories he's going to give them, he wants them to be asking "Why would anybody tell a story like that, what would they be trying to get across?" (Dundon Grammar School, emphasis added)

Of course this apparent strategy of engagement precisely reflects the ways in which religious language is to be embodied in mythic stories, which students are invited to interpret for themselves ('decide what they mean for yourselves'), as if engagement and interpretation were simply to be thought of as preferences. It is seductive to imagine that the central purpose of RE is such personal appropriation of the meaning of religious myth. Indeed, the Scottish 5–14 Curriculum Guidelines (1992) explicitly foreground such appropriation of 'personal' value as central to the task of RE. Significantly, in our study, the impulse to see the content of RE in such personalised terms appeared to lie in anxiety about making substantive claims. Arguably the gradual privatisation of religion in late industrial societies has resulted in confusion between what might be considered epistemic claims and value attachments. In other words, religious propositions lay claim to certain transcendent truths. As theological constructs, sin and salvation, redemption and kenosis, sacrifice and anamnesis are intended to lay claim to a particular feature or features of the world, and the relationship between being in the world and being beyond the world. The verisimilitude of such claims is a second order question, which depends on the more pressing concern of actually understanding the nature of the proposition(s) under scrutiny. However, more often than not, especially in the non-religious school setting, teachers prescind from engaging in such seemingly abstruse discursive practices in favour of descriptions of the social practice. Questions about truth claiming are reduced to interpretation. So it is that teachers feel unable to address the connective tissue of theological description as truth claiming, preferring instead an approach that considers RE to be primarily concerned with meaning making and its concomitant affections. Of course this move has a substantial pedigree going back to the work of R.B. Braithwaite (1968) and beyond, work that considered religion to be centrally concerned with ethics. But Braithwaite's rather subtle analysis of the distinctive ways in which believer and unbeliever approach religious propositions is largely lost in the transactions of the classrooms with which our project engaged. His belief that one has to consider the ways in which religious assertions coalesce into a certain coherent account that joins belief and practice is precisely what is ignored in many classroom transactions. The emergence in the classroom of a perceived interchangeability between religious and ethical propositions allied to the rise of 'postmodern' (Lyotard, 1984) epistemic insecurity has seen teachers resile from a comprehensive engagement with the claims of religion, preferring instead the less contentious route of opinion and voice. Hence, at the more obvious end of the continuum, the following record was not at all atypical of the conversational spaces in the classroom:

Ms Raphael: "You can be as controversial as you like."

Audrey: "What does that mean?"

Ms Raphael: "It means you can say anything you want."

...

Jack: "What about the father of Jesus?"

Ms Raphael: "I'm just gonna put 'Father' [on the board]."

There are a lot of group discussions arising out of students' ideas; this is generating background noise in what is intended as a whole-class discussion. Ms Raphael sits at the front desk, with her arms folded; she looks fed up. "Is it possible to have a discussion with you lot?" (Brockton Community School)

The invitation to 'say anything you want', to be as 'controversial as you like', appears to have little enough foundation in coming to terms with the claims of religion. Indeed, it was precisely this discursive pattern that was made present by the drama students in one of their vignettes. Interestingly, the school students (in our Boal Forum Theatre event) responded by suggesting that they found this form of 'loose' person-centred talk unhelpful. It is certainly the case that students considered that they talked more in RE than in other classes but, in something of a blow to the liberal instincts underpinning such pedagogic strategies, they were much less likely to consider that RE in general or this kind of talk were to be taken seriously. Finally, in this regard, the practices witnessed in our study offered evidence of the repeated failure to present and come to terms with any synoptic whole. There was only a modest sense that religious impulses, beliefs or claims were to be considered in an integrated and coherent manner.

Examination system and religious illiteracy

The problems witnessed in examination papers were symptomatic of a broader set of concerns with examinations and their impact on weak literacy in RE. While performativity in education is hardly new (after all, modern European education is almost entirely a function of the needs of a mass industrialisation over and against those of agrarian economies), its attendant discursive practices have become somewhat shrill and, in the middle to upper reaches of the secondary school, have assumed a dominant note. Teachers repeatedly complained of the corrosive effects of the examination system, and time and again, we witnessed teachers elide difficult or challenging questions on the grounds that taking time out in order to explore these would militate against examination success. So it is that in one school, the head of department discussed the constraints of following the exam syllabus with our ethnographer. In doing so he repeatedly bemoans 'the reductive, instrumental nature of the textbooks and workbooks for each module. The head of department does not feel that they represent good RE but knows that if the pupils do exactly as the books instruct them to do then they will pass/get a good grade' (from ethnographer's field notes). Across a range of schools (denominational and non-denominational) in our study, it was not uncommon to see substantial commitments to a range of rhetorical devices that clearly instrumentalise the study of religion.

On many occasions (and in many schools) the same overriding imperative could be seen in wall charts that exhorted students to get an 'A' at GCSE by following the rubrics, or again, offered reasons why students should study RE that were dominated by claims that success was easier (relatively) to secure than might be the case in other subjects (a belief that received substantial corroboration in our questionnaire responses). As Figure 9.1 (an attempt at seducing students into choosing a longer course of study) well illustrates, this was common practice. RE teachers, under the pressure of an internal as well as external political economy, push their subject hard as an optimal choice for students who want examination success (but which Bonhoeffer (1995) might

Figure 9.1: Persuading students ...

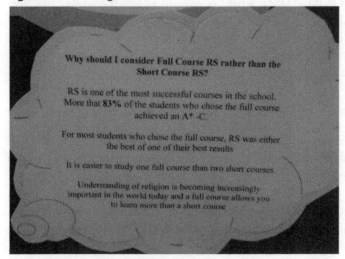

have considered 'cheap grace'). What is of particular interest in this example is the slightly awkward addendum that the subject would help in improving students' multicultural understanding, yet nowhere in this, or many other similar charts/posters in the 24 schools in our study, was there significant evidence that understanding religion or, more importantly, the religious, mattered. Rather, what mattered were the immanent purposes that the subject was required to serve. These included a wide range of social concerns, from civic participation to sex and drugs education.

In this example, the cultivation of religious literacy is indeed subordinated to these other imperatives – exams, and a certain etiolated form of civics. These large board displays were surprisingly common, and most often focused on strategies for examination success. The imperative of understanding religious conceits and concepts was very much a second order entailment, if present at all.

Ironically, the development and expansion of public examinations in RE had been considered by its supporters in the profession to be a catalyst for improved understanding of, and an enhanced engagement with, the subject. In our study this appeared not to have worked. Confusing, as it does, the parts for the whole, it would appear to have had pretty much the opposite effect of that which had been intended. Arguably, the examination system has had a deleterious effect on religious literacy, shaping it through the concern to see religion as a largely immanent resource focused on the here and now. More than this, the examination system produces no requirement that students develop a synthetic understanding of the religious.

Not infrequently the pressure of examinations involved teachers resiling from their educational and human responsibilities to afford students intelligent and fulsome responses to their genuine (if sometimes 'off piste') enquiries. A common response was that there was insufficient time to deal with what was, admittedly, an interesting issue, but "if you come back next year to study AS level we will have time to deal with that." So it was that the pressure to shape teaching and learning in the subject around the imperatives of the examination system was substantial (Conroy et al, 2013) and led to myriad forms of deferral – until they return to engage in further study! In a wide range of the schools in our study we encountered instances of this deferral, about which students expressed significant frustration. The following (indicative) ethnographer's note highlights an important issue in this regard. Of particular salience is the way in which the student, being well rehearsed in the distribution of marks and effort, is able to intervene with the injunction to pay attention to the marking scheme

– that is, the 'thing' that should determine the effort to be put into dealing with this (somewhat complex) issue: "… it's only a ten and two fives"! In this sense the scheme determines the treatment of the topic rather than serving to reflect the capacities of students to elucidate the nature of the descriptive and moral challenge presented by the topic. The second ethnographic note offers some confirmation of this (widespread) practice of 'coaching', and confusion about what counts as success in education about religions, that is, as something determined by the ability to rehearse pre-ordained responses to predetermined enquiries. More than this, the categorisation of teacher 'brilliance' as a good coach is worthy of note given that coaching may not conduce to understanding:

1. The homework consisted off a three-part question based on the broad curricular topic of morality. JR explained that they were practicing for a "timed" from the morality section. She wrote the three-part question down on the board. "You have been asked to take part in a debate on abortion choose one side and present an argument? (10 marks). Explain why abortion is not always a clear-cut issue for Christians (5 marks). Do you think abortion should be available on the NHS? (5 marks)." One boy asked, "Miss, do we do all three of them on the one day?" Rather than JR answering, a girl on his table responded by saying, "yeah sure, it's only a ten and two fives." JR did not answer as she was surrounded by a small group of girls who were getting photocopied GCSE past papers to practice with at home for their revision. JR then highlighted to the whole class that she had papers for anyone who wanted to borrow some so that they, too, could use them to revise with. While many borrowed them, not all did. JR asked one girl in particular if she wanted to borrow any papers. The girl replied "No". (North West School)

2. The HoD [head of department] draws on experience as an SQA [Scottish Qualifications Authority] marker when planning and teaching. "I think it sharpens my practice that I'm a … marker. It means when I'm putting work in place in school and in the run-up to the exam I know what's being looked for, so the sort of phrase I'm expecting the pupils to come out with in the exam I will teach them almost verbatim. Stewarts Melville

always does incredibly well in the exams. They have a brilliant RE teacher and you can tell when you read the kids' works they've been coached." (Wallace School)

This foregrounding of the examination system was manifest not only in the classroom (pedagogical) strategies, but also in the materials to which the students had access. Yet many of these materials (textbooks, exercise books, technological media and so forth) are poorly constructed. These weak constructions take two related forms: the first is highlighted in a recent report commissioned by the former Department for Children, Schools and Families in England (Jackson et al, 2010). It suggests that many of the materials used by teachers were weak and demonstrated poor grasp of theological and religious language and practices; indeed, in a significant number of instances, they contained erroneous or partial claims. Evidence from our own study would suggest that poor resources were not uncommon. In the instance that follows it is clear that teachers are often aware of these weaknesses, yet equally clear that even the most enthusiastic professionals are apt to entertain conceptual confusions. Not infrequently, as in the excerpt below from our field notes, teachers considered that the relevance of the subject was best secured by a focus on contemporary issues and current affairs. Or again, the widespread practice of relying on Google searches offers a weak base for understanding the nature of religion. Hence:

Mrs XXX tells me there is a resource called "perfect papers" which gives example exam papers, she says they are good in the sciences, but very poor for RMPS [Religious, Moral and Philosophical Studies]. She tells me things change very quickly in RMPS, uses the examples of the Pope recently saying that purgatory doesn't exist (which he didn't, it was Limbo) and the Church of England's recent debates about the way it treated Darwin in his own time. You "need to be on your toes ... like Modern Studies." Mrs XXX tries to keep abreast of current affairs as they are a good talking point to get classes interested. (Kinraddie School)

Rise of the personal and gaps between home and school

I now move to the students' own sense of the efficacy of RE in securing their personal religious understanding. In the schools in our study it was not uncommon that students with personal religious backgrounds indicated that the accounts of their faith failed to reflect the actual theological claims and understanding of their faith.

Earlier I suggested that much of the experience of RE in the classroom was shaped by an anxiety to confront the propositional. Here I should like to make some observations about a different, although not unrelated, manifestation of the gap between the formal and the personal. This is of particular significance in those domains where students are themselves, or are assumed to be, religious. In a number of the schools in our study that had significant populations of non-Christian religious adherents, quite significant gaps opened up in the explanatory fabric of the classroom. Sometimes this took the form of different terminology where students within a faith fail to recognise the labels associated with particular practices – of course such labelling is often culturally located. More problematically it frequently took the form of quite significant conceptual or framing gaps between home and school. Hence, in one of the ethnographer's field notes, we find the following description:

> XXXX (student) tells me she was "a bit confused by what's written in the [GCSE text]book" because they use different vocabulary to describe concepts in Islam. She often didn't ask her teachers the reasons for this. Her attitude to GCSE Islam was "Let's just get our GCSE and know this", that is, accept discrepancies between Islam as taught in home and school – school Islam only useful for exam, distanced from lived experience, if she has questions about Islam, more likely to ask family than teachers. This is corroborated by some Year 11 girls' reactions to the treatment of "maha/dowry" in a textbook used in Mr YYYY's class. Only one girl mentioned dowry in her own account of Muslim weddings. Something about the reaction of the girls suggests that this doesn't accord with their own experience. Nonetheless, Mr YYYY tries to offer practical advice to the girls about marriage contracts and divorce. In the same lesson, Mr YYYY prefaces a description of Muslim wedding parties with "Usually, girls ...", the girls' faces are impassive, hard to read, as he talks about Muslim practices, it is hard to gauge how they feel about being "told" about their own faith in this way. (Linden School)

In another instance a student indicated that she found her madrasah more helpful than school because when she asked questions, her imam would answer, but in school she was told that such questions/issues were 'not in the course'. Despite her subsequent observation that this was a common experience for students, it is related, as I have earlier intimated, to the often-baleful influence of a bankrupt examination system.

This reaction was not at all uncommon in our study. Of course it might simply point to the failures of popular or folk religion. After all, in the Christian tradition, all kinds of pieties and practices emerge and/or are reconfigured in the spaces of the local and vernacular. In this regard the work of the comedian and playwright, Dario Fo, is particularly significant in resurrecting the tradition of the *giullare* (jongleur/jester) as a vehicle for not only challenging the holders of power, but also for bringing theological claims closer to the ordinariness of everyday life (Jenkins, 1994). But, I would suggest, more is at stake here. Not infrequently there were instances of teachers having limited understanding of the subtleties of religious practice and their connectedness to the interstices of religious belief and doctrine. Equally, there were instances when students, from a variety of religious and non-religious backgrounds, would ask teachers questions that they felt uncomfortable addressing at home. Often the teachers would respond with formulaic, or potentially inadequate, answers. The gap between home and school often remains unresolved, and may be rather more than manifestations of the gap between 'folk' and 'high' religion. Rather there is often a gap between the ways in which schools dissect and deconstruct religious practices and questions, and the fragility of the conversation in the home. The gap is manifest not only in the quite different explanatory moves made in schools as against those made in students' home environments. This lengthy set of notes from one ethnographic record offers an insight into a not atypical classroom engagement. Hence:

> ... [w]hen engaging with texts, the usual approach is to take brief quotations from the Bible or the Koran. Both teachers and students report to me that the girls feel uncomfortable handling the Koran in class – at home or in the mosque they would be expected to go through *wudu* (ritual ablution) before touching the Koran. The teachers are somewhat dismissive of this concern in the class, leading to some tension at times. In contrast, during one A-level class, one girl has a copy of *Metro* open on top of the Bible. As one example, during an A-level class, Mr Moore asks girls to cut out and match titles, quotes from Calvin's

work and quotes from the Bible on the topics of Baptism, Penance, Reconciliation, Guide, Judge, Resurrection and Love. There are seven Bible quotes given, respectively Acts 22:16, John 19:17-37, John 20:23, John 14:16, John 5:22, Revelation 1:18, Matthew 22:37-40 (related to class handout). Pupils are asked to match the "right" quote to the right title. As a homework task, Mr Moore asks the class to read over the work they have cut and stuck, and list any questions they have. Very few complete the task as homework, but the questions they list include:

"What is the Eucharist ceremony?"
"Reciting of the formula of absolution?"
"What is reconciliation?"
"What is penance?"
"What is redeemed?"
"Jesus as judge?"

– suggesting a possible mis-match of literacy to the complexity of the Christian topic they are studying (Calvin's views on forgiveness and atonement). The teacher begins by asking the class how they would have done if he didn't answer these questions; the class say they would have gone to Google. Mr Moore says that this is a good strategy, "in future, it would be great … just do that." (Bishop Fulton School)

Of course, in so far as it contributes to religious illiteracy, the gap between home and school carries the ongoing twin risks that we either discount the phenomenological experience of *religious people* in the interests of a certain, modally dominant liberal treatment, or we fail to explore RE through the critical lenses afforded by hermeneutics. Falling between both, much that is transacted in the classroom in such circumstances is 'apt to offer a kind of sanctuary to believer and sceptic alike, where they can indulge their hermetically-sealed ontologies and epistemologies, ensuring that the claims of the Other are not simply deemed wrong but are, in fact, radically declassified' (Conroy and Davis, 2007).

Failure to address the 'other'

While the poster (Figure 9.1) suggests that RE is a desirable if not necessary metier for understanding the 'other', much that passes for RE misses the point. In the exploration of the practices of religious communities (note that there was rarely anything that one might consider theology), the dominant mode of operation was morphological. By this I wish to suggest that religions are treated as if their liturgical, social and moral practices were merely locally determined refractions of the same impulses and drives. And these tended to be shaped by a normative liberal discourse. Those features of religion that stand outside such discourse (tricksters, the teleological suspension of the ethical, animal sacrifice, self-harm, the menace of religion as well as its claims to transcendence) tended to be subject to a flattening and ultimately erasure. The rough uplands and valleys of religion were largely ignored. During the work on emergent themes in the Boal Forum Theatre, the drama students identified a substantial collision between, the often impoverished, formal teaching and the actual complexity of religious entanglements. In a lesson devoted to work on Islam, the teacher (back to the class) is proceeding through the standard classificatory techniques, while the students are having a heated and extremely interesting debate on the religious politics and transcendent claims that attend suicide bombing in Islam. At one stage the teacher stops talking to berate the students for not taking the lesson seriously!

Underlying much of this is the desire to construct RE as a form of citizenship education. Given the absence of religious feeling and attachment as well as the substantive claims to religious fealty, there is a strong imperative to regard RE as concerned with matters other than the religious. For example, while there were instances where death was explored, it tended to be within three discrete contexts: the death of Jesus, the psychology of loss and grief, and euthanasia, with the last being the most common. Even where it was being discussed in a religious context, such as the death of Jesus, this tended to focus on the events leading up to his death and the characters involved. For the rest, they were largely concerned with the ethics of care, permission and responsibility with respect to euthanasia. Rarely was there any consideration of teleology or ontology.

One particularly cogent example of the elision between religious and civic categories can be seen in the treatment of festivals. In a number of the schools in our study, Diwali, Hanukah and Chinese New Year are all treated as unproblematically cognate. Similarly, ethnic and religious attributions were frequently treated as interchangeable. This common consideration of the religious as merely one of a series of secular options has its roots in the success of organisations such as the British Humanist Association in securing a place at the table of RE with membership on many Standing Advisory Councils for Religious Education (SACREs) and national organisations such as the Religious Education Council. The argument, which has proved persuasive in such circles, is that humanism represents a life choice equivalent to religion. This equivalence has the effect of establishing religion within the orbit of the immanent – for each religious claim there is a parallel secular claim. Secular humanism sits alongside Christianity, Islam, Buddhism, Judaism … (and their many branches) as one alternative in a pluralist marketplace of alternatives. This is one with the suggestion that religious institutions increasingly face the energies of internal secularisation while maintaining some residual religious practices. This internal secularisation facilitates an occlusion of the distinctively transcendent and theologically grounded epistemic claims and their replacement with a religion of manners more attuned to the requirements of modern social structures, while maintaining their residual symbolism. These, in turn, are transformed into material forms of cultural expression such as art and consumption (Conroy and Davis, 2007). So it is that religious concepts themselves are treated as interchangeable.

Conclusions: underlying causes

I have attempted here to articulate some of the manifestations and explanations of religious illiteracy. I could have peppered this account with the many conceptual and factual errors we witnessed in the classroom, but to do so would do little more than offer a catalogue without a cause. In this final section I suggest three interrelated causes for the failure of compulsory RE to combat religious literacy.

First is the absence of any historical narrative. In her biography of the 18th-century Jewess, Rahel Varnhagen, Hannah Arendt (1957, 1997) argues that without history there is no such thing as personality; without the public there is no private. As she puts it rhetorically, 'What is man without his history? Product of nature – not personality' (1957, 1997, p 85). Religious belief and the education predicated on it require an embedding of religious belief in theological history – how it is that humans come to have the beliefs they have? RE is largely devoid of theological history, and this turns every religious practice into a private practice; every religious sentiment into a private sentiment. Students do not understand the genesis of religious ideas; rather, our obsession with the mistaken cult of relevance reduces religious language to sentiment or ethical attachment in the present. Consequently, RE approaches the religious not as the *mysterium, tremendum et fascinans*, not as hierophantic, but as a psychologised or sociologised epiphenomenon of brute nature. Where history does appear it is not within the discourse of religion but outside, in a different, alternative and morally superior world of reason, with the likes of Bellah imagining that national ideologies and civil religions functionally absorb and recalibrate religious traditions. This is, of course, a key driver in the growing imperative to displace RE with Philosophy and Citizenship. It is also the energy that underpins the delegitimation of RE as a subject that treats its subject, the religious, as already delegitimated as a source of human flourishing. This, in turn, leaves RE as the only subject on the curriculum where core concepts are regularly trashed, both inside and outside the school (Conroy and Davis, 2007).

When we examine some of the practices intimated above, we can see where the second, related, difficulty emerges. In much of the practice that we witnessed there was a significant elision of the distinction between epistemic claim and value attachment. By this I mean (as noted above) that students were rarely invited to consider the merit of a religious claim as a proposition. In this way they did not have to engage with either a theological or historical tradition. Rather, teachers solicited opinions largely grounded in feelings and attitudes rather than description and analysis. The displacement of the historic or communal interpretation must yield to the pre-eminent authority of the individual. There are, of course, parallels in other areas of the curriculum, notably, History and English Literature, in addition to such confused offerings as 'citizenship'. The parallel comprises the contemporary unwillingness to countenance the existence of a canon imagining erroneously that a canon must give rise to the oppressive force of immutability. But of course, a canon can offer a coherent body and simultaneously remain permeable and porous, opening itself up to new contents and interpretations.

Third, there are some key moves in the relationship between the study of religion and the practice of RE that have their roots in the work of Smart (1971) and the educational choices that were made as the subject journeyed in its transition from confessionalism to non-normativity. In the mid-20th century two quite different if related accounts of phenomenology surface. The first, shaped by Husserl (1970), is concerned to foreground the primacy of inwardness. In other words, phenomenology was to serve as a catalyst for enabling the individual to strip away the layers and accretions of experience so as to encounter the-thing-in-itself. Direct apprehension was the goal. The second, grounded in the work of Eliade (1958) and others, gave rise to the focus on the morphological and comparative. While both approaches to the study of religion offer much, the triumph of the latter in the classroom (because it is procedurally and conceptually much easier) has resulted in the triumph of surface engagements.

Given the nature of schooling, it would appear that it is possible for religion to survive only if it adapts to the logic of late industrial society, and contributes to its legitimation. Whereas in the US the absence of RE in the public school has fostered unthinkingness and the consequent growth of fundamentalism; in Britain RE that has failed to pay attention to the relationship between the self and 'religious objects' has also produced an unthinkingness, manifest not as fundamentalism, but as profound disassociation, scepticism and lack of interest. While I have only touched on a few of the manifestations and causes of religious illiteracy in the classroom here, this should not be read as a counsel of despair but as recognition and an invitation to re-think the role of text and history, of propositions of the challenge and attachments in the teaching of RE.

Note

[1] See http://filestore.aqa.org.uk/subjects/AQA-40553-QP-JUN12.PDF

References

Arendt, H. (1957, 1997) *Rahel Varnhagen: The life of a Jewess*, edited by L. Weissberg, translated by R. and C. Winston, Baltimore, MD: Johns Hopkins University Press.

Baumfield, V.M., Conroy, J., Davis, R. and Lundie, D. (2012) 'The Delphi Method: gathering expert opinion in religious education', *British Journal of Religious Education*, vol 34, no 1, pp 5-19.

Boal, A. (1979) *Theater of the oppressed* (translated by C.A. McBride and M.-O.L. McBride), London: Pluto Press.

Bonhoeffer, D. (1995) *The cost of discipleship*, New York: Simon and Schuster.

Braithwaite, R.B. (1968) 'An empiricist's view of the nature of religious belief', in B. Mitchell (ed) *The philosophy of religion*, Oxford: Oxford University Press, pp 72-91.

Conroy, J. and Davis, R. (2007) 'Citizenship, education and the claims of religious literacy', in M. Peters, A. Britton and H. Blee (eds) *Global citizenship education*, Rotterdam: Sense, pp 187-202.

Conroy, J. and Lundie, D. (2015: forthcoming) 'Does Religious Education work? On nested identities', in L. Woodhead (ed) *How to research religion: Putting methods into practice*, Oxford: Oxford University Press.

Conroy, J.C., Lundie, D., Davis, R.A., Baumfield, V. Barnes, L.P., Gallagher,T., Lowden, K., Bourque, N. and Wenell, K. (2013) *Does Religious Education work? A mulitdimensional investigation*, London: Bloomsbury.

Dawkins, R. (2007) *The God delusion*, London: Black Swan.

Eliade, M. (1958) *Patterns of comparative religion*, New York: Sheed and Ward.

Herbert, D. (2003) *Religion and civic society*, Aldershot: Ashgate.

Husserl, E. (1970) 'P. Koestenbaum' (Translation and Introductory Lecture), *The Paris Lectures*, The Hague: Martinus Nijhoff.

Jackson, R., Ipgrave, J., Hayward, M., Hopkins, P., Fancourt, N., Robbins, M., Francis, L.J. and McKenna, U. (2010) *Materials used to teach about world religions in schools in England*, London: Department for Children, Schools and Families.

Jenkins, R. (1994) *Subversive laughter*, New York: The Free Press.

Kerry, T. (1982) 'The demands made by RE on pupil's thinking', in J. Hull (ed) *New directions in religious education*, Lewes: Falmer Press., pp 161-70.

Lundie, D. and Conroy, J. (2012) 'Seeing and seeing through: forum theatre approaches to ethnographic evidence', *Journal of Beliefs and Values*, vol 33, no 3, pp 329-42.

Lyotard, J.F. (1984) *The postmodern condition: A report on knowledge*, Minneapolis, MN: University of Minnesota Press.

Plato (2008) *The Cratylus*, republished ebook (www.gutenberg.org/files/1616/1616-h/1616-h.htm).

Scottish Consultative Council on the Curriculum (1992) *5–14 Religious and Moral Education Guidelines*, Edinburgh: SOED.

Smart, N. (1971) *The religious experience of mankind*, London: Collins.

Voegelin, E. (1952 and 1965) *The new science of politics: An introduction*, Chicago: University of Chicago Press.

Wright, A. (1993) *Religious Education in the secondary school: Prospects for a religious literacy*, London: David Fulton.

Wright, A. (2001) 'Religious literacy and democratic citizenship', in L. Francis, J. Astley and M. Robbins (eds) *The fourth R for the third millennium: Education in religion and vales for the global future*, Dublin: Lindisfarne, pp 201-19.

TEN

Religious literacy in higher education

Stephen H. Jones

In recent years, a number of authors have highlighted the role that universities could potentially play in improving the public conversation about religion and belief (Gilliat-Ray, 2000, p 59; Prothero, 2008, p 173; Woodhead, 2009, p 28). Ford (2004, p 24), for example, has commented that the university is one of the:

> ... few settings in our world where the huge range of issues arising out of [the religious diversity of society], relating to every sphere of life, can be thoughtfully and peacefully addressed in ways that allow for fruitful understanding, discussion and deliberation, leading to negotiation of the sorts of settlements that allow religious and secular civil societies to flourish.

It is easy to see why this is a popular view. Not only are universities pre-eminent centres of knowledge generation, dissemination and exchange, they are also places where people with different beliefs and social backgrounds come into sustained contact with one another. They are situated in specific national and local contexts, but operate on a global level, drawing in students from across the world. They have a huge impact on young people in their formative years – and if today's graduates have a good knowledge of the range of beliefs, then media, politics and society will surely benefit tomorrow.

There also seems to be plenty of scope for improvement in that way faith and belief are publicly discussed. When religious issues are debated in Anglophone contexts, the tone is frequently fractious, and all too often marked by mutual incomprehension. Even though today religion attracts great interest (Knott et al, nd), knowledge of it remains low. The Islamic tradition is perhaps the most obvious case of this. Despite the fact that Islam has been constantly in the media over the last decade, public understanding of it is minimal. According to one recent survey, in the UK 36 per cent of people do not know who the Prophet Mohammed was, and just 20 per cent have come into contact with the Qur'an (Tzortzis, 2010). Another found that, after Muhammad, Osama bin Laden is seen as the individual who best represents the Islamic tradition (Field, 2010). Religious knowledge is often poor even among people who strongly identify with a religious tradition (as discussed in Chapter Four by Stephen Prothero and Lauren Kerby). The sociologist Olivier Roy (2010) has highlighted the recent emergence of what he calls 'holy ignorance' – that is, assertive, often anti-intellectual forms of belief that are based on faith, emotion and spectacle rather than on learning. Universities seem, then, well placed to help provide a remedy to a pressing and intractable problem.

Yet even if higher education (HE) presents a range of possibilities, the recent history of the sector raises complex questions about the ability and willingness of universities to foster religious literacy. Processes of secularisation and neoliberalisation had had a profound impact on universities. Secular vocabularies of understanding have challenged dominant Protestant theologies and become predominant in most Anglophone universities. While this has allowed the academy to become a more inclusive place, it has also resulted in a degree of suspicion of religion – in some institutional contexts at least. Religion can be regarded as a threat to objective scholarship or to collegiality. Even where this is not the case, universities can view themselves as 'above the fray', with religion being perceived as, in Edwards' (2006, p 1) words, something 'out there' in the wider world, rather than something 'in here' that needs to be engaged with in a serious way.

Furthermore, HE has been revolutionised in recent decades, and universities are now pressured by a bewildering range of competing, and sometimes apparently contradictory, demands (Trowler et al, 2005, p 440; Clarke, 2010). Some of these relate to some form of inter-university competition – for research funds, for places in national and international rankings, for students and the income that they help bring in – and others relate to a desire among policy-makers to build a large pool of work-ready graduates. Next to these pressing demands, longer-term concerns about cultural enrichment and conversation across belief can seem of little importance.

In this chapter my aim is to consider what contribution universities can make, realistically and practically, to the improvement of religious literacy. In it I offer an overview of religion in HE, looking at the changing place of religion in the university sector, and describing how it fits into the contemporary academy. My focus throughout is on English HE, where recent reform has been especially radical. (I speak mainly of 'England' in this chapter rather than 'Britain', as elements of HE policy have been devolved in the UK since 1998; different funding arrangements for HE are now in place in Wales, Scotland and Northern Ireland.) I explain how a complex mixture of religious and secular forces have shaped English HE, before going on to outline how recent reform has had an impact on English universities and put under pressure subjects that are not seen as economically valuable. I contend that this reform has not simply furthered the secularisation of the academy. Rather, I suggest that it has prompted new institutional interest in religious *identity* while putting pressure on religious *learning*.

In making this argument I draw on research conducted between 2009 and 2011 with Adam Dinham for the Religious Literacy Leadership in Higher Education Programme. This research comprised 65 interviews with staff in senior management and administrative roles in universities throughout England, along with the observation of a series of events for academic staff on the subject of religion and the university. I draw on this research throughout the chapter before, in the final stages, turning to more practical questions, asking what can and should be done to help modern-day universities meet the challenge of educating society about religion and belief.

Emergence of the modern university

Religion and secularity are, to borrow Ford's (2004, p 24) phrase, 'complexly co-present' in all English universities. Religious faith penetrates the life of universities in a variety of different ways. A wide range of both religious and secular identities can be found within any university's student and body; religious and secular traditions are studied on almost all university campuses; and the built environment, rituals, ethos and character of English universities have been shaped through a complex history in which a wide range of religious and secular forces have played a role.

Since 1800, this history has been one of rapid expansion. As Silver (2003) observes, almost every decade over the last two centuries has been, in some sense, one of transformation of HE. Up until the 19th century there were only seven universities in Britain and only two – the 'ancient' universities, Oxford and Cambridge – in England. In contrast to Germany, France and Scotland, England was slow to develop, but its growth in recent times has been dramatic. After the founding of University College London (formerly London University), Durham University and King's College in the first half of the 1800s, the period between 1851 and 1909 saw the emergence of 'red-brick' universities such as Leeds and Bristol. This was then followed in the 1960s by the creation, following the Robbins report in 1963, of 'plate-glass' universities such as Essex, Kent and Lancaster.

This period of expansion between 1800 and 1970 was also a period of secularisation and of conflict between religious and secular forces. Up until the mid-1800s England's universities were exclusively Anglican; religious tests were only fully abolished at Oxford and Cambridge in 1871, allowing for the first time non-conformists, Jews and Catholics to attend. The expansion of the university sector in the 19th century was in part driven by the desire to establish centres of higher learning that would be open to everyone (Gilliat-Ray, 2000, p 22; Rüegg, 2004, pp 61-4; Graham, 2005, pp 7-9). University College London (established in 1826) – the 'Godless institution of Gower Street', as dubbed by the historian Thomas Arnold – is the most famous example of this, while King's College, London (established in 1829) is equally famous for being founded in order to promote established Anglican values. In the 20th century, too, tensions between religious and secular perspectives were evident. Silver (2003, pp 2, 103-4) highlights how it was common in the mid-20th century for writers to describe English universities as in crisis, and some of the most notable of these – such as Walter Hamilton Moberly (1951) – saw this crisis as spiritual.

Much like the secularisation of English society, the secularisation of HE was not a simple, unidirectional transition. The conflict between religious and secular values within HE can easily be over-simplified and indeed exaggerated. It is worth noting that the most famous advocate of a liberal model of HE, John Henry Newman, was a Roman Catholic cardinal, and that secular writers on the university during the 19th century advocated starkly differing conceptions of HE. Some (like John Stuart Mill) argued that knowledge should be valued as an end in itself, and others (like Thomas Huxley) contended that knowledge should be valued because of its practical uses (Silver, 2003, pp 3-4). Nor is it correct to see the secularisation of HE as a process by which religion retreated to leave an institutionally 'neutral' space. Rather, as Edwards (2008) has said of the American university, gradually various alternatives to the dominant theological knowledge emerged, with the sciences, the social sciences, then the humanities 'declaring their independence' from religion. This, as Wuthnow (2008) notes, has led to a situation in which a complex mix of traditions and philosophies, religious and secular, coexist, for the most part amicably, although not always.

Towards a higher education market

From the late 1970s onwards, the liberal and religious norms predominant in universities in England were profoundly impacted, even to an extent undermined, by a programme of modernisation that was initiated by the Conservative government elected in 1979 and that has not yet come to a conclusion (Trowler et al, 2005, p 440; Clarke, 2010, p 92). This involved a wide range of (often linked) reforms. Perhaps most significantly, the HE sector in England again expanded substantially, with the UK following the international trend (see OECD, 2012) and building a 'mass' HE system. Relatedly, the binary divide between universities and polytechnics was abolished in 1992, causing the number of degree-awarding institutions to almost double overnight (it is, however, still commonplace to refer to universities as 'post-1992' and 'pre-1992' institutions). Major reforms to university funding were also imposed, with the main public funding body for HE, the University Grants Committee (established in 1919), being abolished and replaced with the Higher Education Funding Council for England (HEFCE) and other national funding councils.

Three connected themes stand out in this process: the increasing reliance on student fees to finance universities; the increasing emphasis, in government policy, on universities as crucial to building a flourishing 'knowledge economy'; and increasing competition between universities for students. Gradually, across successive Conservative and Labour governments, England has moved away from a system of universal government grants for tertiary education (which is still favoured in countries such as Norway), and towards a system of fees combined with dedicated financial support schemes and widening participation activity aimed at disadvantaged students (which is favoured in countries such as Australia and the US; see Bowes et al, 2013a). The latest step in this transition occurred in September 2012 when, following the Browne review (Browne et al, 2010) and a government White Paper (BIS, 2011), the teaching grant from HEFCE was all but replaced by student contributions (at the time up to a maximum of £9,000 per annum), supported by loans from the state.

Like many of the reforms that have gone before it, this change was designed to create a link between universities' financial viability and their ability to attract students. Along with the fee increases, some student number limits were lifted in 2012 (with further deregulation planned in future). As a result, for the first time English universities and courses could expand by attracting high student numbers, while at the same time unpopular degrees and institutions were placed at greater risk of failing. Only a small number of supposedly 'strategically important and vulnerable subjects' were cushioned from the effects of this new competition. The door was also opened to new solely privately funded HE providers to enter this nascent HE market (Hughes et al, 2013).

Those courses that were cushioned from the effects of the new market via additional public subsidies were generally selected because they were viewed as important to the development of the 'knowledge economy'. Following the example of the US (see Newfield, 2008, pp 125-8), policy-makers in Britain, over the course of the 1990s, became increasingly focused on the notion that the UK's economic prosperity depended on the growth of high-tech industries and products, and that universities had a crucial role to play in supplying graduates to knowledge-intensive industries (see BIS, 2009; Browne et al, 2010). During the 2000s very few policy documents, even those focusing on social justice issues such as equality of access (see, for example, DES, 2006), were published that did not stress the role universities play in generating economic growth. Accordingly, the 'STEM subjects' – science, technology, engineering and maths – came to be increasingly prioritised and offered special protections in the 2012 fee reforms.

The impact these changes have had on the HE sector has been huge, and it will become greater still as the effects of more recent changes are felt. Universities have undergone a substantial cultural shift, and are now much more focused on performance indicators, student employment outcomes, institutional branding and the provision of a positive 'student experience'. Yet oddly, very little has been said about their effect on religion in HE (Ford, 2004). Notably, the marketisation of HE occurred contemporaneously with a resurgence in publicly active religious movements. The period between 1979 and the present witnessed the end of the Cold War and the widespread 'deprivatisation' of religious traditions and communities of faith through movements such as Solidarity in Poland, the Iranian Revolution and, most notably, the attacks on New York of 11 September 2001 (9/11) (Casanova, 1994; Berger, 1999). These changes have prompted the emergence of a body of literature, most of it focused on the US, that has examined the history of religion in HE (Reuben, 1996; Hart, 1999; Roberts and Turner, 2000), the recent 're-emergence' of religion on university campuses (Edwards, 2008; Wuthnow, 2008), and the implications of increasing religious diversity for teaching and research (Edwards, 2006; Tisdell, 2008; Waggoner, 2011). However, with a few notable exceptions (such as Ford, 2004; Graham, 2005, pp 243-62), recent modernisation has been neglected, with the focus falling on more familiar questions such as possible tensions between theistic and liberal epistemologies, and the extent to which norms of public reason apply to universities. How, then, in this new environment should religion and religious literacy be addressed?

Religion in the university today

The history of HE in Britain has left a complex mix of institutions that differ markedly in their orientation towards religion. Today, a small number of the large research-intensive universities, such as Durham, and the 'ancient' universities, are technically religious foundations, and retain weak links to the Anglican Church. Among the overwhelmingly secular 'post-1992' universities there are also 15 church foundations, most, but not all, of which are also associated with the Church of England. These universities (which have formed into an alliance known as the Cathedrals Group) tend to have closer links with the churches than the older church foundations such as Oxford and Durham, although the exact relationship varies from institution to institution. The vast majority of English universities – and all of the 'red-brick' and 'plate-glass' institutions – are secular. Indeed, *all* publicly funded higher education institutions (HEIs) are secular in the sense that they are open to individuals of all faiths and none. Confessional education that seeks to propagate a particular faith and train religious professionals is rare. Yet even in many secular institutions there are established chaplaincy services and degree-awarding and other ceremonies are often held in religious buildings (see Guest et al, 2013, pp 53-81).

As a subject, Theology and Religious Studies remains fairly marginal, although not negligible by any means. There were just over 7,000 full-time students of Theology and Religious Studies across all years and all degree types in the academic year 2011/12, which represented just under 0.4 per cent of the total students in UK HE at that time. By contrast, 2.8 per cent of full-time students in 2011/12 took English, and 5.4 per cent took Business Studies.[1] Interestingly, recent research commissioned by the Department of Business, Innovation and Skills has shown that religion has a proportionately greater presence within the small but burgeoning privately funded HE sector. An estimated 150,000 students are studying for a higher-level qualification in privately funded institutions in the UK. Most are taking courses in Management, Business or Planning, but a survey of 1,495 students studying at privately funded HE providers indicated that around 12.1 per cent study Religion and Theology (Hughes et al, 2013). The character of privately funded courses is, unsurprisingly, quite different to those in publicly funded HEIs. Liberal and phenomenological approaches to Religious Studies – which seek to remain even-handed between religious traditions – tend to be eschewed in favour of the training of clergy, rabbis and imams. One of the side effects of the secularisation of universities, it appears, is that the privately funded providers now have more of a role in educating religious leaders.

Within publicly funded institutions there is little reason to believe the numbers of students studying Theology and Religion will increase. Indeed, there are threats to subjects such as Religious Studies that have no clear vocational application (or which suggest a career in which earnings are relatively limited). HE in England is now presented to prospective students as an *individual investment*. Students are asked to bear the costs themselves over their working lifetimes, and policy-makers justify this on the basis that graduates can expect significantly larger salaries over the course of their career. As Graham (2005) has observed, the *social* goods that are derived from HE – the benefits of cultural enrichment and improved political conversation – are neglected, while individual earnings are emphasised. The rise in fees in 2012 does not appear thus far to have had a profound impact on applications to university (UCAS Analysis and Research, 2012). However, over the coming years, universities may yet focus on courses geared towards individual earnings and economic growth.

It would be mistaken to say, however, that religion is at risk of being pushed out of the contemporary university. Rather, there are a range of competing pressures, some taking the focus away from religion and others causing more attention to be paid to it. Despite the fact that in Europe traditional forms of religious belief and practice have continued to decline (Brown, 2001; Bruce, 2002), the emergence of publicly active religious movements has meant that media interest in religion and belief has grown substantially over the last 30 years (Knott et al, nd). Religious and secular identities are much more publicly prominent and contested, and this has had a substantial impact on the life of universities, where religion has become more visible. Nationally organised Christian student societies have a long history in the UK (Bruce, 2002, p 127), and the Federation of Student Islamic Societies celebrated its 50th year in 2013. Recently, however, these groups have been joined by the British Sikh Student Federation (established in 2008) and the Union of Jewish Students (established in 2008). Reflecting the emergence of vocal 'young British atheists' (Catto and Eckles, 2013) influenced by 'new atheism', non-belief has become more organised and politically active too, with many universities seeing the establishment of new organised humanist and secular societies – most of which are now members of the Federation of Atheist, Humanist and Secular Student Societies (AHS), a body set up in 2009. As Guest et al's (2013) recent research into Christians students has shown, even if attending university does prompt a proportion of students to no longer attend a place of worship, it can also have the effect of forcing individuals to confront their beliefs more consciously, which in turn contributes to the heightened mobilisation of faith as a marker of identity.

This increasing prominence appears to have affected study patterns in the academy too. Frank and Gabler (2006, pp 92-116) found that in the British Commonwealth countries Theology gave up 60 per cent of its faculty presence between 1915 and 1995. However, unlike other declining disciplines such as Classics, Theology, at least in some contexts, revived from the 1980s on, albeit in new forms focusing specifically on Islam, feminism or the intersection between religion and public life. This shift is reflected in major new programmes of research into religion in Britain and America, such as the Economic and Social Research Council (ESRC)/Arts and Humanities Research Council (ASRC) Religion and Society Programme in the UK, and the US-based Social Science Research Council's (SSRC) programme 'Religion and the Public Sphere'.[2]

Furthermore, new laws and recent HE reforms have led to renewed interest in the faith identities of students among HE managers and administrative staff. Elsewhere, Dinham and I (2012) have identified four separate 'policy arenas' that have encouraged university leaders to focus on faith, with some of these being related to the marketisation of HE. First, legislation introduced over the last 15 years prohibiting discrimination on grounds of religion or belief and prescribing 'reasonable accommodation' of religious practices (see Chapter Eight, this volume) has prompted university staff to consider how best to respond to the religious identities of students and staff. Second, in the academic year 1999/2000, HEFCE introduced funding specifically for widening participation. Universities are given the freedom to determine how this funding – which totalled £368 million across all HEIs and further education (FE) colleges in England in 2011/12 – is spent, and a large number concentrate their outreach activities on their local area (Bowes et al, 2013b). In some localities, especially areas with high levels of religious diversity, outreach and widening participation work has involved new engagement with religious minorities.

Third, concerns about social cohesion and anxieties about extremism and 'hate speech' on campus have caused HE leaders to engage with religious societies and to consider new ways of mediating religious difference (DIUS, 2007). Over the last decade there have been several public crises and controversies relating to extremism on university campuses, which university leaders feel the need to pre-empt while at the same time maintaining a culture of free inquiry and expression. Fourth and finally, increasing competition between HEIs has led to a new focus in universities on promoting a positive 'student experience'. In some institutions, this has prompted HE managers to consider new ways of catering for the full range of students' religious and secular lifestyles. For instance, in two of the universities we carried out research in, chaplaincy was being overhauled and incorporated into a general 'health and wellbeing centre' in which religious observance was provided for, alongside leisure and fitness facilities.

In addition to these four areas, our subsequent research found that the increasing internationalisation of HE (Browne et al, 2010; Wildavsky, 2010) has had an impact on universities' engagement with religious faith. The number of students in British HEIs from non–European Union (EU) nations doubled between the academic years 1997/98 and 2007/08 to one in ten enrolments (*The Guardian*, 2009). In 2007/08 students from overseas accounted for £1.88 billion of UK universities' income, more than they received from government research grants (Shepherd, 2009). This shift has had two notable effects. First, it has forced universities to accommodate new forms of religious diversity, as the following quote illustrates:

> Obviously, like other universities we're looking to recruit as many as we can of international students, and many overseas students come from countries of the Muslim faith.... So the numbers [from different religious traditions] are simply becoming greater in this university. (Head of student services, 'post-1992' secular foundation)

Second, there are indications that religiously affiliated 'post-1992' institutions in particular are beginning to consider religion in their strategy to attract students from overseas. As one of our interviewees explained:

> The issue for us is how, whether, where and when to play the 'Christian card' in terms of whether we target Christian countries or do we target Christian schools in other countries and so forth. (Head of international strategy, 'post-1992' religious foundation)

Finally, there is some evidence that the intensification of competition between institutions is having an impact on the identity of certain universities. One of the most striking effects of the reforms to HE in England over the last 30 years has been the creation of a HE system in which there is increased pressure to be distinctive and to build up a recognisable 'brand'. Universities are searching for a 'unique selling point' to help them attract students. Some of the more recently established religious foundations appear to have responded to this by placing renewed emphasis on their status as institutions with a faith ethos. In our interviews, a number of chaplains based at 'post-1992' religious foundations made comments such as the following:

> I think it would be true to say [this university has] become more self-conscious [about its status as religious foundation] because of the need to be distinctive.... That's not the way that the chaplaincy sees it but I think it's fair to say that's the way [senior management] sees it.

Priorities and challenges for religious literacy in higher education

A number of recent changes, then, have ensured that religion remains a matter of interest for universities. Like many of the changes to HE in England that have taken place in the last 30 years, these have been multifaceted and not without internal tensions and, occasionally, contradictions. Yet there are certain themes that stand out and that can illuminate current challenges for universities in the area of religious literacy. There is now a strong interest in universities – especially in operational contexts such as admissions, recruitment and senior management – in *religious identity*. The internationalisation of HE, the emergence of funding for widening participation, and the emphasis on providing a positive student experience have all increased universities' willingness to listen to the concerns of students and staff and to respond to the distinctive needs of those with a religious faith. Moreover, the new equalities legislation and anxieties about on-campus cohesion have provided universities with an interest in mediating between religious groups and between religious and secular individuals.

The emphasis on *learning religion* within university curricula is, however, more mixed. As we have seen, there has been a response within teaching and learning contexts to the growing interest in religion, with religions starting to appear in a broader range of courses. Yet the pressure on universities to service the needs of the 'knowledge economy' means there are questions about how religiously literate people can be *formed* by universities as they currently stand. A central theme among critics of HE reform in England (see, for example, Collini, 2010; Hotson, 2011) has been its apparent neglect of the responsibility of universities in the formation of persons; the emphasis, it is said, is now on student choice and satisfaction and on individual earning potential and economic growth rather than on the creation of individuals who are well equipped to act as intelligent and responsible contributors to society. This point can be made specifically in relation to religion. University leaders are interested in religion because of legal responsibilities and the need to attract and satisfy a religiously diverse student body. However, even those university staff who are positively disposed toward religious traditions struggle to find the space and resources that would allow them to equip students with the tools to engage with and talk productively about belief. As one of our interviewees observed:

> I'm not sure there are spaces in which [religious issues can be] discussed, issues of faith, no faith, and how they relate to personal behaviour, public issues and so forth. And it's long occurred to me that if want your university to be anything other than just churning out people for jobs, which hopefully it will do, these are big issues and within the university there are people who can come at those issues from a variety of standpoints. But I don't think there is space in the university for that at the moment. (Head of student services, 'post-1992' religious foundation)

In contemporary HEIs, then, religious and secular identities are placed in the foreground, while knowledge of religious traditions and systems of belief is left on the margins. This interest in faith identity is, of course, welcome for a wide range of reasons, yet on its own it offers little assistance in negotiating religious differences, either on campus or in the wider world, through the formation of informed individuals. Willingness in principle to recognise and respond to religious identity has helped to make university campuses more inclusive places, but this is only of limited help in mediating between traditions when conflicts arise. Without a corresponding awareness of the value of *educating* people about faith differences, students are left badly equipped to enter into societies marked by an ever-increasing diversity of belief.

Given that the modernisation of HE is in an advanced state and has involved a number of shifts that are probably irreversible, is there anything realistic and achievable that can be done to foster a HE sector that engages with religion regularly and in a consistently sophisticated way? There have been some proposals in this area made in recent years, although not all of these have been workable. In the US, for example, calls have been made by Nord and Haynes (1998) for mandatory courses in Religious Studies at a higher level. Nord (2008, p 182), in fact, proposes two mandatory courses in Religious Studies for all undergraduates, one historical and one contemporary. Yet it is hard to see how such a proposal could function in practice. First, it would require much more centralised control of university curricula than currently exists in most countries, the UK included. Second, it would require the imposition of degree models that have much more scope for courses not immediately related to undergraduates' primary subjects. Neither of these things would be easy to achieve, and even if they could be achieved, it would be hard to justify Religious Studies getting this attention and not, for example, Politics, History or English Literature.

Ford (2004, p 25), however, suggests a more realistic starting point for practical action. He is in agreement with Nord and Haynes that HEIs 'ought to be taking far more seriously than they do their responsibility' to educate people about the 'simultaneously religious and secular character of our world'. Rather than suggesting mandatory courses in Religion, however, he proposes that the study of religion should be fed into all areas of the university *as well as* being found in departments specialising in the subject. The parallel he draws is with Economics, the study of which is a feature of a range of degrees not based in economics departments. In courses such as Politics, Geography and Development Studies students are likely to encounter the ideas of figures such as Adam Smith, John Maynard Keynes, Friedrich von Hayek and Karl Marx. In much the same way, degrees other than Theology and Religious Studies could give more time to studying, for example, the significance of Protestant theologies on traditions of individualism and the 'work ethic' in the Anglophone world, or the way in which Hinduism and the Deobandi, Barelwi and Wahhabi Islamic traditions were all shaped by Western colonialism.

This approach would have the advantage of taking into account the fact that HEIs, not only in England but the world over, are highly differentiated in their size and subject range. Religion is pertinent to a huge range of academic disciplines. A recent paper by the Quality Assurance Agency (QAA) for Higher Education (2007) listed Anthropology, Archaeology, Area Studies, Classics, Cultural Studies, Economics, Education, Ethics, Gender Studies, Health Studies, History, Languages, Law, Literature, Media Studies, Natural Sciences,

Philosophy, Political Science, Psychology, Sociology, Social Policy and the Visual Arts all as subjects that relate to Theology and Religious Studies in some way. Nord and Haynes actually make a strong case that there are times when relevant religious arguments and concepts are dealt with too lightly, or indeed, not at all. It may be too much to ask students of, say, Civil Engineering to engage with issues of belief, but these questions should be drawn into all subjects much more clearly and consciously where relevant, rather than being left to divinity departments or chaplaincy centres.

There is also an example from English HE that gives a clue as to how forward steps might be taken. In 2007, HEFCE, no doubt influenced by the intense interest in Islam that followed 9/11 and the 2005 London bombings, named Islamic Studies as a 'strategically important subject' (HEFCE, 2008). This was linked to a range of initiatives, including the creation of the Islamic Studies Network by the Higher Education Academy (from 2009 to 2012), as well as efforts to analyse Islamic Studies within and outside the academy (Siddiqui, 2007) and work towards building connections between privately and publicly funded Islamic Studies centres (Geaves, 2012). One of the striking things about these initiatives was that, in addition to considering the development of Islamic Studies within dedicated departments, the Islamic Studies Network endeavoured to gather information and offer guidance on the teaching of Islam in other contexts, such as the Social Sciences, Politics and Comparative Law.[3] The work to build links between publicly and privately funded Islamic Studies centres also involved thinking through how the teaching of private Islamic Studies courses could help students (notably future Muslim religious leaders) engage with contemporary society.

Could similar steps be taken that relate not just to the study of the Islamic tradition, but also to the study of religion as a whole? There is no practical reason why they cannot, although the political will may be hard to build in the absence of the kind of spectacular events that led to Islam being pushed into the public spotlight over the last 15 years. Funding would, of course, be an issue. Yet in the English context, one could argue that extending the focus is needed for reasons of equality: if all this can be done for the study of Islam, why can it not be done for other faith traditions? Indeed, it is possible to persuasively argue that there has been an unhealthy *over-emphasis* on Islam in recent discussions of religion and belief. In recent years, debates have raged within (and beyond) the academy about whether to accommodate Muslims' dietary requirements and gender separation at Islamic society events – without many seeming to notice that these questions are not only relevant to the Islamic tradition. Could it be that opening up a multifaith programme of religious literacy would help rebalance this unhelpful focus?

Conclusions

Of course, another difficulty ought to be mentioned: this suggestion would also almost certainly be met with resistance from those who are wary of religion having a greater role than it currently plays on university campuses. Up to a point, such concerns are easy to sympathise with, for it is genuinely difficult to say when it is and when it is not appropriate to engage with religious traditions and arguments (for an excellent discussion of the contexts in which it may be appropriate to discuss religion in universities, see Edwards, 2008, pp 136-50). Given that religion is for many people not a dry academic subject for detached analysis, but something that provides a purpose and moral framework, it is also easy to see why academics, who occupy a position of authority, may be wary of the area. Any kind of link between universities and privately funded centres of religious learning, such as those being built between Islamic institutions and UK universities, would also have to be carefully negotiated to maintain the independence of both parties.

It would be crucial, therefore, for any proposal to improve Religious Education within HE curricula to be clearly justified as a means to the end of improved encounters between providers and professionals on the one hand, and religiously plural publics on the other, rather than religious indoctrination. While there should always be some space for reflecting on religious truth and practice in universities, the aim of any policy aimed at improving religious literacy must always be the flourishing of civil society. On a practical level, too, it is important to recognise that questions of religion and belief are more relevant in some courses and institutions than others, and that, while religion is relevant to both Arts and Politics degrees, it is relevant in different ways. Any proposal to pay greater attention to faith must be presented as a framework of recommendations rather than a fixed list of things all universities must cover within their curricula.

Nevertheless, this sympathy can only extend so far. Even those who recoil at the idea of a university education altering the religious beliefs of students generally still accept that HE forms people, shaping their convictions, their political and moral positions and their understanding of their place in the world. This includes their attitudes, skills and ability to engage well with the religion and belief identities of those they encounter, whatever their own may or may not be. Indeed, formation is widely seen as one of the primary functions of a university education. Universities would be, in an important sense, abdicating one of their primary responsibilities if they were to shy away from thinking through how they can influence their students in a positive way.

Furthermore, opposition to engagement with religion on campuses is often grounded in understandable and probably justified antipathy toward assertive and/or anti-intellectual forms of religion of the kind that interest sociologists such as Roy (2010). From this antipathy emerges the position that to open up space for religious voices is to risk ceding ground to evangelising movements and 'religious extremists'. In the UK this has been a common response to the on-campus presence of proselytising groups. But this perspective, although it has *prima facie* appeal, is seriously mistaken. One of the strongest points of Roy's writing on 'holy ignorance' is that assertive, anti-intellectual varieties of religion flourish in hostile environments, as new movements set themselves up in opposition to their surrounding culture. This suggests an important corollary: namely, that the meaningful incorporation of religious ideas and traditions into the intellectual life of universities might be an important way of helping reverse the trend toward illiterate, anti-intellectual forms of faith. This aim of fostering improved knowledge of religious and secular traditions, and of fostering more intelligent, more thoughtful varieties of religious and secular faith, is something that all can share and all stand to gain from. The question is whether universities, and the policy-makers in charge of them, can respond to the challenge.

Notes

[1] These figures are based on Higher Education Statistics Agency data. See www.hesa.ac.uk/index.php?option=com_datatables&Itemid=121&task=show_category&catdex=3

[2] For details of these programmes see, respectively, www.religionandsociety.org.uk/ and www.ssrc.org/programs/religion-and-the-public-sphere/

[3] For details, see www.islamicstudiesnetwork.ac.uk, in particular, the 'Resources' section.

References

Berger, P.L. (1999) *The desecularization of the world: The resurgence of religion in world politics*, Michigan, MI: William B. Eerdmans Publishing Co.

BIS (Department for Business, Innovation and Skills) (2009) *Higher ambitions: The future of universities in a knowledge economy*, London: BIS.

BIS (2011) *Students at the heart of the system*, London: BIS.

Bowes, L., Thomas, L., Peck, L. and Nathwani, T. (2013a) *International research on the effectiveness of widening participation*, Bristol: Higher Education Funding Council for England.

Bowes, L., Jones, S.H., Thomas, L., Moreton, R., Birkin, G. and Nathwani, T. (2013b) *The uses and impact of HEFCE funding for widening participation*, Bristol: Higher Education Funding Council for England.

Brown, C. (2001) *The death of Christian Britain*, London: Routledge.

Browne, J., Barber, M., Coyle, D., Eastwood, D., King, J., Naik, R. and Sands, P. (2010) *Securing a sustainable future for higher education: An independent review of higher education funding and student finance*, London: HM Government.

Bruce, S. (2002) *God is dead: Secularization in the West*, Oxford: Blackwell.

Casanova, J. (1994) *Public religions in the modern world*, Chicago, IL: Chicago University Press.

Catto, R. and Eckles, J. (2013) '(Dis)believing and belonging: investigating the narrative of young British atheists', *Temenos*, vol 49, no 1, pp 37-63.

Clarke, J. (2010) 'So many strategies, so little time.... Making universities modern', *International Journal of Higher Education in the Social Sciences*, vol 3, no 3, pp 91-116.

Collini, S. (2010) 'Browne's gamble', *London Review of Books*, 4 November.

DES (Department for Education and Skills) (2006) *Widening participation in higher education*, London: DES.

Dinham, A. and Jones, S.H. (2012) 'Religion, public policy, and the academy: brokering public faith in a context of ambivalence?', *Journal of Contemporary Religion*, vol 27, no 2, pp 185-201.

DIUS (Department for Innovation, Universities and Skills) (2007) *Promoting good campus relations, fostering shared values and preventing violent extremism in universities and higher education colleges*, London: Department for Business Innovation and Skills.

Edwards, M.U. (2006) *Religion on our campuses: A professor's guide to communities, conflicts and promising conversations*, New York: Palgrave Macmillan.

Edwards, M.U. (2008) 'Why faculty find it difficult to talk about religion', in D. Jacobsen and R.H. Jacobsen (eds) *The American university in a postsecular age*, Oxford: Oxford University Press, pp 81-98.

Field, C. (2010) 'Inspired by Muhammad Campaign', *British Religion in Numbers*, 8 June (www.brin.ac.uk/news/?p=334).

Ford, D.F. (2004) 'The responsibilities of universities in a religious and secular world', *Studies in Christian Ethics*, vol 17, no 1, pp 22-37.

Frank, D.J., and Gabler, J. (2006) *Reconstructing the university: Worldwide shifts in academia in the 20th century*, Stanford, CA: Stanford University Press.

Geaves, R. (2012) 'The symbolic construction of the walls of Deoband', *Islam and Christian–Muslim Relations*, vol 23, no 3, pp 315-28.

Gilliat-Ray, S. (2000) *Religion in higher education: The politics of the multi-faith campus*, Aldershot: Ashgate.

Graham, G. (2005) *The institution of intellectual values: Realism and idealism in higher education*, Exeter: Imprint Academic.

Guardian, The (2009) 'Twice as many foreign students at UK universities', 24 September (www.guardian.co.uk/education/2009/sep/24/internationalstudents-students).

Guest, M., Aune, K., Sharma, S. and Warner, R. (2013) *Christianity and the university experience: Understanding student faith*, London: Bloomsbury.

Hart, D.G. (1999) *The university gets religion*, Baltimore, MD: Johns Hopkins University Press.

HEFCE (Higher Education Funding Council for England) (2008) *Islamic Studies: Trends and profiles*, London: HEFCE.

Hotson, H. (2011) 'Don't look to the Ivy League', *London Review of Books*, 19 May.

Hughes, T., Porter, A., Jones, S.H. and Sheen, J. (2013) *Privately funded providers of higher education in the UK*, London: Department for Business Innovation and Skills.

Knott, K., Poole, E. and Taira, T. (nd) 'Media coverage of religion is up, even though traditional religious practice is down', Briefing Note, Religion and Society Programme (www.religionandsociety.org.uk/uploads/docs/2011_03/1301305944_Knott_Phase_1_Large_Grant_Block.pdf).

Moberly, W.H. (1951) *The crisis in the university*, Basingstoke: Macmillan.

Newfield, C. (2008) *Unmaking the public university: The forty-year assault on the middle class*, Cambridge, MA: Harvard University Press.

Nord, W.A. (2008) 'Taking religion seriously in public universities', in D. Jacobsen and R.H. Jacobsen (eds) *The American university in a postsecular age*, Oxford: Oxford University Press, pp 167-85.

Nord, W. and Haynes, C. (1998) *Taking religion seriously across the curriculum*, Alexandria, VA: Association for Supervision & Curriculum Deve.

OECD (Organisation for Economic Co-operation and Development (2012) *Education at a Glance*, Paris: OECD Publishing.

Prothero, S. (2008) *Religious literacy: What every American needs to know – and doesn't*, New York: Harper.

QAA (Quality Assurance Agency) for Higher Education (2007) *Theology and Religious Studies*, Mansfield: QAA (http://qaa.ac.uk/Publications/InformationAndGuidance/Documents/Theology.pdf).

Reuben, J.A. (1996) *The making of the modern university: Intellectual transformation and the marginalization of morality*, Chicago, IL: University of Chicago Press.

Robbins, L. (1963) *Higher Education: Report of the Committee appointed by the Prime Minister under the Chairmanship of Lord Robbins*, London: Her Majesty's Stationery Office.

Roberts, J.H. and Turner, J. (2000) *The sacred and the secular university*, Princeton, NJ: Princeton University Press.

Roy, O. (2010) *Holy ignorance: When religion and culture part ways*, London: C. Hurst & Co.

Rüegg, W. (2004) *A history of the university in Europe: Volume 3, Universities in the nineteenth and early twentieth centuries (1800-1945)*, Cambridge: Cambridge University Press.

Shepherd, J. (2009) 'Overseas students prop up university finances', *The Guardian*, 14 October (www.guardian.co.uk/education/2009/oct/14/international-students-pay-20000).

Siddiqui, A. (2007) *Islam at universities in England: Meeting the needs and investing in the future*, Leicester: The Markfield Institute.

Silver, H. (2003) *Higher education and opinion making in twentieth-century England*, London: Routledge.

Tisdell, E.J. (2008) 'Spirituality, diversity and learner-centred teaching: a generative paradox', in D. Jacobsen and R.H. Jacobsen (eds) *The American university in a postsecular age*, Oxford: Oxford University Press, pp 151-66.

Trowler, P., Fanghanel, J. and Wareham, T. (2005) 'Freeing the chi of change: the Higher Education Academy and enhancing teaching and learning in higher education', *Studies in Higher Education*, vol 30, no 4, pp 427-44.

Tzortzis, H.A. (2010) *Perceptions on Islam and Muslims*, London: Islamic Education and Research Academy.

UCAS (Universities and Colleges Admissions Service) Analysis and Research (2012) *How have applications for full-time undergraduate higher education in the UK changed in 2012?*, Cheltenham: UCAS.

Waggoner, M.D. (2011) *Sacred and secular tensions in higher education: Connecting parallel universities*, New York: Routledge.

Wildavsky, B. (2010) *The great brain race: How global universities are reshaping the world*, Princeton, NJ: Princeton University Press.

Woodhead, L. (2009) *'Religion or belief': Identifying issues and priorities*, Manchester: Equality and Human Rights Commission.

Wuthnow, R. (2008) 'Can faith be more than a sideshow in the contemporary academy?', in D. Jacobsen and R.H. Jacobsen (eds) *The American university in a postsecular age*, Oxford: Oxford University Press, pp 31-44.

ELEVEN

Religious literacy and social work: the view from Australia

Beth R. Crisp

As a Social Work student in Australia in the late 1980s, there was the occasional mention of matters associated with religion when discussing cases involving service users who were Jewish or Muslim. Otherwise, and similar to other Anglophone countries, unless there was a member of the Social Work teaching staff with a particular interest in religion, a curriculum of omission was the norm (Furman et al, 2005; Moss, 2005). The often implicit, but sometimes explicit, message was that there was no place for discussion of religion in Social Work education (Lindsay, 2002). This is perhaps unsurprising given a 1999 survey of Australian Social Work educators that found two thirds claiming no religious affiliation (Lindsay, 2002), at a time when at least three quarters of all Australians identified with a religion (ABS, 2001).

Although the majority of Australians nominally align themselves with a religion, only a small percentage regularly attends religious services (Bellamy and Castle, 2004). For occasional attenders, particularly those going to events where religion and an immigrant culture are closely intertwined, reasons for attendance may be more cultural than religious. With migration resulting in a diversification of religion in the Australian community (Bouma, 2006), unless they are have a particular interest, most Australians rely on the media for knowledge of other religions, and even for news about their own religion. At a time when media interest in religions is often associated with scandals such as the abuse of children by religious officials, or claims that terrorist acts are the work of those with fanatical or fundamentalist religious beliefs, many Australians have little knowledge of the key beliefs and practices of other religions, and sometimes even of the religions they claim as their own.

Despite a lack of knowledge, in recent years it has been argued that Australians are more likely to acknowledge that religion, or more likely, spirituality, has a place in their lives. At the same time, there has been a growing recognition that religion is not just concerned with privatised beliefs, but also plays a prominent role in civic life

(Boer, 2008). Nevertheless, in Australia, the term 'religious literacy' has mostly been confined to debates concerning Religious Education (RE) among school students (see, for example, Goldburg, 2006; Hemmings and Butcher, 2012). This contrasts with the situation in the UK where 'religious literacy' is entering in discourses concerned with the place of religion and religious beliefs in civic life, and the need for community leaders and organisations to have sufficient knowledge to handle the complexities of religious beliefs and practices (see, for example, Dinham, 2011; Dinham and Jones, 2010a, 2010b, 2012).

Religious literacy is arguably useful, if not essential, for a wide range of professionals who work to support the full participation of community members in civic society. This includes social workers, who are the focus of this chapter, and who, I argue, need a degree of religious literacy to work with members of the community, many of whom may be dealing with situations that are at least in part affected by the religious beliefs of either themselves or others. And in the Australian context, large numbers of social workers are employed in organisations that have a religious foundation, and most social workers would engage with faith-based organisations regularly as part of their professional practice. Yet, like most tertiary-educated Australians, social workers have typically had little access to degree-level courses in Religious Studies. While in part this reflects disciplinary silos that allow students enrolled in professional studies few elective choices beyond their main field of study, many Australian universities do not have a Religious Studies programme from which they could choose electives (Boer, 2008).

Looking back, the need for religious literacy was inconceivable to most Australian social workers and social work educators at the end of the 20th century. It is unlikely that we would have predicted that in 2004 a new *Global standards for the education and training of the social work profession* would acknowledge the need for social work education to promote respect for different religions, and for social workers to have some knowledge as to the role religion plays in the lives of social work service users (IASSW and IFSW, 2004).

Evidence of the recognition of an increasing need for religious literacy for Australian social workers comes in a comparison of the 2010 and 1999 versions of the *Code of ethics* of the Australian Association of Social Workers (AASW). The 1999 version included requirements to prevent discrimination on the basis of religion, the need for social workers to remain aware of conflicts of interest on the basis of religion, and the need to be aware of their own religious values (AASW, 1999). While these were retained in the 2010 revisions, a number of additional clauses were added. These include an expectation under the heading of 'Respect for human dignity and worth' that:

> Social workers will respect others' beliefs, religious or spiritual world views, values, culture, goals, needs and desires, as well as kinship and communal bonds, within a framework of social justice and human rights. (AASW, 2010, p 17)

The revised *Code of ethics* also recognised the right for social workers who have religious beliefs to have their beliefs respected within the workplace:

> In carrying out their professional practice responsibilities, social workers are entitled to reciprocal rights, which include the right to ... hold cultural, religious or spiritual world views and for these to be acknowledged in the workplace and professional contexts to the extent that they do not impinge on the other guidelines in this *Code*. (AASW, 2010, p 16)

Another new requirement in the 2010 *Code of ethics* was an expectation that social workers be respectful of faith-based agencies:

> Social workers will recognise, acknowledge and remain sensitive to and respectful of the religious and spiritual world views of individuals, groups, communities and social networks, and the operations and missions of faith and spiritually-based organisations. (AASW, 2010, p 18)

Given mentions of religion in the *Code of ethics* are invariably coupled with references to a 'spiritual world view', their inclusion may reflect a growing interest in spirituality rather than religion per se among Australian social workers (see, for example, Gale et al, 2007; Crisp, 2010; Gardner, 2011). While some have defined 'spirituality' as a distinct dimension to 'religion' (for example, Gray, 2008), others have used these terms interchangeably (for example, Lindsay, 2002). Hence, in some situations, what has been described as 'spiritual competence' (Hodge and Bushfield, 2006, p 101) has some overlap with 'religious literacy', given that the current *Code of ethics* for Australian social workers infers that in order to work either with service users or with colleagues, social workers need to be able to appreciate the role and of religion in the lives of individuals, families and communities that may have differing beliefs and/or practices. However, 'spiritual competence' doesn't usually extend to being able to establish and maintain working relationships with organisations that have a religious identity.

It may well be that the arrival of religion on the agenda for Australian social workers was inadvertent, but multiple references to religion in the *Code of ethics* have resulted in religious literacy now being policy for the AASW. However, it is still unclear as to what is meant, or practically how we do this. To this end, rationales and approaches to religious literacy in respect of working with individuals and organisations are now considered in turn. In terms of organisations, religious literacy is considered at a general level before exploring specific issues for social workers employed in organisations with a faith basis.

Religious literacy for working with others

In North America it has been estimated that approximately one third of all service users presented to social workers with problems in which religion or spirituality was potentially an issue (Sheridan et al, 1992). Holding religious beliefs is one of the most likely reasons for being persecuted (Hodge, 2007). It can also result in discrimination, mistreatment, or being viewed with suspicion, if an individual's religious beliefs or practices are perceived to be outside the mainstream in the community in which they live. Such disincentives to reveal one's religion may be further reinforced in countries like Australia, where there is no state religion, and a widespread belief in the community that religion is a private matter. Furthermore, social workers sometimes call on notions such as the separation of church and state as justification for not discussing issues of religion with service users, particularly if employed in positions that are government-funded (Crisp, 2011).

Social work practice has, on the whole, perpetuated this notion that religion is a purely private matter, with a 'tendency to ignore religion unless it is somewhat exotic or problematic' (Crisp, 2011, p 664), and practitioners often feel inadequately prepared to explore the significance of religion (Horwath and Lees, 2010). The experience in Australia is similar to that which Furness and Gilligan (2010) have described in Britain, where they were told, 'You know, unless a family is really strictly Muslim and it's obvious, the social workers aren't even asking, they're not even looking at it as a topic' (quoted in Furness and Gilligan, 2010, p 36). Furthermore, not only were they not raising issues associated with religion that might be relevant in a particular case, but, as one manager explained, many British social workers were also uncomfortable with the idea of discussing religion with service users:

> My social workers said, "Can we ask that?" I think that they thought that it was too intrusive to ask somebody about religion, but I said, "We talk about relationships, mum and dad, what kind of relationship do they have, do they have time together, do they have time as a couple?" So if we're talking about really personal things, I think we're going to be okay if we ask them about religion. (quoted in Furness and Gilligan, 2010, p 37)

While there is clearly a long way to go, internationally there has been a growing recognition that in order to effectively work with current or potential service users, social workers need an understanding of religion (see, for example, Moss, 2005; Ashencaen Crabtree et al, 2008; Furness and Gilligan, 2010; Crisp, 2011). A few authors have taken this line of argument even further, declaring that failure to address religious dimensions results in unethical practice (Amato-von Hemert, 1994; Hodge, 2005), particularly as religions have at times been implicated in respect of discriminatory behaviour associated with gender, sexual identity and sexual behaviours, as well as being responsible for institutions that have allowed physical, sexual and emotional abuse to flourish (Moss, 2005). However, such arguments by themselves may not be sufficient to encourage social workers to consider whether issues associated with religion might assist them to understand the circumstances of service users. For some social workers, more persuasive is the proposition that religious beliefs and practices can lead to enhanced wellbeing for some individuals and communities (Lee and Newberg, 2005), and that a person's membership of a religious community may be a potential resource (Furness and Gilligan, 2010; Horwath and Lees, 2010).

A low level of religious literacy, particularly in respect of other religions, is also an issue for social workers (Horwath and Lees, 2010). Religious beliefs have been identified as a reason for deciding on a career in social work, both in Australia (Lindsay, 2002) and in a range of other countries including Malaysia (Ashencaen Crabtree and Baba, 2001), South Africa (Sacco, 1996), the US (Rizer and McColley, 1996; Canda and Furman, 1999) and the UK (Cree, 1996). However, having a religion doesn't necessarily mean social workers are able to extrapolate any relevant knowledge they have about their religion and use it in their professional work (Rizer and McColley, 1996).

Nor does being religious guarantee knowledge of religions other than one's own. On a couple of occasions I have been asked by non-Christian colleagues who have read Paulo Freire (1974) to include a mention of liberation theology in papers I have been preparing. I find myself having to explain that there is a wide range of writing that comes under the umbrella of liberation theology, including that which addresses poverty in the Latin American context (Batstone et al, 1997), but which also addresses oppression in Asia (Kyung, 1991), Africa (Oduyoye, 2001), indigenous communities (Pattel-Gray, 1998), as well as forms of oppression that occur in the wealthiest countries of the world, including gender (Reuther, 1983; Russell, 1974) and sexual identity (Althaus-Reid, 2000).

Addressing religious literacy is a vexed question for those of us who teach students who are seeking to qualify as professional social workers, particularly if one has students who are anti-religious, who regard any discussion of religion that does not denigrate religious beliefs or practices as some form of proselytising (Crisp, 2011). In this context, seemingly the most straightforward solution might be to teach the basic tenets of the predominant religions within a region or nation as a set of facts that are regarded as core knowledge for social work. Selectivity is important given estimates that worldwide there are more than 4,000 different religions or variations of religions, each of which not only represents different beliefs, but that have different ways of organising themselves and different expectations on members (Cnaan and Curtis, 2013). Bearing in mind that religion is just one of many aspects of the lives with which social workers must be *au fait*, it has been suggested that:

> It is not a social work task to discern or prescribe the meaning of religious or faith based texts in the way that a leader of a religion might be expected to do. However, it is a social work task to understand, consider and develop religious literacy to work effectively with vulnerable people. (Melville-Wiseman, 2013, p 300)

While some basic knowledge about a religion, or at least an awareness that this needs to be acquired, may assist in responding to specific service users, what may be even more crucial is gaining an understanding as to how their religious beliefs and practices manifest themselves in the lives of *this individual* or *this family*. For example, Scourfield et al (2013), in their study of 60 Muslim families in Cardiff, found a number of differences between families in respect of how they interpreted Islamic teaching about prayer and fasting:

> Amongst the families we interviewed, some parents prayed five times a day, with children joining in when present. Some families only prayed in the mosque. There were debates about what is and is not Islamic and a certain amount of negotiation about religious practice, including different views about when children should start to pray. For example, Sahra Adam (aged 11) told us that regular prayer would start on reaching puberty; Muhammad Jawad (aged six) said he was currently "practising to pray" and would have to do it all the time when he turned seven; and Asad Rahman (aged 11) told us you have to "pray and fast and everything" from 15.
>
> Predictably, we see some variation according to school of thought. One example relevant to children is birthdays. Some families would think it wrong to celebrate a birthday as such, although they might think some kind of gathering is acceptable. Others would happily celebrate a birthday. (Scourfield et al, 2013, p 332)

Despite differences in the detail, Scourfield et al noted a strong continuity in religious tradition being handed down through families. These religious beliefs and practices potentially play a range of functions for individuals and families, including facilitating connectedness, establishing a sense of identity, providing structures for quiet reflection, finding a sense of meaning or experiencing transcendence (Crisp, 2010). Hence, in respect of religious beliefs and practices it has been proposed that for social workers, the key task is to develop an understanding of the function religion plays in the lives of service users (Moss, 2005). In practical terms, knowing the benefits obtained and the issues that arise from religious beliefs and practices may be as useful, or even more so, than knowing someone's religion per se. As one Canadian social worker has suggested when working with service users:

> I say, I'm really interested in understanding what this means for you. And is there anything about your own cultural background, or what this means in your own community, that would be helpful for me to understand, because I may not know that. I'm not going to assume anything.... I'm

going to wait and hear how it's been constructed in their lives. (quoted in Clark, 2006)

For some social workers this might mean a radically different way of working in which religious literacy is conceived not as being the expert about various religions, but rather having the capacity to ask the right questions that enables an individual to articulate what is important for them and the relative importance of religion and aspects of their lives (Dinham, 2011). In doing so, it may be essential to convey to service users that they will not be judged for having systems of meaning, religious or otherwise, particularly if their beliefs are not widely held in the community (Furness and Gilligan, 2010). For the Scottish author John Swinton, this means:

> Rather than beginning by asking "what is wrong with this person", we begin our questioning from a different perspective and ask different questions: "What gives this person's life meaning?", "What is it that keeps them going, even in the midst of their psychological pain and turmoil?", "Where is this person's primary source of value?", "What can be done to enhance their being?" In asking such questions, the person's situation is reframed in a way that reveals hidden dimensions. (Swinton, 2001, p 138)

A religiously literate social worker who works as Swinton suggests should not only have the ability to enable service users for whom it is important to discuss matters of religion, but also to recognise when it is not the time to be asking them more explicit questions about religion, either because religion is not part of their lives, or not a part of their lives that they wish to discuss at that time (Crisp, 2011).

Religious literacy for working with faith-based organisations

In Australia, as in many countries (Ager and Ager, 2011), welfare services are frequently delivered by non-government organisations (NGOs) that have a faith basis (Melville and McDonald, 2006; Swain, 2009). In terms of annual income, all but two of the 25 largest charities are connected with Christian churches (Lake, 2013). Not only are church organisations major employers of social workers (Camilleri and Winkworth, 2004; Holden and Trembath, 2008), but, as in many other countries, even most social workers employed in secular organisations regularly have to liaise with welfare providers that have a religious auspice or religious identity (Edgardh and Pettersson, 2010; Pessi, 2010). Nevertheless, even though it is considered essential that social workers have a good understanding of organisational theory, religious literacy in respect of faith-based organisations often appears to be at most, optional (Gardner, 2006; Ozanne and Rose, 2013).

Faith-based organisations are often stereotyped as having particular values or practices, which may be true of a portion of some faith-based welfare organisations but cannot be generalised to the sector as a whole. Social workers who have had limited contact with faith-based organisations, or only with faith-based organisations of a similar ilk, can often be quite unaware of the variety of practices within the faith-based sector. To this end, Gilligan (2010, p 61) has proposed two contrasting approaches to faith-based practice. In the first, which has he labelled 'liberal or open', religious beliefs are recognised as an underlying motivation to service provision that presents to service users in non-religious language as a commitment to 'care' (Camilleri and Winkworth, 2005; Belcher, 2008; Conradson, 2011). Gilligan has labelled the second approach as 'fundamentalist or exclusive', reflecting a belief that religious salvation is the ultimate imperative (Scales, 2011).

Faith-based organisations in the 'liberal' tradition can be seen as secular organisations in the wider community, by service users and even by staff (Melville and McDonald, 2006). A lack of overtly religious imagery and an absence of religious language often characterises such organisations, at least at the point of service provision. This is particularly so when the work is largely funded by government, and there are usually contractual requirements that funded services will be made available to individuals, to all members of the community, irrespective of their religious beliefs, and should not be actively providing religious teaching or seeking conversions.

For many social workers, it is Gilligan's second grouping of faith-based organisations that is most concerning, especially organisations that act as if procuring the religious conversion of service users is a high priority (De Cordier, 2009). For service users, the experience may range from low-key invitations about which the recipient is made aware that their decision to participate or not in religious activities will have no impact on receipt of services, through to coercive or manipulative attempts involving inducements to participate in religious activities, such as prayers or worship conducted by the organisation (Belcher and DeForge, 2007). However, there are also many faith-based organisations, including those of an evangelical disposition, which would abhor such actions, and understand their purpose as providing services to disadvantaged members of the community with little or no expectation of altering the religious beliefs and practices of those to whom services are provided (Davies-Kildea, 2007). In fact, to guard against accusations of proselytising, there are some faith-based organisations that have made it known to staff that they may face being dismissed from their position if they seek to convert service users (Conradson, 2011).

A second objection to faith-based organisations that is often raised by social workers is that they have reinforced, rather than challenged, social exclusion (Moss, 2005). Religious teaching that has reinforced discrimination and oppression is in stark contrast to the values basis for social work, and it is unsurprising that social workers might be sceptical of organisations that are aligned with religious discourses which deny women access to abortions or effective forms of contraception, which have been unsupportive of women who wish to leave violent relationships or to take employment outside the home, restrict rights for people who are not heterosexual, or are unsupportive of programmes to alleviate poverty. Nevertheless, there are also many faith-based organisations that have strong credentials when it comes to promoting gender equality, running effective anti-poverty programmes and supporting women who do seek to move away from living in violent circumstances. Furthermore, faith-based organisations also have a long history of identifying need and establishing innovative services, particularly those that support the needs of the most disadvantaged in the community (Winkworth and Camilleri, 2004). For example, in Australia, although there is now considerable government involvement in such services, it was the Salvation Army that established the first labour bureau open to all unemployed Australians as well as the world's first programme for released prisoners (Salvation Army, 2013).

Today, faith-based organisations not only continue to identify need and establish services that seek to address these, but are also among the most prominent voices in the community advocating for the needs of those who are excluded, including the poor (Ebear et al, 2008; Swain, 2009), the homeless (Conradson, 2011), and refugees and asylum seekers (Cemlyn and Briskman, 2003). However, in the minds of many Australians, faith-based organisations are intrinsically linked with allegations concerning the sexual abuse of children, particularly in institutions associated with the Catholic Church (Crisp, 2013), although evidence also exists in respect of abuse of children in the care of other religious groups (Family and Community Development Committee, 2013a). As has been found in other countries (CICA, 2009; Shaw, 2011), the abuse of children in the care of Australian religious organisations has often been blamed on inadequately trained staff, and a lack of effective policies and procedures to both prevent abuse occurring and to respond appropriately should it occur. However, while a recent parliamentary inquiry in the State of Victoria has identified cultures of abuse that were once present in some faith-based welfare organisations (Family and Community Development Committee, 2013a), it has also noted some exemplary policies and procedures in some faith-based organisations for preventing and responding to alleged abuse (Family and Community Development Committee, 2013b). Hence, while it is understandable that some social workers will be reluctant to have contact with any faith-based organisations, it is important that such a stance does not ultimately result in service users being denied access to appropriate and ethical services that address their exclusion.

Religious literacies for social workers employed by faith-based organisations

Having put forward a case as to why a basic level of religious literacy in respect of faith-based organisations is needed by all social workers, irrespective of whether or not they are employed in this sector, we now need to consider the issue of religious literacy for social workers employed by faith-based organisations. Some will only employ professional staff such as social workers who are committed to the faith, and who might be expected to have an understanding of the religious beliefs that underpin service delivery. However, in some of the large church-affiliated welfare organisations that employ hundreds of staff, many of the staff do not share the religious beliefs or spirituality associated with their employing organisation. For example, in respect of Catholic social welfare organisations in Australia, it has been observed that:

> Our agencies now operate with a new workforce.... Importantly, in addition to being non-Catholic and non-practising, our workforce is less likely to have had the educational and cultural experiences that might engender some prior understanding of Catholic life and culture. In this context we cannot even assume that some of our very basic assumptions will immediately resonate in the lives of people who make up our workforce. (Quinlan, 2008, p 51)

Similar statements would just as readily apply in many other faith-based organisations in Australia. While it has been proposed that any faith-based organisations should be able to articulate their faith basis in a way that is meaningful to its staff, this does not always occur, and arguably, the observation of British author Helen Cameron applies to some faith-based organisations in Australia:

> It almost seems as if faith-based organizations can be asked about anything except what they believe. There are understandable concerns about giving offense and the inquirers' competence to evaluate the replies, but if faith is their distinctiveness, it must also be open to scrutiny. (Cameron, 2004, p 147)

Elsewhere, it may be recognised that not all staff will share the same religious beliefs or outlook, but there may be expectations of a fit with the organisation's value base or mission statement (Rogers, 2009; Conradson, 2011). In particular, social workers may need to be aware of the place of religious teaching if it results in proscriptions associated with relationships, reproductive health, substance use or medical treatments (Furness and Gilligan, 2010). Furthermore, they need sufficient understanding of the organisation's stance that they are able to balance these with other moral imperatives. For example, workers in faith-based organisations associated with a religion that disapproves of sex outside marriage might nevertheless support individuals such as unmarried pregnant teenagers (Siporin, 1986), or provide contraceptives in situations where not doing so would be harmful. When asked if there were ever any tensions between the values espoused by the organisation and her understanding of social work, a very experienced social worker responded:

> There are probably two answers to that. One would be the official answer and one would be the practice answer, I think. And it's probably most obvious in the area of youth when you are talking about contraception and a lot of talk about safe sex which ... was more of a case of do what you need to do to educate the person and help them to make their own choices and to be safe and that sort of thing. And don't bring too much to our attention that there's a conflict in that. These days I think that the young person's welfare is first and foremost and whatever needs to happen to promote their welfare and give them choices. (Quoted in Crisp, 2014, p 115)

This response is underpinned by a high level of religious literacy in that the speaker was not only aware of the religious teaching about contraception, but also of the imperative to ensure that the welfare of the service user was consistent with religious teaching in that context.

If, as the previous example demonstrates, religious literacy may be important for individual social workers in faith-based organisations, then it is even more imperative for management to have a degree of religious literacy. While individual social workers in large organisations may have little or no contact with the hierarchy of the religion with which an organisation is associated, social workers involved in agency management may have regular encounters with religious officials beyond their organisation. In such roles it may be necessary to 'become "bi-lingual", that is, both theologically literate and professionally literate, such that the same reality can be expressed in two different ways without compromise to either theological or professional discourse' (Ranson, 2008, p 91). As a senior manager in a faith-based organisation explained:

> ... as you get higher up, so there's a number of levels of management and a lot of those levels of management are filled by [religious officials], some who have no social work experience or training whatsoever. So when I started with the [organisation] ... the person who came in to be [senior church official responsible for organisation] had come straight from the church ministry and had no idea. Wasn't social work trained, had no idea of social work. He was a nice person and he did a reasonably good job, but he didn't have any of that training. (Quoted in Crisp, 2014, p 64)

Conclusions

The development of a new *Code of ethics* for Australian social workers, which includes a number of mentions about the need for practice that is sensitive to religious beliefs and practices, has placed the issue of religious literacy as integral policy for the AASW and its members. Yet, although religious literacy is consistent with theories of anti-oppressive practice (Strier and Binyamin, 2010), which have, for some time, predominated in Social Work education in both Australia and the UK, it seems to have snuck onto the agenda rather than emerging from extensive debate within the social work community. Hence, questions such as what does religious literacy entail in respect of Australian social workers, and the many dimensions of practice in which religious literacy may be required, are only just beginning to be asked.

This chapter has suggested a number of reasons why Australian social workers need some religious literacy, both in respect of working with individual service users and in working with or for faith-based organisations. However, many of these reasons may be similarly applicable for professional staff in the fields of health and education, which, like social work, have to work with individuals in ways that are respectful of their religious beliefs, and where professionals may find themselves employed by or working alongside faith-based organisations.

While recognising the need for it, the conversations as to what might represent an adequate level of religious literacy, and how this might be achieved, are still at a beginning point in social work in Australia (Crisp, 2011). With the place of religion in society and in particular, the relationship between religious organisations and the welfare state, as well as different religions being dominant (Bäckström et al, 2010; Crisp, 2014), religious literacy requires social workers being able to respond to, and advocate for, the needs of religious people in the specific societal contexts in which they live, work and participate in civic life. While arguably social workers require a base level of knowledge about each of the major religions present in the communities where they work, more importantly, they should have an awareness that religion is an important facet of people's lives, which may need to be acknowledged when responding to the needs of individuals and communities.

Dinham and Jones (2010b) identified 22 challenges requiring religious literacy for the leadership of higher education institutes (HEIs) in the UK, and undoubtedly this was just a sample of the many issues that could have been identified. Like HEIs, organisations employing social workers may potentially have to respond to a myriad of issues in which religious literacy may contribute to better decisions for the organisation, staff and members of the organisation, and others, including service users. Religiously literate social workers won't necessarily have all the answers, but they will be able to work from a framework that enables them to ask questions about the role of religion in a particular situation, and to identify a range of options and resources that take seriously the religious issues at play (Dinham and Jones, 2010b).

References

AASW (Australian Association of Social Workers) (1999) *Code of ethics*, Canberra, ACT: AASW.

AASW (2010) *Code of ethics*, Canberra, ACT: AASW (www.aasw.asn. au/document/item/740).

ABS (Australian Bureau of Statistics) (2001) *2001 Census of population and housing, religious affiliation by sex*, Canberra, ACT: ABS (http://abs.gov.au/websitedbs/censushome.nsf/home/historicaldata2001?opendocument&navpos=280).

Ager, A. and Ager, J. (2011) 'Faith and the discourse of secular humanism', *Journal of Refugee Studies*, vol 24, no 3, pp 456-72.

Althaus-Reid, M. (2000) *Indecent theology: Theological perversions in sex, gender and politics*, London: Routledge.

Amato-von Hemert, K. (1994) 'Should social work education address religious issues? Yes!', *Journal of Social Work Education*, vol 30, no 1, pp 7-11.

Ashencaen Crabtree, S. and Baba, I. (2001) 'Islamic perspectives in social work education: implications for teaching and practice', *Social Work Education*, vol 20, no 4, pp 469-81.

Ashencaen Crabtree, S., Hussain, F. and Spalek, B. (2008) *Islam and social work: Debating values, transforming practice*, Bristol: Policy Press.

Bäckström, A., Davie, G., Ergardh, N. and Pettersson, P. (eds) (2010) *Welfare and religion in 21st century Europe: Volume 1, Configuring the connections*, Farnham: Ashgate.

Batstone, D., Mendieta, E., Lorentzen, L.A. and Hopkins, D.N. (eds) (1997) *Liberation theologies, postmodernity, and the Americas*, London: Routledge.

Belcher, H. (2008) 'Explaining a paradox: church and health policy in the 1940s and 1970s', *Australasian Catholic Record*, vol 85, no 3, pp 259-73.

Belcher, J.R. and DeForge, B.R. (2007) 'Faith-based social services: the challenges of providing assistance', *Journal of Religion and Spirituality in Social Work*, vol 26, no 4, pp 1-19.

Bellamy, J. and Castle, K. (2004) *2001 church attendance estimates*, Sydney, NSW: NCLS Research.

Boer, R. (2008) 'The new secularism', *Arena Journal*, vol 29/30, pp 35-57.

Bouma, G. (2006) *Australia's soul: Religion and spirituality in the twenty-first century*, Melbourne, VIC: Cambridge University Press.

Cameron, H. (2004) 'Typology of religious characteristics of social service and educational organizations and programs: a European response', *Nonprofit and Voluntary Sector Quarterly*, vol 33, no 1, pp 146-50.

Camilleri, P. and Winkworth, G, (2004) 'Mapping the Catholic social services', *Australasian Catholic Record*, vol 81, no 2, pp 184-97.

Camilleri, P. and Winkworth, G. (2005) 'Catholic social services in Australia: a short history', *Australian Social Work*, vol 58, no 1, pp 76-85.

Canda, E.R. and Furman, D.L. (1999) *Spiritual diversity in social work practice: The heart of helping*, New York: The Free Press.

Cemlyn, S. and Briskman, L. (2003) 'Asylum, children's rights and social work', *Child and Family Social Work*, vol 8, no 3, pp 163-78.

CICA (Commission to Inquire into Child Abuse) (2009) *CICA investigation Committee report* (www.childabusecommission.com/rpt/pdfs/).

Clark, J.L. (2006) 'Listening for meaning: a research-based model for attending to spirituality, culture and worldview in social work practice', *Critical Social Work*, vol 7, no 1 (www1.uwindsor.ca/criticalsocialwork/listening-for-meaning-a-research-based-model-for-attending-to-spirituality-culture-and-worldview-in-).

Cnaan, R.A. and Curtis, D.W. (2013) 'Religious congregations as voluntary associations: an overview', *Nonprofit and Voluntary Sector Quarterly*, vol 42, no 1, pp 7-33.

Conradson, D. (2011) 'Values, practices and strategic divestment: Christian social service organisations in New Zealand', in C. Milligan and D. Conradson (eds) *Landscapes of voluntarism: New spaces of health, welfare and governance*, Bristol: Policy Press, pp 153-71.

Cree, V.E. (1996) *Social work: A Christian or secular discourse?*, New Waverley Papers, Edinburgh: University of Edinburgh.

Crisp, B.R. (2010) *Spirituality and social work*, Farnham: Ashgate.

Crisp, B.R. (2011) 'If a holistic approach to social work requires acknowledgement of religion, what does this mean for social work education?', *Social Work Education*, vol 30, no 6, pp 657-68.

Crisp, B.R. (2013) 'Can the church be good news for survivors of sexual abuse?', *Crucible: The Christian Journal of Social Ethics*, July, pp 33-40.

Crisp, B.R. (2014) *Social work and faith-based organizations*, London: Routledge.

Davies-Kildea, J. (2007) *Faith in action: A study of holistic models care, for highly disadvantaged people, which have been established in faith-based communities*, Brunswick, VIC: The Salvation Army (www.salvationarmy.org.au/Global/State%20pages/Victoria/Brunswick%20Corps/faith%20in%20action%20report.pdf).

De Cordier, B. (2009) 'Faith-based aid, globalization and the humanitarian frontline: an analysis of western-based Muslim aid organizations', *Disasters*, vol 33, no 4, pp 608-28.

Dinham, A. (2011) 'A public role for religion: on needing a discourse of religious literacy', *International Journal of Religion and Spirituality*, vol 2, no 4, pp 291-302.

Dinham, A. and Jones, S.H. (2010a) *Religious literacy leadership in higher education: An analysis of challenges of religious faith, and resources for meeting them, for university leaders*, London: Religious Literacy Leadership Programme/Higher Education Funding Council for England.

Dinham, A. and Jones, S.H. (2010b) *Religious Literacy Leadership in Higher Education: Leadership challenges: Case studies*, London: Religious Literacy Leadership Programme/Higher Education Funding Council for England.

Dinham, A. and Jones, S.H. (2012) 'Religion, public policy and the academy: brokering public faith in a context of ambivalence', *Journal of Contemporary Religion*, vol 27, no 2, pp 185-201.

Ebear, J., Csiernik, R. and Béchard, M. (2008) 'Furthering parish wellness: including social work as part of a Catholic pastoral team', *Social Work and Christianity*, vol 35, no 2, pp 179-86.

Edgardh, N. and Petterson, P. (2010) 'The Church of Sweden: a church for all, especially the most vulnerable', in A. Bäckström, G. Davie, N. Edgardh and P. Pettersson (eds) *Welfare and religion in 21st century Europe: Volume 1, Configuring the connections*, Farnham: Ashgate, pp 39-56.

Family and Community Development Committee (2013a) *Betrayal of trust: Inquiry into the handling of child abuse by religious and other non-government organisations, Volume 1*, Melbourne, VIC: Parliament of Victoria.

Family and Community Development Committee (2013b) *Betrayal of trust: Inquiry into the handling of child abuse by religious and other non-government organisations, Volume 2*, Melbourne, VIC: Parliament of Victoria.

Freire, P. (1974) *Pedagogy of the oppressed*, Harmondsworth: Penguin.

Furman, L.D., Benson, P.W., Canda, E.R. and Grimwood, C. (2005) 'A comparative international analysis of religion and spirituality in social work: a survey of UK and US social workers', *Social Work Education*, vol 24, no 8, pp 813-39.

Furness, S. and Gilligan, P. (2010) *Religion, belief and social work: Making a difference*, Bristol: Policy Press.

Gale, F., Bolzan, N. and McRae-McMahon, D. (eds) (2007) *Spirited practices: Spirituality and the helping professions*, Crows Nest, NSW: Allen & Unwin.

Gardner, F. (2006) *Working with human service organisations: Creating connections for practice*, South Melbourne, VIC: Oxford University Press.

Gardner, F. (2011) *Critical spirituality: A holistic approach to community practice*, Farnham: Ashgate.

Gilligan, P. (2010) 'Faith-based approaches', in M. Gray and S. Webb (eds) *Ethics and value perspectives in social work*, Basingstoke: Palgrave Macmillan, pp 60-70.

Goldburg, P. (2006) 'Critical religious literacy: a challenge for secondary religion studies', *Religious Education Journal of Australia*, vol 22, no 2, pp 9-13.

Gray, M. (2008) 'Viewing spirituality in social work through the lens of contemporary social theory', *British Journal of Social Work*, vol 38, no 1, pp 175-96.

Hemmings, M. and Butcher, J. (2012) 'The needs for a school–parish approach to religious education: lessons for a religious literacy project', *Religious Education Journal of Australia*, vol 28, no 2, pp 22-8.

Hodge, D.R. (2005) 'Spirituality in social work education: a development and discussion of goals that flow from the profession's ethical mandates', *Social Work Education*, vol 24, no 1, pp 37-55.

Hodge, D.R. (2007) 'Advocating for persecuted people of faith: a social justice imperative', *Families in Society*, vol 88, no 2, pp 255-62.

Hodge, D.R. and Bushfield, S. (2006) 'Developing spiritual competence in practice', *Journal of Ethnic and Cultural Diversity in Social Work*, vol 15, no 3/4, pp 101-27.

Holden, C. and Trembath, R. (2008) *Divine discontent – The Brotherhood of St Laurence: A history*, North Melbourne, VIC: Australian Scholarly Publishing.

Horwath, J. and Lees, J. (2010) 'Assessing the influence of religious beliefs and practices on parenting capacity: the challenges for social work practitioners', *British Journal of Social Work*, vol 40, no 1, pp 82-99.

IASSW (International Association of Schools and Social Work) and IFSW (International Federation of Social Work) (2004) *Global standards for the education and training of the social work profession*, IASSW and IFSW (www.ifsw.org/cm_data/GlobalSocialWorkStandards2005.pdf).

Kyung, C.H. (1991) *Struggle to be the sun again: Introducing Asian women's theology*, Maryknoll, NY: Orbis Books.

Lake, M. (2013) *Faith in action: HammondCare*, Sydney, NSW: University of New South Wales Press.

Lee, B.Y and Newberg, A.B. (2005) 'Religion and health: a review and critical analysis', *Zygon*, vol 40, no 2, pp 443-68.

Lindsay, R. (2002) *Recognizing spirituality: The interface between faith and social work*, Crawley: University of Western Australia Press.

Melville, R. and McDonald, C. (2006) 'Faith-based organisations and contemporary welfare', *Australian Journal of Social Issues*, vol 41, no 1, pp 69-85.

Melville-Wiseman, J. (2013) 'Teaching through the tension: resolving religious and sexuality based schism in social work education', *International Social Work*, vol 56, no 3, pp 290-303.

Moss, B. (2005) 'Thinking outside the box: religion and spirituality in social work education and practice', *Implicit Religion*, vol 8, no 1, pp 40-52.

Oduyoye, M.A. (2001) *Introducing African women's theology*, Sheffield: Sheffield Academic Press.

Ozanne, E. and Rose, D. (2013) *The organisational context of human service Practice*, South Yarra, VIC: Palgrave Macmillan.

Pattel-Gray, A. (1998) *The great white flood: Racism in Australia*, Atlanta, GA: Scholars Press.

Pessi, A.B. (2010) 'The church as a place of encounter: communality and the good life in Finland', in A. Bäckström, G. Davie, N. Edgardh and P. Pettersson (eds) *Welfare and religion in 21st century Europe: Volume 1, Configuring the connections*, Farnham: Ashgate, pp 77-94.

Quinlan, F. (2008) 'Common challenges for health, education and social services', in N. Ormerod (ed) *Identity and mission in Catholic agencies*, Strathfield, NSW: St Pauls Publications, pp 39-58.

Ranson, D. (2008) 'A service shaped by Catholic identity', in N. Ormerod (ed) *Identity and mission in Catholic agencies*, Strathfield, NSW: St Pauls Publications, pp 83-99.

Reuther, R.R. (1983) *Sexism and God-talk: Towards a feminist theology*, London: SCM Press.

Rizer, J.M. and McColley, K.J. (1996) 'Attitudes and practices regarding spirituality and religion held by graduate social work students', *Social Work and Christianity*, vol 23, no 1, pp 53-65.

Rogers, R.K. (2009) 'Community collaboration: practices of effective collaboration as reported by three urban faith-based social service programs', *Social Work and Christianity*, vol 36, no 2, pp 326-45.

Russell, L.M. (1974) *Human liberation in a feminist perspective: A theology*, Philadelphia, PA: The Westminster Press.

Sacco, T. (1996) 'Spirituality and social work students in their first year of study at a South African university', *Journal of Social Development in Africa*, vol 11, no 2, pp 43-56.

Salvation Army (2013) *Foundation of Salvation Army social services* (www.salvationarmy.org.au/en/Who-We-Are/History-and-heritage/Foundation-of-Salvation-Army-social-services/).

Scales, T.L. (2011) '"Accepting a trust so responsible": Christians caring for children at Buckner Orphan's Home, Dallas, Texas, 1979-1909', *Social Work and Christianity*, vol 38, no 3, pp 332-55.

Scourfield, J., Warden, R., Gilliat-Ray, S., Khan, A. and Otri, S. (2013) 'Religious nurture in British Muslim families: implications for social work', *International Social Work*, vol 56, no 3, pp 326-42.

Shaw, T. (2011) *Time to be heard: A pilot forum*, Edinburgh: Scottish Government.

Sheridan, M.J., Bullis, R.K., Adcock, C.R., Berlin, S.D. and Miller, P.C. (1992) 'Practitioners' personal and professional attitudes and behavior toward religion and spirituality: issues for education and practice', *Journal of Social Work Education*, vol 28, no 2, pp 190-203.

Siporin, M. (1986) 'Contribution of religious values to social work and the law', *Social Thought*, vol 12, no 4, pp 35-50.

Strier, R. and Binyamin, S. (2010) 'Developing anti-oppressive services for the poor: a theoretical and organisational rationale', *British Journal of Social Work*, vol 40, no 6, pp 1908-26.

Swain, S. (2009) 'Welfare work and charitable organisations', in J. Jupp (ed) *Encyclopaedia of religion in Australia*, Melbourne, VIC: Cambridge University Press, pp 685-94.

Swinton, J. (2001) *Spirituality and mental health care: Rediscovering a 'forgotten' dimension*, London: Jessica Kingsley Publishers.

Winkworth, G. and Camilleri, P. (2004) 'Keeping the faith: the impact of human services restructuring on Catholic social welfare services', *Australian Journal of Social Issues*, vol 39, no 3, pp 315-28.

TWELVE

Religious literacy and the media: the case of the BBC

Michael Wakelin and Nick Spencer

Given the ever-growing salience of religion as a political, social and cultural factor in global affairs, even in comparatively secular Western Europe, *and* the ubiquity and importance of the media, now present in almost every area of our lives, one would have imagined that religious literacy among those who report news and make programmes would have been of paramount importance. Discussing or depicting religion inaccurately today risks not only misleading the public (which is bad in itself) but provoking suspicion, tension and, at its most egregious, outright hostility within and between communities. There is no sector of society – whether politics, business or sport – that actively seeks erroneous or flawed coverage of its dynamics and structures, but there are few where the stakes are higher. When it comes to people's core identities – the ideas, objects and practices that they hold in special consideration, indeed, hold as 'sacred', and the values by means of which they navigate shared public space – it is essential that we understand them as fully and seriously as possible. Understanding does not necessarily mean sympathise, still less agree with – we should not impose consensus where there is none – but it does mean placing ourselves in a position from which we can make the truest and fairest judgement of the people among whom we live. This chapter examines religious literacy in the British media, outlining its history, focusing at first on the BBC as the longstanding dominant feature on the national religious broadcasting landscape in this particular context, and then analysing its current condition, in the process outlining why religious literacy matters in the media, and what can be done to improve it.

Understanding the background: the BBC and religious broadcasting

From its outset in 1922, the British Broadcasting Corporation (BBC) was married to religious broadcasting, which initially comprised almost exclusively Christian content. Lord Reith, the son of a Scottish Presbyterian minister, was himself a committed Christian and was convinced that his fledgling organisation could play an important role in keeping Christian values as a central part of the life of the nation.

The churches, after an initial problem with the whole notion of broadcasting the sacred to the masses (there were concerns that the viewing public would not treat the most sacred moment of the 1953 Coronation with due respect in their living rooms) soon saw that here was a great opportunity to use the BBC as a platform for continuing to propagate the traditional form of Christianity they believed the country wanted and needed. There was a conviction, at least in some quarters, that if the BBC were regularly to broadcast the Church of England's Book of Common Prayer on the wireless, the nation, the depth and solidity of whose Christianity had been a cause for worry since at least the turn of the century, would be reconnected with its Christian (that is, Anglican) values, and perhaps even flock back to already half-empty churches. Many believed the BBC was there to do its job, and at least initially there was a tacit, if not active, agreement from the Corporation with this strategy.

This was the beginning of an unhealthy relationship in which the churches in general, and the Church of England in particular, felt that they had some special status and would always be considered in any decisions the BBC made. It was a status quo in which the BBC management colluded for a long while, at least up until shortly after the Second World War. The churches became complacent as their right to be on the air was unchallenged, regardless of whether the programmes were interesting or relevant to an increasingly diverse audience, who could not only exercise their choice over the on-off switch, but also increasingly, over the years, move the dial to another station.

Alongside this privilege, the churches also insisted that there should be a protection clause around any discussion of religious scriptures, and the banning of anything that might alarm the delicate faith of the audience. BBC managers went along with this in the early days, deferential to episcopal concerns. Far from protecting them, however, such paternalism, in fact, paved the way for a degree of disillusionment among the audience, and perhaps even bred a lasting attitude to religious broadcasting that it was in some ways different, not as 'grown up' as other programme genres.

The relationship began to change, albeit slowly, in the 1960s, when Christianity lost its position as the default cultural assumption of those in authority. It was no longer self-evident that religion, which still then predominantly meant Christianity, needed special treatment. Indeed, given the at times highly fractious relationship between the BBC (and Independent Television or ITV) and the National Viewers' and Listeners' Association, led by the Christian values campaigner Mary Whitehouse, there emerged a class of media professionals, some of whom were actively antagonistic towards religious presuppositions. When, therefore, in the 1980s and 1990s, a more self-consciously secular leadership emerged in the BBC, they were minded to circumvent the earlier, tacit agreements between the Corporation and the Church, and no longer prepared to see broadcast media as an outpost of Christianity. Moreover, the fact that the genre had not been given the chance to grow up and adapt to the already fast-changing media scene left religious broadcasting vulnerable to cuts and marginalisation.

The withering significance of religion at the BBC is well illustrated by the Central Religious Advisory Committee (CRAC). This once all-powerful body shrank, both in terms of the stature of its members and the weight of its influence. During the 1980s, the Director General and the Head of Television regularly attended these meetings. However, by 1996, when one of the authors attended as Head of Religion at the BBC, it was a smaller and almost insignificant affair, attended, on that occasion, by the Bishop of Norwich and the three other members who had bothered to turn up.

The BBC's decision in 1992, under the then Director General John Birt, to move the Religious Broadcasting Department out of London to the northern English city of Manchester was pivotal in the history of British religious broadcasting. It has proved to be a negative step for the group of specialist producers and programme makers who, now being out of sight of the London-centric media, were largely out of mind. Despite firm promises, the department lost major factual output when two distinguished religion documentary strands (*Everyman* and *Heart of the Matter*) were axed, and the budgets and timeslots never regained.

Since that point, there has been no comparable, serious evening television space to deal in depth with contemporary religious issues. After the move, the Religious Broadcasting Department lost respect and, in turn, religiously literate programme makers. Without this talent it was hard to win new commissions in the marketplace. It became a vicious circle, as fewer commissions tempted less talent, which generated less profile, which led to fewer commissions. The decision to outsource Sunday morning religious television programmes to an independent TV production company and then to BBC Belfast had a further damaging impact on the department, which was left only with *Songs of Praise*, a long-running and popular Sunday evening programme of hymns and features which, while judged with affection by the British public, is distinctly homely in its tone and content.

Perhaps more seriously, at least for the long-term future of religious literacy in the British broadcast media, these structural and cultural changes within the nation's biggest single broadcaster helped to restrict the pipeline of emerging religiously literate talent which, in turn, meant that when it came to replacing senior executives, there were a limited number of highly experienced, religiously literate applicants.

View from the inside

The consequence of these changes was to starve an industry of religiously literate executives at just the moment when religious literacy emerged as being a particularly important qualification for understanding the modern world. The Hungarian–British author and journalist, Arthur Koestler, remarked of the 1940s that it was a tragedy that the age of mankind's greatest technological achievement happened to coincide with the age of his lowest moral capacity. The sentiment is appropriate, albeit without its apocalyptic weight, for the status of religious literacy and the media in the early years of the 21st century. It is troubling that the time of greatest need for religious literacy has coincided with the time at which religious literacy in the media is at a low ebb – for what has happened to the BBC, despite it no longer being the sole or even primary presence on British broadcast media landscape, is indicative of the wider status of media religious literacy. While the religious output of the BBC is low, that of ITV is non-existent, and Channel Four no longer has any specialist commissioner.

This decline is not matched by general decline in coverage of religion over recent years. Indeed, there is evidence to suggest that there has been an *increased* interest in religion of late, particularly in print media. Ian Mayes, former reader's editor for the British left-leaning newspaper *The Guardian*, responding in 2005 to several readers who wrote to him complaining about the paper's increased coverage of religion, wrote that, 'there is undoubtedly more discussion of religion in the pages of the paper but that reflects its increasing importance in politics' (Mayes, 2005). A crude measure of this is the number of stories in *The Guardian* that mention the word 'Christian': in 1985, 770; in 1995, 1,221; and in 2005, 2,341. A search for the word 'Muslim' showed: 1985, 408; 1995, 1,106; and in 2005, 2,114 (Mayes, 2005).

More recently, a research project into portrayals of religion in the British media compared the amount of religion in the media in 2008–09 with a similar period in 1982–83, and found that there was more Christian coverage, much more coverage of Islam, and also much more coverage of secularism and atheism (Knott et al, 2013). Another study, analysing the spectrum of the press over the last 40 years in its coverage of religious matters, found that there is a general persistence in coverage in the broadsheets, *The Times* and the *Independent*, increased interest (and hostility) in *The Guardian* and a right-leaning broadsheet, the *Telegraph*, marginally increased interest in new-age tendencies in the right-wing tabloids, the *Mail* and *Express,* and low-level interest and considerable hostility in the left-of-centre tabloids, *The Sun* and *The Star* (Gill, 2012).

Religion thus remains eminently newsworthy. For all the declining content in the visual media, the problem lies less with quantity and more with quality, or more precisely, with the level of religious literacy with which religion is covered and portrayed. Religious specialists in broadsheet journalism are few and far between, the vacuum created by this absence often being filled by those who believe that because they write well on social, cultural or political affairs, they necessarily write equally well on religious ones.

It is not, however, ignorance of religious affairs that is the most important factor in the realm of media religious literacy. Well-informed commentators are self-evidently better than ill-informed ones, but better-informed commentators would not necessarily 'solve' the problem of media religious literacy. It is important that there is recognition that religious faith is not simply a thing, an object to be studied, but a living identity to be experienced. Few media executives would consider reporting or making programmes on social poverty or exclusion drawing solely on sociological data and analysis, ignoring the *experience* of poverty altogether. In a similar fashion, no one would make programmes on immigration that simply spoke of changing national trends and the composition of local populations, while ignoring the sense of threatened identity among host communities, or the sense of fear and isolation among immigrant communities. It is often second nature in these areas to understand that there is a subjective as well as objective aspect to these issues, that there is a story from the inside, which is equally as valid and relevant as that from the outside. Religion is no different.

One of the reasons for this difficulty in seeing religions from the inside perhaps lies in a disconnection between those who work in the media and those to whom they speak. The BBC's own research, for example, has revealed that its audience is twice as likely to be religious as the people in the Corporation providing the content (BBC, 2011). The problem with this should be obvious. No one would imagine that having an entirely white class of professionals making programmes for and reporting on the affairs of black or Asian communities, or vice versa, would be appropriate. Given that religion is arguably, today, as or more central to social and cultural identity as ethnicity, it is hard to see why this situation is acceptable.

A more subtle and arguably more significant reason for this resistance to 'the story from the inside' lies in the preconception that to show what being religious is like from the inside is to risk proselytising. If religion from the inside is attractive – and it certainly appears to be for many millions of people in the UK, and many billions across the world – showing it as attractive, without any objective commentary or critique, risks turning the media into an evangelistic enterprise.

This fear, we would suggest, is misplaced or at least exaggerated. No one seriously thinks mainstream media should imitate the God channels that lurk deep down the satellite TV running orders. If there is one thing worse than ill-informed religious broadcasting by secular people, it is ill-informed religious broadcasting by religious people. But that is a fear extreme in its proportion. If covering religion from the inside shows it to have its attractions, so be it. That is merely a fair and accurate depiction of its dynamics. It is only when covering religion shows it to be obviously, uncomplicatedly and incontrovertibly attractive (cf the God channels) that there is a problem.

Why religious literacy is important

Treatment of religion and belief within the media suffers, then, from three key problems: low output and presence; low levels of religious literacy; and nervousness about exploring religion from the inside, perhaps borne of a disconnection between producers and consumers. This would matter in any sphere but, to return to Arthur Koestler's point earlier, it is an especial problem at a time when there is a particular need for religious literacy. The reasons for this have been well rehearsed elsewhere: the British religious landscape is more plural now than at any time in its past; globally, religion is on the political agenda in a way that few thought it would be two generations ago; questions of religious identity, particularly among religious minorities, are now closely intertwined with those of ethnicity and migration, as unprecedented numbers of Muslims, Hindus, Sikhs and others have settled in Britain in the postwar period; and although intertwining of this nature has some precedent, for example, in the period of Catholic migration in the later 19th century, it is on a greater scale and arguably more complex today. As Grace Davie suggests in her Foreword to this book, self-consciously secular and explicitly non-religious identities are now major and sometimes muscular elements in discussions of public morals and values.

The consequences of a lack of religious media literacy are potentially significant and can be seen in a number of different ways. The greatest risk is of intemperate and ill-informed media storms. Rowan Williams' 2008 lecture on 'Civil and religious law in England' is an extremely intelligent and nuanced, if dense and complicated, analysis of a difficult subject. More importantly, however, it was commenting on a subject wholly alien to many in the media and those who read their indignant reporting of it. The question of 'supplementary' (which is not the same as 'parallel') legal jurisdictions – or 'minority legal orders' as they are also known – is neither new, nor exclusively about Islam (for examples, see the Roman Catholic Church's Code of Canon Law, or the Jewish Beth Din), nor even exclusively about religion (Native American communities have been granted supplementary jurisdictions in Canada, with a similar power of civil disputes). To some specialists on law and religion, there was some astonishment at the subsequent furore. Religious illiteracy presents the danger of religion being re-narrated according to other priorities. This was the background to Williams' 'shari'a' lecture, many media outlets and commentators using the lecture to engage in a certain sort of rhetoric about Islam that would have been more difficult in other circumstances. It would be wrong, however, to imagine that Islam is the only point of tension here.

Confusing religion and the far right

Key among other points of tension is muddle, anxiety and confusion about religious extremism and the far right. In 2012, the religion and society think tank, Theos, published a research report entitled, *Is there a 'religious right' in Britain?* (Walton, 2006). Its origins lay in the awareness that the phrase 'US-style religious right' was appearing with greater frequency in media commentary on the state of Christianity in Britain. The phrase is a specific and loaded one, indicating a large-scale, well-organised, well-funded network of groups that has a clear and limited set of policy aims – broadly, anti-abortion, anti-gay rights, pro-Israel, pro-religious freedom, anti-evolution, anti-big government – which are deemed as 'Christian' or 'Judeo-Christian' and which these groups seek to deliver through the vehicle of a particular political party (in the US, the Republican Party). One may quibble with the details of this definition – certainly not all 'religious right' groups would support all of these causes with equal fervour – but the term 'religious right' clearly indicates something with at least what the philosopher Ludwig Wittgenstein termed a 'family resemblance' to these characteristics.

Given everything that this phrase indicated, it was clearly important to assess the claim that Britain was developing a 'religious right' carefully and empirically. The Theos report found that, *on the surface*, the claims appeared to be justified. There was evidence of greater coordination among Christian groups with a strong socially conservative commitment, in particular, relating to human sexuality, marriage, family life and religious freedom, about which they were vocal and often willing to resort to legal action. This is a familiar picture within the US political and religious scene. However, it went on to outline why this picture was superficial, and why the current trends within British Christianity did not constitute the emergence of a US-style religious right, and why such a phenomenon was unlikely to emerge in Britain. For demographic, economic, party political, ecclesiological and (ironically) media-related reasons, Britain was not likely to follow the US path.

The report's conclusions were covered widely in the media, including by *The Guardian*, a reporter from which had participated in a round-table discussion at which the report was launched and discussed. Unfortunately, the conclusions were either not covered fully or simply ignored, *The Guardian* headline declaring 'Britain's religious right is on the rise' (Quinn, 2013). The narrative of an ominously emerging religious right was too strong, and perhaps too useful, to be dislodged. Religious illiteracy – in this instance, in the teeth of an attempt to improve religious literacy – led to the false depiction of a religious landscape.

At its most egregious, such deliberate misunderstanding can come perilously close to hate-mongering. The 2008 Theos Annual Lecture was delivered by Mark Thompson, then Director General of the BBC, on faith, morality and the media. Following the lecture, Thompson was asked whether there was any truth in the comedian Ben Elton's claim that the BBC consciously treated Islam differently to Christianity. Thompson gave a long and thoughtful reply, which intimated that the Corporation was conscious of the social and, in particular, ethnic dimensions among and between different religious groups in Britain, and treated them accordingly. This was reported as an admission of blunt preferential treatment by some newspapers the following day, and was picked up by the tabloid newspaper, the *Daily Star*, on the following day (no journalist from which had been present at the lecture), and given a front page that read 'BBC BOSS PUTS MUSLIMS BEFORE YOU'.

All news – political, environmental, economic, just as much as religious – is susceptible to re-narration, artificial confrontation and manipulation. Much of this is undoubtedly due to the basic need to sell papers that necessarily prioritises not only the unusual, but also the conflictual and the personal. Just as 'Dog bites man' is not a story but 'Man bites dog' is, so 'Church publishes a report' is not a story whereas 'Church attacks government' might be, and 'Archbishop attacks Prime Minister' usually is. Religion stories are no more immune to the basic pressures of the media world than any other, and we should not imagine that perfect coverage of religion in the media – whatever that might actually entail – is an attainable goal. That acknowledged, it is precisely religious literacy that makes bad reporting or outright manipulation more difficult. The more a journalist, a commentator or their audience knows about and understands religion (or politics or environmental science, etc), the harder it is to engineer media storms, press personal agendas or stage-manage social provocations such as *The Star*'s – or simply to misreport for more basic economic reasons. This is precisely why religious literacy is needed in the media.

Finally, it is vital to acknowledge that better religious literacy does not preclude criticism of religion. Recent research, looking at British press coverage of religion over recent years, has shown that the number of hostile articles has grown considerably (Knott et al, 2013). This is perhaps unsurprising given some of the key events of the last 15 years, as Grace Davie and Diane Moore have pointed out earlier in this book. But religious literacy should ensure that criticism is better informed, researched and evidenced. It ought to enable religions to be better covered, better depicted and better understood by commentators and programme makers, and by those to whom they speak.

References

BBC (2011) *Development of a BBC Diversity Strategy: Summary of responses to public and staff consultations*. Available at: http://downloads.bbc.co.uk/diversity/pdf/diversity_strategy_consultation_report.pdf.

BBC (2013) *2013 Impartiality Review: Breadth of opinion in coverage of religious issues*, London: BBC.

Gill, R. (2011) 'Religion, news and social context: evidence from newspapers', in J. Mitchell and O. Gower, *Religion and the news*. Basingstoke: Ashgate, pp 45-60.

Knott, K., Poole, E. and Taira, T. (2013) *Media portrayals of religion and the secular sacred: Representation and change*, Farnham, Surrey: Ashgate.

Mayes, I. (2005) 'Open door: the readers' editor on ... a charge that the paper is no longer secular', *Guardian*. Available at: http://www.theguardian.com/world/2005/dec/05/religion.commentanddebate.

Quinn, B. (2013) 'Britain's religious right is on the rise: recent opposition to abortion and same-sex marriage suggests a Christian, socially conservative bloc is a very real presence', *Guardian*. Available at: http://www.theguardian.com/commentisfree/2013/feb/01/britain-religious-right-on-rise.

Walton, A. (2011) *Is there a 'religious right' emerging in Britain?*, London: Theos.

Williams, R. (2008) 'Civil and religious law in England: a religious perspective'. Available at http://rowanwilliams.archbishopofcanterbury.org/articles.php/1137/archbishops-lecture-civil-and-religious-law-in-england-a-religious-perspective

THIRTEEN

Religious literacy and chaplaincy

Jeremy Clines with Sophie Gilliat-Ray

Introduction

For chaplaincies to succeed in becoming more religiously literate, this requires some self-understanding about the history of their development, and also the ways chaplaincy can, by default, operate *without* being religiously literate. Developing religious literacy within the chaplaincy and collaborating with others in an organisation can improve the way a setting – whether educational, healthcare, military or penal – can be responsive to the breadth of religion and belief identities of its constituents.

Chaplaincies across many sectors, typically, are wanted (by the institution and by at least some of its constituents) to be places that are religiously plural and accommodating to all faiths and none. This common assumption goes with the territory of most chaplaincies, which are based within organisations that are usually without a religious foundation. Some chaplaincies within a religious foundation, for example, certain church school chaplaincies, may be a typical – but not universal – exception, since religious pluralism in society has an impact on admissions and appointments in nearly all settings. Despite this, there are many ways in which provision across the different sectors is heavily inflected – perhaps even determined – by the history of Christian provision and the accompanying resources and models for how to organise spiritual services and pastoral care.

An initial pair of obstacles that impede any development of religious literacy in chaplaincies is the need for two key shifts: one in the chaplaincy's self-understanding, and a second in the institution's understanding of its chaplaincy. In many contexts there is a mutual acceptance between chaplaincy and organisation (however reluctant) that the chaplaincy becomes an isolated repository of 'religion', rather than serving a purpose to integrate religion and belief identities into the complexities of institutional life.

This chapter outlines how chaplaincies have been established, and then explains their sizes and shapes. It continues by exploring both the needs and the risks chaplaincies face in becoming more religiously literate with and for the organisations where they are based.

The second and main part of this chapter is an exploration of four key challenges that chaplaincies that want to be more religiously literate are likely to face. These are:

- Uses of religious diversity as a catalyst for faith development, considering how successful or not this is as a method for change.
- How chaplaincies can be responsive to people of many religion and belief identities and none; and yet how chaplaincies must also be part of a wider organisational response.
- Inequalities within religious and multifaith spaces; many organisations and their chaplaincies have such spaces, but equality cannot be achieved by space alone.
- The imbalance between 'multifaith' aspirations and Christian-funded chaplaincies: rather than providing alternatives, the complexity of this reality is identified and mapped.

In the third and final section of the chapter, further suggestions are made about methods for chaplaincies seeking to become more religiously literate.

How and where chaplaincies have been established

The formation of prisons, military units and hospitals as state institutions has, in most cases, included a requirement for a chapel and chaplain. In the more independent setting of higher education institutions (HEIs), whether a chapel and chaplain were requisite depended on the foundation and purpose of the organisation. In British HEIs, the armed service, prisons and hospitals historically, it would be a minister of the state church (England, Wales or Scotland) who was appointed (unless the place was founded by a different Christian denomination). Most of these chaplaincies became ecumenical in provision before they became multifaith, although this depends in part on the time at which a chaplaincy was established.

As with higher education (HE), schools have followed a similar route. In the case of other chaplaincies, such as airports, the railways, shopping centres and city centres, emergency services and in sport or other specialist contexts, provision is dependent on the choices made by the organisation. If there was no specific religious foundation to the chaplaincy provision, most chaplaincies will have been established as Christian provision, and in these more contemporary settings, it is more common that ecumenical arrangements occurred from the outset.

Existing shapes, sizes and models of chaplaincy

Many salaried chaplains are funded in one of four ways: by the state church; by another religious group or denomination; in conjunction with the organisation where they serve; or solely by the institution.

Most of these salaried posts have been Christian. Consequently chaplaincy has often followed a Christian model, by default, until recent times, and still does in many contexts. Where a Christian model remains, even one person can be the person who is both chaplain and chaplaincy department for the whole place (Oxford and Cambridge colleges, smaller hospices and military units are all examples of places where a chaplaincy is, in effect, one chaplain).

Where the size of organisation is larger, chaplaincies have broadened, initially, to represent different Christian denominations, with chaplains and other staff being appointed (salaried or voluntary) to serve different types of Christian belief. Where religious pluralism has influenced the development of a chaplaincy, representatives, nearly always from some or all of the world religions and from other belief positions, are part of what is typically called a 'multifaith' team of staff, some of whom may be called chaplains or faith advisers.

Along with the staffing structures of chaplaincies, spaces for prayer and worship are often built by the organisation (sometimes with assistance from external religious groups). Historically these would have been Christian chapels; more recently multifaith spaces and Muslim prayer rooms and rooms set apart for quiet and reflection all appear. These are sometimes part of a chaplaincy's domain or the chaplaincy is involved with them by using them or having some oversight for how the spaces are managed.

The need for religiously literate chaplaincies

Any change in existing provision that improves an institution's religious literacy is going to need to involve an organisation's chaplaincy. Additionally, any change will depend on a deepening sophistication in the religious literacy of the chaplaincy itself. Recent 'Religion and Belief' legislation (Religious Literacy Leadership in Higher Education, 2011) means that in the future, institutions and their chaplaincies will need to be responsive, not just to 'all faiths and none', but rather, to be attentive to a range of religion or belief identities, where and when reasonable needs and requests arise (or are anticipated). What legally constitutes a 'Religion and Belief' identity has been demonstrated to include, for instance, a person who holds deeply held views on environmentalism (McVeigh, 2009).

This change means that however inclusive a chaplaincy is in providing a service for everyone, the organisation and chaplaincy must reflect on the equality of its provision not just for some, but most (if not all). How a chaplaincy is responsive has to intersect with the way an organisation responds to the intersections between 'Religion and Belief' and other matters of equality included in law (such as gender, disability, sexuality, race and ethnicity).

In this chapter ideas are presented, both for chaplaincy teams and organisational leaders, which can help a movement towards a more religiously literate chaplaincy, that is, a chaplaincy that recognises and responds to the pluralities of religions and beliefs present where it is situated. A religiously literate chaplaincy will also recognise its own limitations, because those working within it will have a committed faith position, may well have something distinctive to offer rather than being all-inclusive, and the chaplaincy alone cannot be responsive to all needs. Thus, the challenge is for chaplaincy and its organisation to develop a new range of responses to 'Religion and Belief' identities.

Risks

Chaplaincies face multiple challenges – with their manifold forms and functions – in maintaining current provision as well as achieving change, not just within their own service, but also with and on behalf of the organisation they serve. These are discussed in depth in a report commissioned by the Church of England (Clines, 2008) and summarised here. Some meta-challenges are: the organisation's resistance to change; the funders of chaplaincies resistance to change; an increased risk of accentuating inequality of existing provision; and pressure on chaplaincy staff leading to an inability to change.

These resistors occur, even when both an institution and those staffing a chaplaincy are committed to being inclusive of an even broader range of identities. A principle difficulty is the mismatch between what can be resourced, the pluralistic sensibilities of an institution, and a chaplaincy's automatic commitment to giving space to distinctive expressions of a variety of singular faith, religious and belief positions.

Weighing up the risks involved leads to a further inhibitor of change: the risk of an organisation being drawn towards making the bare minimum of provision as the only way of being equally responsive to religion and belief identities (so as to make sure there is no inequality in provision). The incentives to lead a 'secular or neutral' organisation may be compelling (Dinham and Jones, 2010, p 18).

There are, however, disadvantages of diminishing an organisation's responsiveness to the spiritual, pastoral and belief needs of its members; these are best articulated by naming the benefits of doing more rather than less. These include: being attentive to the interests of an organisation's members demonstrates a more holistic attitude; supporting and understanding members improves organisational resilience; being religiously literate helps towards an organisation's 'quality enhancement'; promoting healthy 'work–life balance' includes esteeming full identities; community engagement is stronger when religion and belief are understood; and equalities legislation encourages a fuller attentiveness to the wide range of religion and belief identities.

Succeeding with such an endeavour is bound to have to include dialogue and the fostering of mutual understanding. This will, in consequence, establish a different kind of institutional culture that will need the efforts of the chaplaincy, but always in conjunction with others. Because chaplaincies are likely, in many contexts, to be called on to act as significant, if not principal, agents to bring about change, a range of challenges must be examined.

Four challenges for improving religious literacy in chaplaincy

Using religious diversity as a catalyst for chaplaincy development

For the longest period, when there were only Christian chaplains, chaplaincy development took shape in the mutuality that is expressed between an organisation and its Christian minister. Religious diversity has provided a catalyst for much greater change, but this has not always led to a deepening of religious literacy by chaplaincy staff or organisation. As this section demonstrates – with the example of the assimilation of Muslim chaplains into Christian chaplaincies – there is variance in how much a chaplaincy changes to accommodate different beliefs compared to how much those of different beliefs must self-adjust to fit into the existing chaplaincy context.

Christian chaplains have, over many centuries, understood their pastoral work as a basic tenet of a place's raison d'être because so many hospitals, prisons, schools and colleges required a chaplain as part of their foundation. The 'cure of souls' is a principle – although not a universal concept among Christian denominations – that carries, in its meaning, some of the common understandings that Christian ministers have a responsibility to all people in their care, not just the Christians. This means that, previously, pastoral care for everyone was guaranteed from one source, however partisan, whereas a more religiously literate response would be aware that people may want support from a source akin to their own beliefs rather than standing over and against the person's identity.

In contrast, there is no tradition of institutionalised chaplaincy in other faith and belief traditions. Although there is an implicit theology that supports and encourages what might be called 'pastoral care', neither of the other 'Abrahamic' faiths, Judaism and Islam, have followed the same trajectory of developing a professional ministry in which the pastoral role is central. Similarly, the myriad religious specialists within the Indian religious traditions do not incorporate an explicit pastoral focus in their work in a way that equates to the 'chaplaincy' role. Meanwhile, the findings of the 2011 Census show that the number of people who describe themselves as having 'no religion' continues to increase (approximately a quarter of the population in England and Wales, that is, 14.1 million), and recent decades have seen the emergence of 'humanist' chaplains who offer spiritual support to people with non-religious world views. Set against this background, the emergence of professional Buddhist, Jewish, Muslim, Hindu or Humanist chaplains in Britain today is clearly a relatively novel development, both for British society, as well as for many faith and belief traditions themselves. It is a development that indicates the way in which other faith traditions and world views can become embedded within, and can contribute to, public life and human flourishing in new contexts.

However, this raises the question as to how (if at all) Christian models of chaplaincy have informed different faith and belief communities in developing *their* own provision. To what extent have they been influenced by the centuries of Christian tradition that have shaped the chaplaincy profession? This section considers these questions in more depth, and with particular consideration of the emerging role of Muslim chaplains in Britain, which was the subject of a research project from 2008 to 2011, the findings of which are given in greater depth in Gilliat-Ray et al (2013). The research team carried out extensive qualitative research, including shadowing chaplains, and holding focus groups. They also interviewed 65 Muslim chaplains (around 15 per cent of the total number), both male and female, from a range of sectors, including full-time, part-time, sessional and voluntary staff.

This focus on Muslim chaplains derives from the fact that they now constitute a sufficient critical mass (approximately 450 in Britain today, including part-timers and volunteers), and they serve the second largest religious group in the UK after Christians. They are increasingly serving as full-time chaplains and managers of chaplaincy services, and in achieving these senior roles, they have often had to navigate their way through a distinctive set of historical and institutional assumptions about chaplaincy itself.

Before examining some of the distinctive ways in which Muslim chaplains have been influenced by Christian models of pastoral care, largely through the influence of Christian chaplains with whom they work, it is worth noting that there are particular challenges faced by chaplains from minority faith and belief traditions.

First, the relative novelty of their roles means that there is often significant educative work to be done, to inform prison, hospital or university staff about the particular religious or spiritual needs of their clients. In an interview with Reverend Michael Binstock, Director of Jewish Prison Chaplaincy for The United Synagogue in London (see www.theus.org.uk), he describes some of the ways in which prisons accommodate the needs of Jewish prisoners:

> For example, I was once informed that a female prisoner had requested permission to light candles for Shabbat but this presented concerns about health and safety in the cell. I advised that the prisoner should be escorted to the multifaith room each week to perform the lighting there under supervision. This was granted. In Wandsworth, we were permitted to supply a pop-up sukkah for a Chasidic prisoner and each day of the festival, he was escorted to the grounds so that he could eat one meal per day and thus fulfil the mitzvah. He was also given a room so that he could blow the shofar on Rosh Hashanah for himself and other Jews on his wing. Yet another Jewish prisoner coming towards the end of his sentence in an open prison was permitted to walk to Shul each week for Shabbat services. (The United Synagogue, 2012)

This short extract contains a range of religious terms that would be unfamiliar to many prison officers. Thus, many chaplains from minority traditions will often find themselves acting as 'translators' and educators in relation to the meaning of a new religious vocabulary. Although Census data indicates that the number of people identifying as 'Christian' is falling in the UK, nevertheless, there is a likely to be a degree of latent understanding of some Christian traditions (if not beliefs and doctrines) in public life more broadly. For example, Christmas and Easter, and the manger, carols and the cross might be recognisable symbols or expressions for many. Consequently, Christian chaplains probably need to spend less time engaged in this kind of religious education compared to their non-Christian counterparts.

Second, many minority faith chaplains have to be willing and able to provide religious and pastoral care to clients from a range of 'traditions' and perspectives *within* their faith community. Although many Christian chaplains, regardless of denomination, are also expected to provide pastoral care to people of 'all faiths and none' (a phrase that is now woven into the fabric of discourse about religion in public life), nonetheless, there are well-established structures and personnel able to provide religious support for the distinctive needs of denominations such as Roman Catholic, Free Church or Pentecostal Church clients. In contrast, the diverse practices and world views within other major minority faith traditions (with the exception of different Jewish traditions) usually have to be accommodated via a single individual. A good example of this can be found on the website of 'Angulimala, the Buddhist Prison Chaplaincy', founded in 1985. Those with an interest in serving as a Buddhist chaplain:

> … must have knowledge of Buddhist schools other than the one to which he or she belongs and be willing to help and encourage interest in and practice of those schools when required. (Angulimala, nd)

The relative novelty and infancy of chaplaincy within other major religious traditions is such that we are yet to see internal diversity reflected within religious and pastoral care provision: 'one size fits all' in most cases. This situation is unlikely to be sustained, however. During the 'Muslim Chaplaincy' project at Cardiff University, the project began to receive inquiries from solicitors representing Shi'a clients who felt that their particular religious practices were not sufficiently supported by Sunni chaplains. Meanwhile, the Prison Service Chaplaincy was simultaneously taking steps to ensure greater diversity among its Muslim chaplaincy provision (including encouragement to Shi'a organisations to develop chaplaincy skills among its clerics).

A third issue that has challenged the development of minority faith chaplaincy is the question of 'what counts' in terms of qualifications, and 'who decides' the validity of those qualifications or experiences that might indicate competence to undertake chaplaincy work. The development of Christian chaplaincy has emerged in relation to the structures of authority and hierarchy within the Christian churches. In contrast, minority faith chaplaincy has developed without reference to a 'sending church', or an authorising religious figure (for example, an individual equating to a bishop). Public institutions in Britain are familiar with the idea that chaplains have usually undertaken a Bachelor's degree in Theology as part of ordination training, and this qualification, validated by a recognised university and subject to formal quality control processes, guarantees minimum educational standards (Gilliat-Ray, 2001). Furthermore, many degree programmes that lead to Christian ordination and ministry include a pastoral placement of some kind (for example, working in a prison chaplaincy). Currently, few minority faith traditions (again, with the exception of British Jews) have acquired validation of their professional religious educational programmes in the UK, and de-centralised systems of authority and governance often raise questions about who is best placed to 'authorise' a prospective chaplain.

Despite these educational and structural challenges, chaplains from minority faiths and beliefs have become embedded within the religious and spiritual care provision of many large publicly funded institutions in Britain. The extent of their presence and incorporation is often a reflection of local religious demographics and infrastructures. This means that in some large towns and cities with well-established and diverse religious communities, chaplains from these various traditions may have acquired over 15 years of experience as professional chaplains. Among this growing community of non-Christian chaplains we can begin to see some of the ways in which the influence of Christian models of pastoral care and practice intersect with systems of faith and belief derived from other traditions.

This is perhaps clearest among experienced Muslim chaplains, who now constitute the largest 'minority' within professional chaplaincy work. In the Cardiff University research, we saw how Muslim chaplains have been susceptible to influences from beyond the Islamic tradition. For example, irrespective of sector, many have learned a new set of attitudes as a result of their experiences. While they often tend to start with normative, didactic approaches that are directed towards their co-religionists, their experiences of working with all kinds of people in a multifaith environment seems to inculcate within them attitudes of

245

empathy, person-centeredness, equality, broad-mindedness, openness, approachability, supportiveness, tolerance, non-judgementalism, non-directiveness, compassion, patience and humility. This short interview extract is a particularly good illustration of a narrative that we heard from numerous chaplains.

> Interviewer: To what extent do you feel that your practice of chaplaincy has changed over time?
>
> Chaplain: I think 100 per cent. I think when I graduated as an 'alim [Islamic scholar] I had never thought that this is the kind of work I would be doing ... that I would be sitting down with the Christian colleagues or Buddhist. I think that I've learnt [...] that it's been a lost identity of Islam of how to work with other faiths and other people. And so, I have over a period of time changed by values, my values have changed, code of ethics has changed, my behaviour patterns has changed to accommodate and facilitate this secular organisation ... how you need to be working in that organisation as an effective imam [full-time male prison chaplain]. (Gilliat-Ray et al, 2013, p 176)

Along with these kinds of changes has come an adoption of counselling and listening techniques that are already commonplace in Christian pastoral care (Pattison, 2000). This is challenging because in most Muslim communities over the course of history, 'pastoral care' has consisted of people fulfilling clear Islamic obligations towards their immediate and extended family members. A real innovation in Islamic chaplaincy practice – which mimics Christian pastoral care traditions – is the visiting of complete strangers, and, once there at the bedside or in the cell, offering non-judgemental listening. But Muslim chaplains have also been influenced by their Christian colleagues in more subtle ways – the carrying and use of 'prayer cards' at the bedside of a hospital patient being one example. We met several Muslim chaplains who had created small laminated pocket-sized 'cards' carrying words of comfort deriving from Islamic sources that they could give to patients as a 'gift' ... not the kind of artefact that an imam would typically carry.

Perhaps one slightly unexpected aspect of chaplaincy practice is that it deepens some chaplains' sense of being a Muslim. As one prison chaplain told us: "working in an environment like this makes you value your Islam". The multifaith environment makes chaplains very aware of what it means to have a distinctive Islamic identity, helping them to see Islam, as it were, from the outside. They also learn the potential for establishing common cause with chaplains of other faiths, and the value of cooperative working as fellow religious professionals.

The changes experienced by Muslim chaplains shows that the shift to religiously pluralistic chaplaincies does not automatically guarantee religiously literacy within any particular chaplaincy, or within the host organisation. The findings may indicate that a Muslim chaplain assimilates themselves into the existing provision, more than the chaplaincy changes to accommodate its new plurality.

How chaplaincies can be responsive to people of many religion and belief identities and none

Organisations and their chaplaincies that are developing their religious literacy to be more responsive are well aware of two traditional approaches that require transformation: chaplaincies as repositories of religion on behalf of the organisation; and the organisation as remaining relatively neutral about religion for much of the time (with exceptions for certain religious festivals, especially Christmas).

Neither of these approaches is without merit, but they are only starting points to improve on. Chaplaincy has worked best where it is understood by its institution as a place that can offer resources, training and advice, where the chaplaincy is seen as a department that collaborates with a variety of areas within the organisation to shape policy and practice (as well as providing a specialised support service). There are a variety of ways an organisation may want to find answers, create policy and respond specifically, to a range of religion and belief needs, both in planning and in reaction to issues that arise.

Whether the chaplaincy is the best place for an institution to guarantee a responsiveness, for example, to the legal requirements of equalities legislation depends partly on how well equipped the chaplaincy is, and who else in the organisation has oversight for equality, diversity and inclusion. It must also require an honest assessment of how possible it may be for a chaplaincy, especially when heavily populated by Christian staff, to respond to questions of equalities, religion and belief in a unilateral way within an organisation. It is also incumbent on the organisation to recognise that multilateral responses to equalities, including religion and belief, can be a catalyst for both collaborative practice and an improved environment.

Quite who is included and excluded within a chaplaincy setting has its roots in the dynamics of who chooses. As Gilliat-Ray's study of the way belief positions were included at the Millennium Dome observes, this was dependent not on inclusive, but rather on excluding criteria:

> [Although some of the] ... strongest religious currents in society today flow outside any easily identifiable faith. (Arthur, 2000, p 11, cited in Gilliat-Ray, 2004, p 474)

What has more typically happened in the shaping of a chaplaincy and organisational response to religion and belief is that:

> ... what "counts" as religion in public life, and the extent to which particular faiths are visible (or not) depends upon criteria which can do more to *exclude* than include. These criteria are rarely subject to critical evaluation because they are part of a taken-for-granted *modus operandi* that is implicit and assumed to be unproblematic. (Gilliat-Ray, 2004, p 469)

Historically, where an organisation has wanted a chaplaincy to do the work, on its behalf, to develop a response to religion and belief issues, Christian perspectives are likely to have been normative, simply by being dominant. Places with Jewish chaplaincy and more recently Muslim chaplaincy have enabled a change in perspective on how chaplaincy itself is done and perhaps, in the future, will have more influence on responsiveness to a variety of belief identities becoming 'more critical of some of the models and assumptions that it has ingested from outside itself' (Gilliat-Ray et al, 2013, p 173).

New thinking is required about how to be responsive to the religious and belief identities of an organisation's constituents. New structures are needed too, that do not give primacy to those who have an explicit rather than an implicit spiritual identity. The challenge, Pattison argues, is one of 'equality and justice (Pattison, 2013, p 200). Pattison, in mapping this out in relation to a health-care setting, argues that:

> ... the ordinary but only implicitly "spiritual" person is less likely to have their needs identified and met, eg, by chaplains and health care staff, than the overtly religious person? (Pattison, 2013, p 200)

Chaplaincies are more than likely to want their spiritual care to be something that is useful to and ordinarily accessed by people who do not understand themselves as explicitly belonging to a specific and singular religion. To be responsive, however, will mean gaining new levels of insight that can be offered by the implicitly spiritual to those running chaplaincies. This would result in those who are implicitly spiritual being provided with a better service, largely, although not entirely, from an explicitly Christian standpoint.

One area where progress has been made is the relatively recent resituating of some chaplaincies within the health and wellbeing framework. This allows a more obvious opportunity for collaboration between religious and non-religious practitioners to support and promote a holistic programme of support. This change alone, however, can obscure the need for a much wider wholesale shift in attentiveness to different belief identities by both organisation and chaplaincy.

Religion specific and multifaith spaces

Many institutions that are reluctant to fund faith-specific roles within their staff teams may more readily construct physical spaces that are provided to meet the needs of those practicing a religion. Historically these have tended to be religion-specific and most usually a Christian chapel aligned with a particular denomination of the church. These constructed spaces are provided for the convenience of those present in the environment (and in some contexts, to enhance the experience or to express a purpose of the organisation). More recently there has been a large increase in the number of multifaith spaces: 1,500 such places already exist in Britain (Crompton, 2013, p 475).

Similarly to the challenges outlined in the previous section, multifaith space is, typically most useful to those with the most explicit religious identity and requirements. In the last 20 years both multifaith space and prayer rooms for the purpose of Islamic prayer have been built. This change has been documented in an example from HE, Clines' report on chaplaincy in HE (2008, pp 15-17), where 35 per cent of HEI chaplaincies reported both at least one Christian chapel and one Muslim prayer room. This heavily outnumbered those with just a Christian chapel (5 per cent). Fifty-one per cent had at least one Christian chapel, 57 per cent at least one quiet or multifaith space, and 65 per cent had at least one Muslim prayer room. Those with two or three types of space made up 65 per cent of all HEIs; only three institutions had nothing at all by way of prayer room, quiet space or chapel (Clines, 2008, p 18).

Although Clines recommends that consultation is a useful first step in developing spaces that are attentive to an 'equivalence of provision for adherents of different religions' (2008, p 29), it is clear this will not result in consensus, which is 'unrealistic' (Clines, 2008, p 31).

Clines argues that there are other ways to respond more evenly to the breadth of religious and belief identities within an organisation than by diversity of chaplaincy staff and provision of space, with many finding 'their identity is respected and affirmed through having their needs met' (Clines, 2008, p 20), with different groups having 'differing levels of need and aspiration for some of the following':

- social space
- appropriate living accommodation
- prayer facilities
- sacred spaces and places to store religious symbols and writings
- facilitated opportunities to meet people from their own religion
- an active interest in the individual
- a willingness to enter into dialogue
- an emphasis on the people, not on places. (Clines, 2008, p 29)

Where these topics are given attention, this means there is a multifaceted response to religion and belief identities that leads to a higher likelihood of establishing a successful equivalence. Where the primary focus, apart from staffing, is spaces for prayer, problems will be perpetuated by: the disparate kinds of need; the risks of providing something that isn't fair; and mixed messages that such spaces communicate.

There are multiple risks in establishing any specific spaces for people's religion or belief activities. First, the physical structure or room established may be fit only for a limited range of purposes. It can build in bias (and at times, obsolescence). Second, it gives primacy to groups of people whose religion or belief will be advantaged by design (while others will be disadvantaged). Third is the risk that such spaces serve as a convenient way for an organisation to believe they have 'done' their 'religious duty' by making provision. Finally, this can result in a siphoning-off of religious expression within an organisation into both a 'safe space' but also a 'hidden corner' that is removed from the more 'secular' notions of what an organisation is truly about.

There is evidence, too, of some positive outcomes of establishing such spaces, especially when they are left undescribed, and made available for the purposes of all-comers. Such places may, at best, become spaces to be 'politically and spiritually "appropriate" in a society of religious diversity [...] and for individuals whose personal journey might also reflect the religious diversity of society' (Gilliat-Ray, 2005b, p 364).

Gilliat-Ray also shows how many such spaces, such as the Prayer Space at the Millennium Dome, became not the preserve of religious professionals, or even religious adherents, but attractive for 'those people in society who might embody the Heelas/Woodhead shift from "religion" to "spirituality"' (Heelas, 2002, cited initially in Gilliat-Ray, 2005b, p 363, and subsequently, 2005b, p 365). These 'usually "unsupervised" sacred spaces' become, instead, places where 'users of the space largely mediate their own experience rather than rely upon a religious professional to do it for them' (Gilliat-Ray, 2005b, p 365). Such spaces are sacralised in a way that is very different to how a place of worship is set apart. Unlike places of worship, sacred spaces in non-religious public institutions 'can still be considered "sacred" on account of the rituals and activities that take place within them' (Gilliat-Ray, 2005b, p 368).

Even so, when places that are apparently for all-comers are established, with sacralising patterns that come not from a religious group but from the organisation that establishes the space, 'Christian churches' try to 'assert and maintain some sense of ownership over sacred space, even where the space might be called a "Prayer Room"' and even 'where it has been newly produced, rather than adapted from a Christian Chapel' (Gilliat-Ray, 2005a, p 298). When there is a conversion of a Christian space to a multifaith space, some chaplains and 'possibly others, will struggle to find ways of resisting that process, perhaps by retaining, for example, a central table, with a cloth over it – in other words, an altar of some kind, in all but name [...] there are almost inevitably "winners" and "losers" in the process' (Gilliat-Ray, 2005a, p 303).

A religiously literate organisation would want to take a look at the spaces it has created for religious needs, consider who is managing them, and what belief identities they are communicating as being most aligned with. It is not that chaplaincies are the natural obstacle to enabling such spaces to be used equally, but there can be challenges to overcome from chaplaincies that might experience 'outright resistance, wearied resignation, obedient compliance, to wholehearted enthusiasm' (Beckford and Gilliat, 1996, quoted in Gilliat-Ray, 2005a, p 303).

Neither is it that removing responsibility for such spaces from a chaplaincy helps, since multifaith spaces 'represent a new form of socio-material configuration' (Hewson and Brand, 2011, p 4). Part of the ironic comedy of creating blank canvasses for religious and non-religious activities is that they are architecturally puzzling (Crompton, 2013, p 491). Crompton explains that the oddness of making such non-spaces reflects a mode not dissimilar to the 'theatre of the absurd' genre, epitomised and established by Samuel Beckett in 'Waiting for Godot' (premiered in 1953), where the play's duration explores a nowhere place, inhabited by some very lost and confused people waiting for what they don't know, except the name is 'Godot', and never finding it. Creating a place that is no particular place results, Crompton argues, in an:

> ... architecture [that] has caught up with Samuel Beckett. Inside a windowless multifaith room we are in limbo, like the non-place where the action of a Beckett play occurs. (Crompton, 2013, p 492)

The imbalance between the 'multifaith' aspirations and Christian majority-funded chaplaincies

In many settings, chaplaincies that were established as places of Christian ministry within an organisation are still in many regards primarily and predominantly Christian, even where faith advisers and multifaith spaces have been set up for the use of many. In a society where the largest religious grouping is Christian, as in Britain, there are some justifications for some weighting towards Christianity within an evenly established service. Even more significant than this is the resource that the Christian churches have historically offered to such work, where voluntary or externally funded assistance is appreciated and welcomed.

In Clines' report (2008), the weight of numbers of Christians serving in the 102 chaplaincies included in the survey (2008, p 5), is overwhelming, '78% of all religious appointments to chaplaincies are Christian', then it is Muslim and Jewish appointments (both 6 per cent), and fourth, 'posts where religion is not role related (5%) [...] such as administrators, cleaners and gardeners' (Clines, 2008, p 13). As to full-time salaried staff, 95 per cent have a Christian role (usually as a chaplain or chaplaincy assistant), whereas of the voluntary staff, '66% (245) are Christian, 33% (124) represent religions other than Christianity, 1% (2) are where religion is not role related, and less than 1% (1) is a post where the person's religion is not stated' (Clines, 2008, p 13).

When all contributions to multifaith chaplaincies are taken into account, at least in HEIs, the scope of the work and representation of people of different religions and beliefs remains unrepresentative of society.

Even where there is a higher proportion of those serving in chaplaincy who are not Christian, there have been many obstacles to those coming in part time and voluntarily when entering an inherently

Christian chaplaincy environment, and an organisation that is not automatically hospitable to religious identities that had previously been left out. Many of those working in Muslim chaplaincy in prisons have 'suffered the consequences of direct and indirect exclusion because of the financial, structural and procedural life of their institutions' (Gilliat-Ray et al, 2013, pp 100-1).

Conclusions

Organisations and chaplaincies are challenged to take a more even-handed approach to the breadth of religion and belief identities they could be responsive to. Greater sharing of a chaplaincy's responsibility for religion with its wider institution is an important challenge. Religious literacy needs to result in an improved 'service level' (a guaranteed provision of service) for a much wider range of people. Clines emphasises that this will succeed where institutions and chaplaincies comprehend a 'dynamic equivalence' (2008, p 29) between different needs, a level which 'translates into something similar' rather than something identical for the next group or person. In 2008, Clines, speaking of HEIs, argued that this 'is a challenge that is yet to be met in nearly every' setting, but that places which 'model such strategies will gain more than advantage in the sector. They will have ensured that their response relates to identified or anticipated needs rather than being based on assumption' (Clines, 2008, p 29).

Improving chaplaincies and their organisation's religious literacy

Improving chaplaincies in relation to religious literacy requires a more attentive deconstruction and reconstruction of chaplaincy identities that recognises the unevenness of funding provision and how the history of support for such services has affected its delivery. Additionally, when a chaplaincy does enable, or contribute, to improved religious literacy in an organisation, this provides a two-way flow of benefits between chaplaincy and organisation in terms of a new type of strategic engagement for the organisation and a deeper level of strategic engagement for the chaplaincy.

Organisations need to understand the case for supporting religion and belief identity, through chaplaincy, and vice versa, the role of the chaplaincy as one actor among others in any organisational context. Chaplaincies work for religious literacy least when they are the 'go to' focus for anything thought 'religious'. Also, those of different faiths, beliefs and non-beliefs need, themselves, to generate much more fluid ideas of chaplaincy if they are to engage better with the real religious landscape in Britain which is simultaneously Christian, plural and secular.

Explaining change

For a chaplaincy to succeed with newly introduced and positive shifts, some clear explanation of change is needed that can be articulated in a way that both the institution and chaplaincy practitioners can understand. This will include:

- how a chaplaincy can explain what it is not providing;
- how an organisation can see chaplaincy as part of its response to religion and belief;
- how equality, diversity and inclusion teams and chaplaincies can, by working together, be of mutual benefit;
- how a more flexible and lightweight physical structure and/or setting can enable a greater responsiveness to presenting needs within an organisation.

Chaplaincies as a religious literacy catalyst and helper

Religious literacy presents chaplaincies with three challenges. First, there is a challenge to seek to be inclusive rather differently than simply having a 'cure of souls' from a single Christian perspective. Second, there is a range of new opportunities to present chaplaincy not simply as a repository of knowledge, advice and religiousness from which comes pastoral care, but rather a place that seeks to support, investigate and resource both individuals and organisations in a quest for a fuller understanding of human identities. Third, there is the issue of chaplaincies having the ability to move from the margins to the centre of an organisation's purpose by providing both expertise and practical skills in shaping a holistic environment that promotes the wellbeing of everyone. Alongside this is the challenge to organisations more widely to take responsibility for religion and belief alongside their chaplaincies, rather than leaving them to it and/or sending all the 'religion' issues that way when they arise. A really religiously literate organisation would work with its chaplaincy to take responsibility for such issues in a way that is broadly owned.

References

Angulimala, the Buddhist Prison Chaplaincy (nd) 'Buddhist prison chaplain – job description (www.angulimala.org.uk).

Arthur, C. (2000), 'Exhibiting the Sacred', in C. Paine (ed), *Godly things: Museums, objects and religion*, Leicester: Leicester University Press.

Clines, J.M.S. (2008) *Faiths in higher education chaplaincy*, London: Church of England Board of Education.

Beckford, J.A. and Gilliat, S. (1996) *The Church of England and other faiths in a multi-faith society. Report to the Leverhulme Trust*, Warwick: University of Warwick.

Crompton, A. (2013) 'The architecture of multifaith spaces: God leaves the building', *The Journal of Architecture*, vol 18, no 4, pp 474-96.

Dinham, A. and Jones, S.H. (2010) *Religious Literacy Leadership in Higher Education: An analysis of challenges of religious faith, and resources for meeting them, for university leaders*, York: Religious Literacy Leadership in Higher Education Programme.

Gilliat-Ray, S. (2001) 'The fate of the Anglican clergy and the class of '97: some implications of the changing sociological profile of ordinands', *Journal of Contemporary Religion*, vol 16, no 2, pp 209-25.

Gilliat-Ray, S. (2004) 'The trouble with "inclusion": a case study of the faith zone at the Millennium Dome', *Sociological Review*, vol 52, no 4, pp 459–77.

Gilliat-Ray, S. (2005a) 'From "chapel" to "prayer room": the production, use, and politics of sacred space in public institutions', *Culture and Religion*, vol 6, no 2, July.

Gilliat-Ray, S. (2005b) '"Sacralising" sacred space in public institutions: a case study of the prayer space at the Millennium Dome', *Journal of Contemporary Religion*, vol 20, no 3, pp 357-72.

Gilliat-Ray, S., Ali, M.M. and Pattison, S. (2013) *Understanding Muslim chaplaincy*, Aldershot: Ashgate.

Heelas, P. (2002) 'The spiritual revolution: from "religion" to "spirituality"', in L. Woodhead et al, *Religions in the modern world*, London: Routledge, pp 357-77.

Hewson, C. and Brand, R. (2011) 'Multi-faith space: towards a practice-based assessment', Paper presented at the International RC21 conference, Amsterdam, 9-11 July 2011, Session 14: Religion and Urban Space.

McVeigh, K. (2009) 'Judge rules activist's beliefs on climate change akin to religion', *The Guardian*, 3 November (www.theguardian.com/environment/2009/nov/03/tim-nicholson-climate-change-belief).

Pattison, S. (2000) *A critique of pastoral care*, London: SCM.

Pattison, S. (2013) 'Religion, spirituality and health care: confusions, tensions, opportunities', *Health Care Analysis*, vol 21, no 3, pp 193-207.

Religious Literacy Leadership in Higher Education (2011) 'Religion and Belief: Summary of legal requirements' (www.religiousliteracyhe.org).

United Synagogue, The (2012) 'Interview with Rev Michael Binstock: Director of Jewish Prison Chaplaincy', You & Us (http://youandus.theus.org.uk/chesed/project-chesed/interview-with-rev-michael-binstock-director-of-jewish-prison-chaplaincy).

FOURTEEN

Religious literacies: the future

Matthew Francis and Adam Dinham

The preceding chapters have laid out ways in which religious literacy is pressing, and how it can be, is, or should be, applied in various public settings. What is clear from the outset, are the sheer complexities referred to by the 'religious literacy' idea, and the challenge of pinning it down. It is a fluid notion.

This book also helps us to understand that different cultures, derived from national, institutional and specific sector identities, colour and shape the religious literacy problem, as well as the solutions. How religious literacy is defined is at the heart of the challenge, and this has been a central theme of the book as a whole. It turns out to be an idea that is specific to the contexts in which it plays out. One size will not fit all. In the US, for example, Stephen Prothero and Lauren Kerby (Chapter Four) point to a crisis of religious knowledge defined in relation to a need to understand the nuances and distinctions between Christian theologies that have informed contemporary American culture, whereas in Chapter Six, Adam Dinham makes a call for a religious literacy characterised by the religiously plural marketplace of welfare provision in the UK. And then again, at the institutional and sector level, Jeremy Clines and Sophie Gilliat-Ray (Chapter Thirteen) show how a very specific history of state-church chaplaincies in Britain has led to a peculiarly Anglican model of professional pastoral care, within a variety of faith and non-faith traditions. These examples are echoed throughout the book.

Religious literacy, then, is a stretchy, fluid concept that is variously configured and applied in terms of the context in which it happens. We argue that this is very much how it should be, and as we expected it to be from the settings in which we ourselves have worked to date. Religious literacy is necessarily a non-didactic idea that must be adapted as appropriate to the specific environment, such as those that the chapters in this book have sought to explore and define.

But even allowing for the differences in settings and definitions, there are also clear areas of overlap, where core distinctions and lessons can be drawn out as to what religious literacy is and how it might be applied.

257

These are what make the idea appealing across boundaries. These cores and overlaps render religious literacy a *framework*, to be populated in detail in relation to the context in which it finds itself. In this closing chapter we outline some of those points of consensus, and try to bring in to focus this framework. We want to explore how religious literacy might be defined, developed and applied in the future and in other settings. In this sense this chapter brings the book full circle, to engage, iteratively, with the chapters that contest the idea of religious literacy at the beginning. We hope that the journey is instructive.

A modern problem: plurality and ignorance

As outlined in the opening chapter, building religious literacy in contemporary Western societies is an urgent challenge. Secular assumptions, whereby religion is either assumed to have no relevance to a modern, enlightened age, or is seen as increasingly irrelevant due to diminishing memberships of its formal institutions, have led to people paying less attention to religious debates, and taking less interest in religious knowledge. The resulting gap is problematic, not just because people often lack an understanding, but also because they assume that this deficiency is not an issue. This line of thought can have practical disadvantages across contemporary society, for example, for Muslim students negotiating summer exams during Ramadan, as well as legal ramifications (for example, in the UK, following the Equalities Act 2010). And writing from an Australian perspective, Beth Crisp (Chapter Eleven) shows that, despite policy about social work training requiring some sort of engagement with the spiritual, there remains a serious deficiency in the religious literacy of practitioners and their educators.

Disinterest about religious dimensions of the public realm is another common outcome, and can quickly translate into more interest than is helpful. It has sometimes led to striking problems, as the chapters here have highlighted. For example, Prothero and Kerby point to attacks on Sikhs after the terrorist attacks in the US in 2001. Perpetrators of the violence couldn't distinguish between Sikhs and Muslims, making false assumptions based not just on ethnicity, but also head coverings. They also remember the events surrounding the Branch Dravidian group in Waco, Texas in 1993.

In similar vein, in Chapter Seven Matthew Francis and Amanda van Eck Duymaer van Twist point to how brainwashing and radicalisation became popular terms for the ways in which predominantly religious (and allegedly dangerous) groups were assumed to be accumulating new members – assumptions that led to headlines and even policies that damaged relations between religious communities and the government.

Indeed, several of the chapters show that ill temperedness frequently inflects the conversation. Rebecca Catto and David Perfect (Chapter Eight) develop a point highlighted in the introductory chapter, that religious differences and disagreements tend to produce more heat than light – sometimes in the form of litigation, which is costly and divisive, being used to resolve issues where knowledge and positive engagement are lacking. Their chapter also highlights another important issue, that assumptions of secularity and poor knowledge about religion have come at a time when issues of religion or belief have become far more complex. Despite the positions taken by *Eweida* and *Ladele*, two of the cases Catto and Perfect discuss, it is by no means true, for example, that all Christians feel it is a necessity to wear a cross or crucifix, nor are all Christians morally opposed to same-sex relationships or marriage. Where religious positions were once assumed to be homogeneous and orthodox (although note that, as mentioned by France and van Eck, assumptions of religious homogeneity in the recent past, at least in the UK, are probably over-stated), there is now a very clear sense, as Diane Moore (Chapter Two) puts it, of 'internal diversity' within religious traditions.

This point is echoed throughout. Catto and Perfect refer to the multidimensional nature of religious communities, Francis and van Eck to the complex make-up of religious traditions and Barnes and Smith (Chapter Five) to the innate diversity of factors between believers of similar faiths. These indicate a common point of connection in all the chapters, which sees religious literacy as focused as much, or more, on religion and belief as *identity* than as traditions. Religion and belief are, for all the authors, lived, contested and shifting. They are, in this sense, *real* rather than ideal, and it this reality that religious literacy requires to be understood. Religious literacy therefore thrives in what David Ford and Mike Higton (Chapter Three) call a 'conversational mode', which enters into the experience of religion and belief. At the same time, the approach to such conversational modes differs, so that while for Ford and Higton it is through Theology, for Michael Barnes and Jonathan Smith, it is encounter, and for Stephen Jones (Chapter Ten) and James Conroy (Chapter Nine), it is education.

Of course this diversity isn't limited to religious beliefs, as we acknowledge in the introductory chapter, and this stretches the 'religious literacy' idea still further. Non-religious identities are just as complex, and assumptions that all non- or areligious people conform to a standardised form of atheism is as misleading and damaging as assumptions about Islam or Christianity that ignore centuries of debate, contest and conflict between differing understandings. The recognition of non-religious beliefs in a legal setting, noted by Catto and Perfect, points to a further challenge, salient in all the Anglophone countries discussed in this book, but equally applicable elsewhere. Of course, the increasing religious plurality of societies also further extends the notion of religion that needs to be addressed. Francis and van Eck, while pointing out that religion in the UK was never so homogeneous as is often assumed, also highlight the huge influx of traditions that have either been imported to the West, or the new religious movements that have grown out of, alongside, or in competition with existing faiths. This point is echoed elsewhere, for example, by Jeremy Clines and Sophie Gilliat-Ray, in their discussion of the necessarily multifaith nature of modern chaplaincies, and by Dinham, in the plural nature of religious provision of welfare services, alongside or replacing the previously privileged places of church and state. It isn't just new religious traditions that need to be engaged in contemporary society, but also other belief identities, be they spiritual, areligious or a complex combination of various other beliefs.

This, too, has been recognised in law through cases such as *Grainger v Nicholson* (as indicated by Catto and Perfect), where environmental beliefs were recognised as receiving protection alongside established religious beliefs. The legal dimension, more recently in the UK and Europe, but a longer-standing issue in the US, adds a further need for greater religious literacy. This is demonstrated in the chapter on UK equalities law by Catto and Perfect, as we have seen, but is also evidenced through the impact of legal cases on religious literacy in the US, outlined in Prothero and Kerby. Legal definitions of religion matter, but change over time, as Francis and van Eck highlight in the case of Scientology in the UK. These can be problematic as they sometimes harden religious boundaries and serve to marginalise women or children, for example. While laws are useful and necessary means to legislate against discrimination, the ability to navigate within these laws without recourse to litigation is a useful skill which itself requires greater religious literacy.

A modern solution: understanding and engagement

The way in which Ford and Higton suggest that religious literacy should be applied is one good place to start in considering how this book has developed our sense of what religious literacy is as a solution. Ford and Higton's call for more theology is atypical in the definitions proffered here, and this is a useful reminder that what we are discussing might reasonably be called 'religious literacies', plural.

In our introductory chapter and at the beginning of this chapter, we have highlighted how religious literacy is context-sensitive. What works for British universities might not work for the media, and likewise, what works for British universities based on religious foundations might not work for British, Australian or US universities with secular foundations. Thus, while we will draw out, in the next section, some concrete suggestions about what religious literacy might look like as a practice or a method, it is nevertheless important to recall that these chapters describe specific settings and situations, which allow us to explore the richness of 'religious literacies' through both the differences and similarities of the ideas expressed.

As Moore argues, religious literacy shines a light on the lenses through which religious people engage with the world around them. It highlights the fluid, socially constructed and contested norms of religion, and is reliant on a basic understanding of religious forms of belief to discern the religious dimensions of policy, economics and other aspects of society. Her account is based on a tradition of Religious Studies which recognises, understands and analyses the fluid nature of religious belief, and understands how it is embedded in all aspects of culture, not existing as a separate category with tangential and fleeting connections with other features of modern life. She supports the arguments laid out in Francis and van Eck (Chapter Seven), through her analysis of features of violence, challenging the misleading assumption that extremist religion is a perversion of faith, which itself is an outcome of a religiously illiterate understanding of belief.

Although also arguing from a US perspective, Prothero and Kerby's (Chapter Four) account of religious literacy argues that it is a moral, not an intellectual, accomplishment. This sharp distinction lies in their grounding of religious literacy as a need to re-engage with the Christian values that underpinned the creation of many US institutions and that continue to play a prominent (if often shallow) role in public political discourse. In order to be effective US citizens, religious literacy is needed, they suggest, so that Americans can effectively decode and understand the Christian values of the US, but also develop a deeper understanding of the religious dimensions of world affairs. In light of the former of these two aims, it is not surprising that Prothero and Kerby's religious literacy draws heavily from Christianity, and could be seen as a form of biblical literacy. In this they share a point highlighted in Ford and Higton, that through developing a clearer understanding of one faith tradition (in this case Christianity), it is possible to better understand other faith traditions.

In contrast to Moore, Ford and Higton derive their enthusiasm for religious literacy from a theoretical perspective that might be said to predate religious studies, and which is found within Theology. While Moore draws on the academic study of religion, Ford and Higton work from the academically messier discourse between Theology and Religious Studies, highlighting how the interiority of Theology enriches the exteriority of comparative studies of religion. Religious literacy is more than just learning about religion; it is understanding religious reasoning and engaging with this. This doesn't require religious faith, nor even that faiths cannot be argued against, but does require attention to a discourse developed and sustained by those who believe. The argument is controversial in an age when Theology is under attack by secularists and under pressure in university priorities, but is a clear defence of our claim in the opening chapter that religious literacy enriches a public discourse dominated by rationalist enlightenment thought.

This unabashed connection with religious reasoning and knowledge is further developed by Michael Barnes and Jonathan Smith in Chapter Five. Through their engagement with the concept of *lokahi*, they demonstrate how religious literacy can open up religion (religious thought, practice and communities) as a source of opportunities, rather than as a problem to be managed. The examples they use to explore this aspect of religious literacy are challenging, including the Pakistani Taliban and the interface between the UK police and Islamic communities in the effort to counter terrorism. In these case studies they also draw out important aspects of religious literacy that are also found in other chapters, for example, that religious belief does not guarantee religious literacy, a point made by Jeremy Clines and Sophie Gilliat-Ray in Chapter Thirteen in relation to multifaith chaplaincies, but also made by Barnes and Smith in relation to the Taliban. In this instance, members of the Taliban were encouraged to develop a deeper understanding and engagement with their religious tradition.

Knowledge in this respect was not enough, and Barnes and Smith also highlight this in their case study on UK police, where they demonstrate that a knowledge of diversity was not enough to ensure religious literacy, but also required an engagement with it (a point echoed from a similar example in Francis and van Eck's chapter). While these particular examples were drawn from positive policing at a local level, the need for engagement is no less pressing, if more difficult in practice at the more abstract level of legislation and justice, as shown in Rebecca Catto and David Perfect's chapter.

Catto and Perfect's vision of religious literacy is one of dialogue and accommodation, firmly defined within the legal parameters of British and European equalities law. While the picture of religious literacy that emerges from their analysis of legal cases is one of necessity brought about by complicated and often controversial laws, it nevertheless builds on the theoretical approaches laid out in the earlier chapters in suggesting that it is grounded in knowledge and dialogue. However, the operationalisation of the concept here is more similar to that laid out by Moore than Ford and Higton, with a sociological approach to religious literacy that recognises how it is embedded throughout culture, but where knowledge of religion is learned rather than experienced. While Ford and Higton's account would no doubt lead to a richer interaction between differing world views, Catto and Perfect's is undoubtedly more practical for the legal consideration of workplace settings, which is their focus.

Francis and van Eck continue in this vein, focusing less on experience and more on knowledge. However, where Catto and Perfect stress the need for knowledge about beliefs in order to anticipate and engage with potential workplace issues, Francis and van Eck highlight the need for a better structural understanding of the nature of religion. While most of the chapters reference the internal plurality within religious traditions, Francis and van Eck take pains to emphasise this immense complexity, which highlights the range of conflicts and diverging opinions that can exist within what to outsiders are often assumed to be one single community. The policy implications are spelled out here, as they make clear how power structures can lead to the marginalisation of sections of communities, where they are assumed to be homogeneous. The influence of power structures are also raised as an important reason why religious literacy is needed within Moore's chapter, but this analysis is absent in Ford and Higton's chapter, whose experiential approach necessarily privileges the role of individual voices potentially (although not necessarily) at the expense of an awareness of their interaction with others. This tension between individual and communal beliefs (that is, those articulations of belief that somehow stand for the various versions of them which individuals live) is woven through the chapters focusing on policy. In particular, Catto and Perfect, as well as Francis and van Eck, highlight the necessity of recognising that individual experiences and expressions of religion and belief may be even messier than their communal counterparts. They want religious literacy to enable policy and law to recognise this.

This tension is only really resolved at the level of practice, which the remaining chapters tackle. Education and welfare have traditionally been the two sectors where religion has most actively participated in the past and continues to do so to this day. Conroy's critique of the role of religion within school education demonstrates how a failure to engage with religious history on the one hand, and its truth claims on the other, leaves students ill equipped for a religion-inflected reality. For him, the problem is embedded in an increasingly religiously illiterate culture that is less and less confident to recognise, let alone address, the challenge.

Perhaps more than any other chapter, Jones' demonstrates just how important both the sector and institutional context of religious literacy is, and the differences that can arise between settings. Still within the education sector, Jones draws out the contrasting ways in which different institutions historically and presently deal with religion, with very different outcomes for a space and role for religious literacy. His discussion also draws out the important distinction between religious identity and religious learning. This crucial point echoes explicitly a theme common throughout the book wherein, while religious identity is foregrounded, teaching about religions and beliefs languishes on the margins. This disconnection between demand and supply means that while institutions like universities, and technically the UK (and other countries) as a whole, are becoming more open to religious diversity, they often lack the means through which to practice this openness, leading to and exacerbating tension and conflict.

The concern about teaching about religion in universities often centres on the desire to avoid altering the religious beliefs of students. While many institutions adopt (institutionally and/or at individual levels) an assumption of universities as repositories of secular enlightenment thought, they often recoil at the possibility of religious proselytising. Of course, as all the authors are very clear, there is no reason for religious knowledge, as instruction or experience, to lead to belief. Indeed, such an assumption is ironically an indicator of the irrational fear of religion that is encapsulated within many instances of secular 'rational' thought. Indeed, as Jones suggests, the location of the study of religion within universities is perhaps the best place to ensure that anti-intellectual, equally religiously illiterate, religious ideologies are explored and challenged.

For Dinham, changes in welfare provision since the Second World War have also played a significant role in the decline of religious literacy, in the UK at least. As churches have become disconnected from their role as local welfare providers, so the general population has lost the language of faith that connected worship on Sundays with other days of the week. His focus on the withdrawal, primarily of the Church of England, from the civil sphere in this regard is an important, although often neglected, strand of the story of how the relationship between religious providers, secular government and the development of public healthcare and welfare has changed over the last century. But his analysis of the contemporary situation highlights the way in which such a relationship never was, nor is, so simple. 'Religious providers' is a simple term for organisations that may vary, from having religious foundations to being entirely staffed by active believers, and the notion of a secular marketplace is undermined by the multitude of faith identities of users, and their complex infusion across the public sphere. This is another sense in which it makes no sense to talk of a secular–religious binary. So Dinham's notion of religious literacy is explicitly targeted at this messy, complex mix of needs and identities, in both the supply and demand ends of welfare provision. In doing so, he reminds us of the religious heritage of many of the institutions and services that are assumed to be secular today, implicitly reminding us of the need for a historical awareness of our culture that celebrates and understands its religious past, in order to properly understand its complexly secular and religious present.

Jeremy Clines and Sophie Gilliat-Ray (Chapter Thirteen) also highlight the historical development of institutions in relation to religious literacy, this time through the lens of chaplaincies. Focusing on chaplaincies in UK organisations, such as hospitals, prisons and universities, they note the particular role of church-based professionals and how this has changed over time, with increasing numbers of voluntary staff providing similar services to non-Christian communities. They highlight how chaplaincies can be champions for increasing religious literacy within their host organisations, although note, as does Beth Crisp (Chapter Eleven), that just because staff might have religious knowledge, this does not mean they are religiously literate. This is an important point to remember, as it could seem counter-intuitive. But Crisp is clear that from her vantage point within Australian social services, believers often do not have the skills to apply their beliefs to their work: they cannot extrapolate that religious knowledge in a way that it can be helpfully utilised. Nor, of course, does having knowledge of their faith tradition mean that they are any more likely to be religiously literate about other faith traditions. Learning to reason religiously, as Ford and Higton outline, is more than knowing a tradition. It is learning the skills to interrogate that and to consciously (not unthinkingly) engage with it. This requires attention to the connection between service and faith – religiously literate service providers, in social services, welfare, education and other sectors, need to become bilingual, that is, professionally and religiously literate in order to apply religious reasoning in useful everyday contexts.

Religious literacy can help this through developing a level of 'background understanding', so a person may be able to grasp the inner meaning of users' needs, political events or public actions, as well as the history that has shaped particular public institutions or national norms. As the contributions to this volume suggest, religious literacy lies in having the knowledge and skills to recognise religious faith as a legitimate and important area for public attention, a degree of general knowledge about at least some religious traditions, and an awareness of and ability to find out about others. Its purpose is to avoid stereotypes, engage, respect and learn from others, and build good relations across difference. In this it is a civic endeavour rather than a religious one, and seeks to support a strong multifaith society, that is inclusive of people from all faith traditions and none, within a context that is largely suspicious and anxious about religion and belief.

Looking forward: a religiously literate world?

The elements of a religiously literate framework uncovered in this book suggest that religious literacy is generally concerned with seeking to inform intelligent, thoughtful and rooted approaches to religious faith that countervail unhelpful knee-jerk reactions based on fear and stereotype. Schools and universities are shown to be particularly well placed to inform this, while methods such as theological reasoning (Ford and Higton) and celebration of diversity (Barnes and Smith) provide ways to enrich the process. All of the chapters demonstrate how the formation of today's learners in religious literacy, in education or already in the workplace, will enable a vastly improved quality of conversation about religion in wider society, underpinning better encounter in partnerships, service provision and active citizenship between religious and non-religious actors alike.

They also show that religions deserve to be articulated publicly, not only so their positive aspects are acknowledged and engaged with, but also so they can be criticised constructively, and any risks identified and addressed (Francis and van Eck). In doing so it has the potential to mediate cultural, moral and cognitive differences, and to broaden intellectual, social and cultural horizons. It can also challenge any attempt to close down debates with 'conversation-stopping' certainties and absolutes.

But the contributions to this book also show that building religious literacy is a challenge: partly because of disinterestedness, partly just because the world is increasingly diverse, people often find that religion and belief are poorly understood. This can lead to resistance – even violence – against them (and by them) and to missed opportunities to enrich experience. In order to overcome these challenges it is important to realise, as shown here, that religious literacy is a method or practice *and* a theory. It can't be started without first being rooted in social scientific analysis – as stressed in the chapters by Moore, Catto and Perfect, and Francis and van Eck. It is necessary to be clear about some of the misconceptions and misunderstandings that surround religion, for example, whether it has a special connection with violence, or whether it exists as a dichotomous 'other' to a secular neutral realm. Understanding that secularity does not imply value neutrality and garnering basic knowledge about different faith traditions are options open to all. Some chapters suggest routes such as theological engagement or scriptural reasoning, which are, by their nature, limited in scope to those trained, interested and willing to engage at that intellectual level.

What they have in common is a sense of religious literacy as a journey from the lamentable quality of conversation talked about by Davie, to a high quality engagement, variously envisaged. The chapters in this book suggest that this resides in a progression in four main parts: beginning first with an examination of religion as a category, drawing on the social scientific, theological, philosophical and critical to locate how religion is characterised and problematised in the first place. A key part of this is also in understanding the secular, and understanding the real religious landscape; second comes an engagement with disposition. It is critical to identify personal and organisational stances, both emotionally and intellectually, towards religion and belief as a category, including understanding one's prejudices, expectations and the road blocks to forward thinking. Challenging sub-conscious assumptions is crucial, even if surfacing them leads to the same conclusions; third, only then can religious literacy arrive at engagement with content, and this is located in both knowledge and language. What can – and needs to – be known about religion and belief? But also, what languages are needed to swim well in these waters? And finally, we come to skills. In the religious literacy idea, these are derived as a response to the understandings developed in the earlier three stages. This is what makes religious literacy context-specific. What is my stance on the place of religion in this space? What are the intellectual and emotional obstacles to thinking well about this? How can they be addressed and engaged?

And then, what do I need to know in order to produce religously literate practice in this setting? In the end, it is practical and concrete: what skills should my workforce, student body, community group, or neighbour be equipped with in order to encounter religious plurality and diversity well in a world which turns out to be full of religion, belief and non-belief after all?

Regardless of the routes taken or the nature of application of religious literacy to fit different contexts, these chapters suggest some benefits that could be consolidated through extending religiously literate approaches in other settings. Rebalancing assumptions that religion is bad (Francis and van Eck) could lead to more positive policy development, and more constructive diplomatic engagements internationally as well as within multicultural societies. Understanding that religion is religion, not race or culture, but also that these and other aspects are complexly intertwined, can lead to more meaningful academic and practical engagement too. While religion should not be reduced to race or culture, nor should it be studied in isolation of them. An analysis of the kind Moore set out in her chapter will lead to more productive social analysis, including of the power relationships that intentionally and unintentionally marginalise sections of communities due to ignorance of religious difference.

We learn, too, that religion or belief are real for a majority of people in the world. This is so despite many religious institutions being in sharp decline, and many individuals openly diverging from significant tenets of their (at least nominal) faith communities. Whether because of a historical legacy of religious world-building or a continued and active (if messy and complex) engagement with one or amalgams of different belief systems, people still encounter religious symbols, ideas and people on a daily basis. So long as this is the case, there is a need for religious literacy.

Summary

The chapters in this book have explored religious literacy as a fluid and context specific idea. We detect it operating in the chapters here at three key levels, which, taken together, represent a journey from idea to practice.

First, there are challenges about how to see religion. As several contributions argue, a social scientific and sociological engagement with ideas about religion as a category is crucial, if otherwise sceptical or disinterested parties are to see the point in the first place. Grace Davie sets the important points out very helpfully in the Foreword, and they have been highlighted throughout: this is a landscape that has become both more secular and more religious; the binaries of religious/secular and private/public are increasingly thought to be distractions from the reality; there are growing social and political imperatives for engaging with religion and belief; and formal, traditional religion exists alongside a burgeoning in informal modes too, which stretch ideas of religion and belief, as UK law has recently recognised. Also crucial is an understanding of the real religious landscape as it is revealed in data and experience.

For Ford and Higton, and for Conroy, a deep engagement with the Theology that inheres is also valuable, alongside the sociological. What people believe and practice is an inherent part of religious literacy. Taken together, these elements constitute the conceptual level of religious literacy.

Second, there are questions about what religious literacy is for. Again, throughout the chapters, the question of purpose is posed. Various answers are given: that it is for cohesion and good citizenship; the avoidance of extremism; strengthening the encounter between public professionals and religiously plural publics; aligning policy-making and the real resources that inhere within faith communities; and even for the excitement of positing alternative logics of person and society, drawing on the wisdoms that reside in religions and beliefs. All seem feasible and valuable. The lesson we take is that it is crucial to know what religious literacy is for in the instance in which you undertake it. In this way, concepts and purposes must also be aligned.

Third, there are questions about how to do religious literacy. What does it look like as a practice? Since religious literacy is established throughout as pressing and urgent, and is put forward as a response to contemporary deficits in the conversation, it seems reasonable to assume that action is key, and implementation matters. Ideas of religious literacy are of little use if they cannot be connected to practices. Our projects in higher education, schools and with employers and providers are an attempt to close the gap. Religious literacy audits, as have been undertaken by the Religious Literacy Leadership in Higher Education Programme, are one tried and tested method involving a review of policies and practices in specific spaces and places, so as to identify the key challenges and opportunities. These are translated into packages of training that relate to the issues that arise. And they are illustrated with case studies of biting points and controversies that form the basis of discursive searches for solutions, undertaken in small groups in workshops.

Likewise, David Ford's Cambridge Interfaith Programme has developed the practice of scriptural reasoning as a way of implementing the vision for Theology as religious literacy set out in Ford and Higton's chapter. This involves deep engagement in scriptural text between people of different faiths and none, often in the original language.

By contrast, the *lokahi* approach set out in Chapter Five emphasises dialogue for harmony. A number of other initiatives take similar approaches, inflected for their own contexts and goals.

The journey from concept to practice is at its most difficult at the start – at the level of conceptualisation. This is the point at which religious illiteracy is at its most pervasive and the muddle at its worst. Clearing the debris of a century of declining religious talk and increasing assumptions about 'the secular', in all its forms, is the number one challenge, and this is the point at which sociological and social scientific approaches have most to contribute. It is closely followed by the need to understand the real religious landscape, and the ideas that accompany the change that is revealed. This, too, depends on sociological and social scientific methods. From there it might take any number of ways forward, depending on the purposes in mind and the methods that align. We hope that this book has shown not only why religious literacy is pressing, but also that it is best understood as a framework to be worked out in context. In this sense, it is better to talk of religious literacies in the plural than literacy in the singular.

Index

S

Sabaoon Centre for Rehabilitation 91–92
Sandberg, R. 139, 143, 147, 149, 153, 154
Sangharakshita (Dennis Lingwood) 124
Schein, Edgar 126
schools, challenges for religious literacy
delegitimisation of religion 183
disaggregation and extrapolation 168–171
examinations, focus on 170, 173–177
gaps between teaching at home and at school 177–180
historical narrative, lack of 182–183
legal and constitutional issues (US) 55, 56, 65, 67
personal interpretation, emphasis 171–173
resources and support, lack of 66, 177, 179–180
secularisation of religion 181–182
Scourfield, J. 213
Scriptural Reasoning 51
Scriven, John 145
Scurry, Richard 73
Second Great Awakening 57
secondary schools *see* schools, challenges for religious literacy
sectarianism, lack of in US 56–57, 59–64, 74
secularisation
as European exception viii–xi in growth of vii, viii–x, xi
neutrality of, as assumption 4, 5, 85
in schools 181–182
Sentamu, John 139
September 11 attacks
attacks on Sikhs after 56
Iraq invasion, linking of to 35
religion and extremism, linking of after 110
religion, role of in x
as trigger to interest in religious literacy 30, 65, 114, 192, 200
Singer, Margaret 126–127
'situatedness' 31–32
slavery, Galtung on 33–34
Smart, N. 183
social capital of faith groups 87, 105–106
social enterprises 108
social exclusion and religion 216–217
social work, religious literacy in 207–220
challenges to
faith-based organisations, issues with 215–217
opposition to religion 212

perception of religion as private matter 210–211
in faith-based organisations 214–219
knowledge of basic tenets *vs* deeper meaning 212–214
lack of 207, 208
need for 207, 208–214, 219
Society for the Study of Theology 47–48
'soft neutral' attitudinal group 8
Songs of Praise (TV programme) 229–230
Southern Baptist Convention (US) 29
spirituality, compared to religion 209
St Mellitus College 49–50
St Paul's Theological Centre 50
stand-alone Religion courses 70–71
Star, The
hostility to religion 231
mis-reporting on religion 234
stereotyping of faith groups 81
Stetson, Chuck 73
structural violence 33
Stuart, H. 140–141, 144–145, 147–148, 149–150, 152
Sun, The, hostility to religion 231
superdiversity 84
surveys and polls
attitudes of Christians in UK 155, 195
beliefs in the UK 12–13
US, religious literacy in 55
Swinton, John 214
Syria, war in 36

T

teacher training and guidance 67–70, 71, 73–74
Telegraph, The
coverage of religious rights cases 140
increasing coverage of religion 231
Temple, William 101–103
terrorism *see also* extremism; September 11 attacks
as trigger to interest in religious literacy 30, 65, 67, 114, 192, 195–196, 200
use of term 35–36
textbook trials 66
Thatcher administration 108
Theology
definitions 39–40
institutional settings for 47–52
public argument and 41–45
Religious Studies and
combination with 39–40, 193–194
comparison to 45–46, 262
requirements for students of 41, 45
Theos (think tank) 233–234
Thomas, Oliver 67
Thompson, Mark 234
tolerance and religious education 72